W9-AKB-291

Jac

One Ranger

H. Joaquin Jackson,
Texas Ranger (Ret.) and
David Marion Wilkinson

One Ranger

A Memoir

UNIVERSITY OF TEXAS PRESS, AUSTIN

Photo still of Joaquin Jackson and Tommy Lee Jones in *The Good Old Boys* reprinted by permission of Turner Network Television. © 2002 Turner Network Television. An AOL Time Warner Company. Photo by Erik Heinila.

The authors wish to extend their gratitude to photographer Dan Winters for his permission to use his photograph of Joaquin Jackson on the cover of this book. © 1994 by Dan Winters.

The authors wish to thank Larry McMurtry for his permission to quote from *In a Narrow Grave*; © 1968 by Larry McMurtry; renewed 1996.

Thanks to the estate of Alan Le May for the authors' fair use of a short quote from *The Searchers* (1956), Warner Bros. Motion Pictures.

The authors wish to thank Michael Ives for his gracious permission to reprint his image of Joaquin Jackson.

Requests for permission to reproduce material from this work should be sent to Permissions, University of Texas Press, P.O. Box 7819, Austin, TX 78713-7819.
www.utexas.edu/utpress/about/bpermission.html

⊚ The paper used in this book meets the minimum requirements of ANSI/NISO Z39.48-1992 (R1997) (Permanence of Paper).

LIBRARY OF CONGRESS CATALOGING-IN-PUBLICATION DATA

Jackson, H. Joaquin. 1935–
    One ranger : a memoir / H. Joaquin Jackson and David Marion Wilkinson.—
1st ed.
        p.   cm.—(Bridwell Texas history series)
    ISBN 0-292-70259-0 (alk. paper)
    1. Jackson, H. Joaquin. 1935–   2. Texas Rangers—Biography. I. Wilkinson, D.
Marion. II. Title. III. Series.
HV7911.J28A3   2005
363.2'092—dc22   2004019566

For Shirley

And the boys:
Don Joaquin, Lance Sterling, Tyler Joaquin, and Adam Michael

 # Contents

 # Prologue

Most everyone has heard the story in one form or another. Some say it's a myth. Others claim it's as certain as Noah's flood and Sherman's march to the sea. Doesn't really matter because the tale speaks to the truth. The definitive version is sometimes attributed to one man, but I've always felt like it pertains to us all. Of the countless variations told and celebrated since I was a boy, this is the one I always liked best:

The sheriff paced up and down the rail depot, waiting for a train. A few days before, a riot had broken out in his Spindletop-era boomtown. His bootstrap resources overwhelmed, he placed a frantic call to his governor in Austin. Don't worry, he was told. We're sending the Rangers down to sort it out. He hung up the phone and breathed a little easier, hoping he could hold off the mob and the looters just a while longer.

Finally came the day of the sheriff's salvation. He stood at the railhead, chain-smoked handrolls, and compulsively checked his pocket watch. He finally heard the whistle, then the squeal of the brakes. He stubbed out his cigarette with the toe of his boot and waited for the train to coast to a stop.

He waited for a dozen or more confident, well-armed, hard-eyed men to climb down from the passenger car, assess the situation, and then decisively restore order. Several unlikely candidates emerged with their luggage in hand and, without any eye contact, drifted away from the station. The sheriff's resolve faded as he noted that the last man to exit had a silver badge stuck to his dusty lapel.

He couldn't believe his eyes. Had he not explained the seriousness of his situation to the governor? Surely there were more officers. The tall, raw-boned traveler could pass for a cowboy if not for his tie. His slacks were tucked neatly into the shank of his boots. His spurs were probably packed away in the saddlebags he had slung over his shoulder. He seemed oblivious to the sheriff's despair as he offered him his hand. His duster fluttered open to reveal twin engraved Colt .45's hanging on each hip.

"Only one Ranger?" the sheriff said.

"Well, there's only one riot," the Ranger said.

That's one story. There are countless others that belong to the hundreds of men who are part of a proud tradition close to two centuries old. I am only one Ranger out of those who came before me and those who will ride on ahead. Only one story belongs to me.

ALL RISE! I snapped out of my trance when the bailiff demanded our attention. I stood as I've done a thousand times before. Soon the judge swept in, his black robes flowing. He had an academic look about him, accentuated by the horn-rimmed glasses that saddled the bridge of his nose. When he peered over the top of his specs and scanned the courtroom, I sensed a tinge of arrogance that told me he liked his job. He'd probably learned to sleep well at night with the power he lords over people. I never did.

Normally the judge and I are allies, equal partners in the justice system. My kind round them up and the judiciary sorts them out. The owlish New Mexico judge and I didn't come close to seeing eye-to-eye on this case, though we were both deeply disturbed by the crime. I could tell by the way he set his jaw and spoke through clenched teeth that he was angry about what happened. But me, I was torn apart.

I squirmed in a creaking chair that in no way was designed to accommodate my six-foot-five-inch frame. I've spent years in these places, and they all have the same stale feel. The architects had tried to warm this Albuquerque courtroom. There was plenty of lacquered wood paneling and trim to impart a reverent air; acoustic ceiling tiles to absorb random wailing; microphones everywhere to make sure everybody heard the horror of what was being said; padded seats in the jury box like you'd find in a fancy movie theater. But the designers failed. This was a sad, cold place where every day the countless variations of human tragedy played out their last act. Build courtrooms as fancy and modern as you like, I'd rather be anywhere but inside one. Especially on that day in February 1992.

Sitting at the defendant's table in his prison coveralls was a deeply troubled twenty-eight-year-old man on trial for a senseless, unpremeditated double homicide. Local authorities had found two boys shot to death in the desert, and they wanted this third one to pay for it. Both victims were homosexuals, which allowed the prosecutors to up the ante and classify the offense as a hate crime. Local authorities had apprehended two suspects. One proved to be the faster talker. The other sat in chains in front of this judge. The defendant and I flinched when the judge pounded his gavel.

I've put hundreds of people in the defendant's predicament, but never in New Mexico, a place that has always been special to me. In the 1950s, I cowboyed on the Bell Ranch in the state's northwest corner. I worked cattle operations like it on the sea of grass that stretches across the Southern Plains. I broke horses, branded yearlings, and rode fence as I entered manhood, steeped in the culture and legends of the American West. While Eisenhower was still president, economic circumstances dictated that I had to leave that world behind.

Thirty years later I returned to the lonesome places, the Big Country of southwest Texas. I make my living there now and I don't expect I'll ever leave it. While I watched this trial run its course, though, I was hundreds of miles out of my jurisdiction, hundreds of miles from home.

I didn't know it, but I was about a year away from retiring in protest. I didn't see that coming any better than I had imagined my appearance at a murder case in New Mexico.

I was struck, despite years of my best efforts to connect with the defendant, by how little we had in common. The only thing we could agree on was that he had probably thrown his life away.

I knew better than most how ruthless the justice system could be. The judge was going to drop the boom on that kid. Still I prayed for the court's mercy. In fact, I took the oath and testified to several reasons the defendant deserved it.

In 1992 I was an active officer in the oldest and most legendary law enforcement agency in the United States. As a Texas Ranger, I have always understood that I was part of a rich, proud tradition. I'd drain the last drop of blood from my body to uphold it. The Rangers have been the most effective, independent law enforcement agency in history. We evolved perfectly attuned to our time and place—for Texas has long been a sort of human Galapagos, an unsettled country of conflicting cultures and social contradictions, a rugged, ragtag region born with wars raging on two disputed borders. Young Texas battled her enemies for five straight decades, pausing only to send her sons to fight in America's wars. The Tejanos, the pioneers of Mexican descent, fought horse Indians for over a century before Anglos ever set foot in this country. Such violence created a special breed.

Unlike most of the American West, the Texas frontier wasn't settled by trappers, miners, and mountain men. The family farmer settled Texas, often in neighborhoods claimed in blood by the Comanche, Kiowa, and Lipan Apache, setting the stage for one of the most desperate and horrific racial and territorial contests in human history.

West of the Colorado River the rain played out. After the farmers defeated the plains tribes, the droughts rose up and thunderheads gave way to clouds of pale dust. Such harsh conditions bred the best and worst of humankind. Weary of all the bloodshed, the people demanded order before law. In a tradition dating back at least a thousand years, the young and the brave hunted down their people's enemies wherever they were. In the 1870s, such men wore a silver star cut from a Mexican cinco peso coin. In 1966, I pinned one on my chest.

Change came quickly for the Rangers during my tenure. Texas evolved into an urban society. My children's generation seemed to care less about traditions that were sacred in the house where I was raised. In the 1960s, the long-disputed Texas/Mexico border erupted in the fight for civil rights. The drug culture gave rise to drug lords, ruthless killers with more money and power than many Third World countries. Nothing in my Depression-era upbringing on the High Plains had prepared me for any of this. And yet there it all was, snarling at every Texas Ranger straddling the past and present.

Mix all that social commotion with your run-of-the-mill crimes in the Texas borderlands—contraband whiskey and dope smuggling, armed robbery, gambling, prostitution, livestock rustling, burglary, gangs, and murder—and you can see why my plate was full.

Then this New Mexico murder case took possession of my life. Suddenly I was way out of my league. I should have been consoled by the many blessings that came my way. How many country-boy cops make it to the movies? I played the sheriff in Tommy Lee Jones's production of *The Good Old Boys*. I had a cameo role as an air force officer in *Blue Sky*. I posed for one of the most successful covers of *Texas Monthly* magazine. I was featured in articles in *Life* and *Rolling Stone*. I spent three weeks preparing Nick Nolte for the lead role in *Extreme Prejudice*. His costume for that movie was an exact replica of how I dressed every day for work. I didn't care much for the movie, but, by God, Nolte looked great. Folks began to recognize me after all this. I looked around and it appeared that I had become a little bit famous. My job as a Ranger laid all of that at my feet.

In the mid-1980s I was transferred to the Big Bend country. I patrolled the largest and by far the most beautiful jurisdiction of any Ranger in the state. My family had everything we had ever hoped for. My wife and I bought a home with a view at the base of the Del Norte Mountains. She earned two master's degrees and settled into a fulfilling career in education. After overcoming the tragic accidental death of his best boyhood friend, my oldest son was thriving in the Marine Corps. My youngest boy was a student athlete and scholar, and would soon join me in law enforcement.

My career was at a pinnacle. My life seemed full. I felt like I had accomplished something in this world, that my work had made a difference. I looked out my window and saw God's hand at work all around me in the form of an ocotillo cactus in full bloom after a rare summer shower or a black chin hummingbird damn near pecking at my nose. And I was a part-time movie star, too. Who could ask for more?

But being a good Ranger exacted a price. The phone always rang. I slept little. I drove a lot. I spent days away from home on manhunts and stake-outs. I slept under a canvas saddle bedroll as often as I did next to my wife. I missed far too many important moments in the lives of my handsome sons. As I sat in that New Mexico courtroom awaiting the judge's ruling, I was crippled with guilt. I couldn't help but wonder if maybe my job had asked too much of me; if maybe I'd been away from home too often; if I loved being a Ranger more than being a husband and father.

I don't believe this judge listened to a word of my testimony. I guess I don't blame him. As is so often the case, the crime contaminated the lives of people beyond its initial victims. I understood the anger of the families who lost their loved ones. I was certain that their terrible grief held more sway with the bench than my pleas for mercy. The judge glared at the young defendant and ordered him to rise.

It was a tough year for my family and me, but I would soon see worse. We were losing the War on Drugs. The crimes on the border grew more violent. My cherished Texas Rangers were about to be diminished by political meddling, a slap in the face to me and my fellow officers and to the Ranger tradition itself. Before my head cleared, a trusted colleague who I thought was my friend—and who had once been such a comfort to me when my family was in crisis—betrayed me. Because of our close association, his crimes cast a long shadow over my reputation at a time when I leaned on it most.

Worst of all, my wife and I had to watch helplessly as the justice system was unleashed against our home. As the judge leveled his stare at that lost young man, I remember thinking that maybe it wasn't healthy for a kid to grow up in a world where his dad's best friends carried guns as often as they wore shoes. Having failed at balancing the two most important roles I chose to play in this life, I should be the one to pay for that.

The young man staring a death sentence in the face was Don Joaquin Jackson. He was my oldest son.

A lot happened between coming of age on a farm on the Southern Plains during the Great Depression and waiting to learn if my boy would go to the electric chair or spend his best years in a New Mexico prison. The weight of this and all those other burdens combined would drive me from a world I loved more than my own life. But even this is not the end of the story. I got through it. I went on.

ON MY FIRST OFFICIAL DAY as a Ranger my captain ordered me to report at five A.M. sharp to his ranch home outside of Carrizo Springs, Texas. Captain Alfred Allee Sr. was almost sixty-five years old by then. He had been a Texas Ranger since 1931. But he was still a human dynamo of energy, grit, and swagger. In my day we would say that he was a hell of a man. I don't know how that plays anymore.

I slid into the passenger seat of Captain Allee's tan unmarked 1966 Plymouth Fury I Pursuit state vehicle as he hugged his wife, Miss Pearl. Then, with his jaw set for business, he stormed my way. He groaned as he squeezed behind the steering wheel, bit down hard on a cigar, and cranked all eight throbbing cylinders of that 383 cc V-8 Commando engine. Each piston sat cocked and locked at a stout 10:1 compression ratio. A Carter AFB four-barrel carburetor perched atop the gasping intake manifold, mixing the most potent combination of air with 105-octane gasoline back when some cops used to run down bootleggers by goosing the gas tank with a healthy splash of airplane fuel.

The Pursuit Commando engine didn't idle as much as it boiled like a witches' brew. Dual sets of points ensured that the spark plugs fired long and hot. Dual exhausts shot the spent fumes beyond the rear bumper with a menacing hum. Once the engine ignited, Captain Allee reined back 330 wild horses chomping at the bit to run. He slammed the transmission into drive and stomped his polished boot on the accelerator, and one of the most powerful automobiles to roll out of Detroit exploded out from its parked position. The sudden thrust nearly gave me whiplash.

"Let me show you some of this country," Captain Allee said as he rocketed down the two-lane blacktop at triple-digit speed toward the breaking dawn. I already understood that he intended to introduce me to the thirty-nine-county jurisdiction of Ranger Company D. The surprise was that he meant to do it before noon. He never bothered to mention that we were on our way to a riot. Nevertheless, new to the job, I had arrived nervous. I felt only terror by now.

Captain Allee blew past the cars on the road as if they were parked. He was giving me all sorts of good practical advice based on his three decades of Ranger service, but it wasn't really registering. For all its power, the Plymouth Fury Pursuit didn't handle well. The frame was cursed with a long, narrow, unstable wheelbase, and was burdened by too much American steel fabricated with nine welds to the inch. The rudimentary suspension system waffled under all its weight. There was no power steering and no power brakes. You didn't drive the Pursuit; you sailed it. There was an art to keeping it between the lines at high speeds. At Allee's rate, safe navigation was nothing short of a miracle. Although I was proud to have made Ranger, I had hoped that the position would last for more than one day.

Captain Allee was passing yet another rancher petering along in a lumpy old Dodge pickup when another vehicle emerged from around the bend heading straight for us. I clamped both hands on the dash to brace myself for a head-on collision and glanced over at my captain.

His boot never touched the brake. Instead, he moved his cigar to the other side of his mouth and plowed ahead at 120 miles per hour. The distance between us closed in three frantic beats of my heart. Captain Allee refused to yield. The other car, horn blaring, swerved onto the shoulder at the very last second. I saw clearly the horror in that man's eyes at the peak intensity of the Doppler effect.

I whipped my head around as the driver skidded into the bar ditch. He fought to keep his rear bumper from overtaking his front grill and hurling his vehicle into a death roll. After a few hundred yards he finally came to rest and stayed there.

Captain Allee tooted his horn to signal his displeasure. The sun was nearly up now, driving a gray haze to horn depth on the cross-bred Brahma cattle grazing in the South Texas pastures. It was a beautiful day. And I was still alive to enjoy it. Captain Allee said nothing as he hurled on at blinding speed, still puffing on that stubby cigar. We had thirty-eight more counties to see.

"Never let the sons of bitches bluff you out, Joaquin," he said after several minutes of silence.

"Amen to that, Captain," I said. I had already accepted the fact that I was in for a long, wild ride. Captain Allee chomped his dentures around a fresh spot on his disintegrating cigar and plunged deeper into the ranch country that had spawned his special breed.

Looking back after retirement on my career as a Ranger, I still recall the value of Captain Allee's advice. Whenever personal and professional problems closed in on me, I always heard those few calm words echo in my head. *Never let the sons of bitches bluff you out, Joaquin.* I'd like to think that I never did.

One Ranger

CHAPTER ONE

Ice in August

LIFE IN THE TIME IT NEVER RAINED —

IN THREE PARTS

1935–1953

MY DAD, A FARMER BY TRADE, devoured the Sunday sports section of the *Lubbock Morning Avalanche.* When football season rolled around, he kept an eye peeled for any articles about the University of Texas Longhorns. In the fall of 1935 the *Avalanche* allegedly ran a stirring feature about one particular contest. I don't know which team UT played that weekend, but the journalist's gripping description of the gridiron battle inspired my father during one of his hopeless vigils for rain to name his firstborn son after the game's standout player.

In those days, football was a far more brutal game. Collegiate rivalries adopted the fervor of a blood feud. The stakes were always high, because in Texas bragging rights were everything. UT's lettermen were lionized throughout the state. Many athletes were endowed with entertaining nicknames, like "Potsy" Allen, "No-No" Reese, "Bully" Gilstrap, "Snaky" Jones, "Hook" McCullough, "Mogul" Robinson, "Big-Un" Rose, "Ox" Higgins, "Stud" Wright, and, my absolute all-time favorite, the University of Oklahoma's "Cactus Face" Duggan. Old Cactus Face must have been quite a looker.

For modern eyes, looking at the 1935 *Alcalde,* the University of Texas yearbook, is a sobering experience. So many of these ambitious, smooth-chinned faces graduated out of the deprivations of the Great Depression and were hurled into the meat grinder of the Second World War. The Korean conflict soon followed. Survivors lived under the perpetual threat of the Cold War, the McCarthy era, the Vietnam War, social upheavals of the 1960s, and on through the second half of America's most chaotic century.

Joaquin Jackson with his grandfather, Haynie Lollis, Lamb County, Texas, 1936

Only the strongest could have mustered enough enthusiasm and faith to sustain them through all that.

As I flipped through the pages in search of my namesake, I wondered which among the best and brightest of my parents' generation went on to live contented lives. Seventy years have passed since the senior class of 1935 competed for life's glories. The youngest would now be in their late eighties. Whether the individual players of the 1935 Longhorn football team went on to fulfill their greatest ambitions or failed at every turn, they are either gone from this world or nearly so.

I was also bothered by what you don't see in the 1920s and 1930s *Alcalde*. There are few Hispanic surnames and not one mention of an African American underclassman. The football program did not appear to have a single Mexican American on the squad, a reminder that higher education was once a pursuit limited to the Anglo population of Texas.

But, by God, somebody nicknamed "Joaquin" played one hell of a game sometime in the fall of 1935. He impressed the *Lubbock Avalanche* sportswriter, who unilaterally branded him with All-American potential in his Sunday morning recap. At least that's what my dad always said.

The facts say otherwise. The University of Texas at Austin would not boast of an All-American until the 1940s, long after I was born. No player named Joaquin ever lettered in the sport.

There were, however, two great players from that era named Jack. Back in the days when most of these boys literally came off the ranch, one of these fellows probably hung around the vaqueros enough to be nicknamed Joaquin. My dad loved the Texas Longhorns. Once he read the name of the promising player, it stuck in his head like another molar. I'm just grateful that he wasn't a fan of the fashion pages.

So, why am I named Joaquin? I've always told everyone who asked—and so many did—what my father told me. During the writing of and research for this book, I've followed my father's lead until the trail went cold. I tracked down a squad of young ghosts leering back at me. I thumbed through a decade of yearbook mug shots and I couldn't find my man.

I'm more confused than disappointed. As far as I'm concerned, the name worked out just fine for a Texas Ranger and was suited to a time when the racial barriers in Texas were tumbling down. I've always had an affinity for the Mexican American culture even if I didn't have any Mexican American blood. If the arbitrary name that my father picked for me encouraged the Mexican American community to risk a tidbit of faith in the Texas Rangers at a time when they had little or none, it served a far grander purpose than my poor father could have ever imagined. I have always been Joaquin. I have always been proud of the name. The true story of how I came by it, however, was buried with my father.

I came by the knowledge of my ancestry and earliest years by the same flawed oral tradition. My family talked on those rare occasions when there was no work to do. Even though we were assigned chores of our own, my sisters and I listened as best we could. What we were told will have to do.

PART I

The snow piled close to six inches in the winter fields and up to a man's knee in the drifts beside the house, barn, and outbuildings. On a gray, darkening afternoon, my daddy reeled on the telephone crank to ring the family doctor. "We need you out here, Doc," he said. "Baby's coming; and my wife's hurtin' awful bad."

The old man cared enough about his patients' welfare to make the drive through flurries of snow and sleet from Littlefield, Texas, out to the little farming community of Anton. And then he drove three miles more until he coasted to one mailbox nearly swallowed up by drifts of early winter South Plains snow. He read "Jackson" in black, hand-scrawled letters.

James Holcomb Jackson was a lean, tall, twenty-three-year-old man, dressed in starched khaki from his neck to his lace-up brogans, his shining blue eyes shaded by a short-brimmed, sweat-stained felt fedora. He watched his young wife endure the agony of labor, but he didn't show any worse for his worries.

James Jackson was a farmer, the same as his father before him, and on back as far as anyone could remember. Farmers learn early not to fret over what they can't control, which included nature in all of her manifestations except rain. On the High Plains dry farmers prayed for rain ahead of salvation. Other than that, they let nature ride on as she would, in birth as in all other things. For James's kind there weren't too many to cry for him if he couldn't bear the agony of a farmer's life. You bucked up, got through another day, and went on. He expected the same of his young bride.

Virah Jones was sixteen when she married James Jackson. Now barely eighteen, she was about to give birth to the first son of the handsomest young farmer in Lamb County. The old doctor arrived to examine his patient, clearly in the advanced stages of labor. Small woman, big baby. Nothing about this cold night would come easy.

The Jacksons were Scotch-Irish and English by blood. They came to America hungry like most of their kind, poured through the Virginia settlements like somebody's dishwater in search of cheap land. Each generation migrated farther west until they numbered seven—and none of them to my knowledge escaped the poverty that drove them deeper still. The Jackson clan eventually spilled into Texas, and there, east of the Colorado River, some of them dug in to stay.

James Austin "Jim" Jackson was born in Marble Falls, Texas, in 1878. My sisters and I called him "Papa Jackson." His daddy dragged him back down to a farm near Granger, Texas, near the junction of the Missouri, Kansas, and Texas Railroad, where he spent much of his life. His wife bore him four daughters and one son before she was burned alive in a house fire. Papa Jackson's second wife, Mississippi-bred Zelma Dean Holcomb, married him because his sister told her she ought to—to care for the motherless children if nothing else. The mercenary marriage worked out anyway. Zelma soon brought two boys of her own into this world. The oldest was my father, James Holcomb Jackson, born in 1912.

Folks around Granger said that the tall, thin, serious-faced boy was born to go places in this world. Turns out Papa Jackson had other plans. The Southern Plains of Texas were opening up farms of virgin soil far to the north of any country Papa Jackson had known. He could cash out his place in Williamson County for a larger spread on the prairie and have plenty of money on hand to endure the lean years. The old man didn't have to ask James to go with him.

Not that Papa Jackson was much on asking. When he needed help getting the crop in he ordered James to quit his senior year. If there was no crop, there was no money, and what good was his schooling unless they were teaching him how to make a stew out of them books? After that, James Jackson was destined to be a farmer whether he liked it or not. As things turned out, he didn't like it at all.

James's bitterness ate at him long before his father dragged him off to Lamb County to dry farm a half-section of land carved out of the Old Spade Ranch, sandy loam pasture that had never been scratched by a plow. Papa Jackson reaped bushels of hope from new country, believed in the promise of abundance to come. He strapped on his Dickie overalls, hitched up his Georgia mules, and led his boys James and Clarence into the fields.

James Jackson inherited his father's willingness to gamble everything on one good year—and he'd see it happen, too, in the early 1950s. But by then his bitterness and temper had consumed him and his marriage. He didn't know that he was already alone in the world, with his hip fat with cash money he'd gleaned from the dirt and his labors. But we'll get to that in its time.

If Papa Jackson was a severe man, I didn't see it. He may have thwarted my father's ambitions, but he always encouraged mine. I never understood how such a large, tough man as big as a barn could have been so tender with his grandchildren. Maybe seeing his daddy give what James never got ate at my father, too.

By that early November snow, father and son were both in Anton, working on land my grandfather owned, butchering hogs for winter lard and smoked bacon and Christmas hams. The house was no place for them once the doctor arrived. They probably didn't say much of anything as they stood under the dim, golden light of the coal oil lantern. The barn and outbuildings were still new enough that they smelled of pine sap on humid nights. The men were busy making quick strokes with skinning knifes, hanging bloody quarters from rafters in the smokehouse, listening to the wind to see if it carried a baby's cry.

Inside the clapboard house, labor pains wracked the body of a brown-haired, small-boned woman, born Virah Alice Jones in Pioneer, Texas, in

1917 and raised in the town of Comanche. Her parents, Ruby and Homer Jones, had divorced back when the act was akin in the social conscience to a bank robbery. Ruby took up with a wonderful concrete and masonry contractor named Haynie Lollis. She got around to marrying him in 1950, which speaks for itself when it comes to how my mother's side of the family cared for social conventions.

Daddy Haynie, as we called him, always turned over our dinner plates just before it was time to eat. When we set them right, there'd be a buffalo nickel or a mercury dime shining back at us. Sometimes he left a Peace silver dollar even though he'd worked half a day to earn it. I carry his name, just as my maternal grandmother wished—*Haynie* Joaquin Jackson.

Grandmother Ruby knew how to make much out of little, and there was always plenty to eat when she was around. Helping Virah with my birth detracted from her work as an Avon lady and a Stayform lady's undergarments agent. But with her first grandbaby coming, she didn't mind. She dipped Garrett snuff between sales calls, careful to pick the little particles out of her teeth with an elm twig. She sipped a little Mogen David wine when the mood caught her. She had Cherokee blood, too. She was as full of life as my daddy was taciturn.

This diverse and volatile group huddled together to await my birth. Some called them wanderers, dreamers, rebels, misfits, clodhoppers, dirt-farming folks born with more stubbornness than good sense. I called them my family. I first laid eyes on them on November 12, 1935.

Whatever the differences between my various kin, they were all astonished by my size. Father and son Jackson took one look at the long, fat baby and hauled their firstborn out to the cotton scale. When the needle passed ten pounds and rising, the doctor said, "That's enough! Take 'im off. She don't want to know!"

Papa Jackson slapped James on the back and said, "Look at the size of 'em, son! He'll tote a bale by himself 'fore he's twelve."

I can imagine my father's pride at holding me—the first thing that belonged only to him. The relief on his face that I was born big, strong, and healthy. I can see Virah, exhausted and pale, reaching for me with her twiglike arms. Grandmother Lollis snatching me away from my father, telling him he's a fool to weigh a newborn on a cotton scale in the cold, and handing me to my mother to cradle at her breast.

I wish I had a photograph of the moment when my mother and father stared into each other's eyes and understood that they had a baby to bind them when they were just a step or two beyond childhood themselves. I'd like to carry the image of my parents when they were young, healthy, fearless, and, with their arms wrapped around their firstborn child, hopelessly in love. I know there was a time when it was true.

Instead, other images come to mind—some warm and comforting, and others I wish that I'd never seen.

PART II

See a boy of three or four bouncing beside his grandfather on a cotton wagon pulled by two black Missouri draft mules. The stout, square-headed old man holds the reins, the skin of his fist rough and dry like an August dirt clod. They ride down the graded dirt roads that cut through country where you can see farther than you could afford to go, to Anton or maybe Littlefield. In the winter, after a crisp blue norther wipes the skies clean, you can see almost to the mountains of New Mexico.

The man loads the month's sugar, coffee, beans, lard, and salt when he notices the boy standing there in his Sunday shorts and tie, staring at the jar of rock candy. The old man flips a Mercury dime on the worn counter of the Mercantile.

"Well, go on," he says to the boy. "And get yourself a Nehi, too. But don't you tell nobody, 'specially your ma." The boy claps his hands together before he runs his index finger through the loop of string and pulls the candy out of the jar. His grandfather pops the cap on an orange soda and hands it to him. They walk out and climb back onto the wagon.

A BOY ABOUT THE SAME AGE and his blonde-haired sister board a train. She looks like a little angel in the dress her mama sewed out of a Gladiola flour sack. He looks like any other big-eyed, scuff-kneed boy. They sleep in the same bed, inseparable both night and day. They tickle each other as the green rows fly by on their way from Littlefield to Amherst.

SEE JAMES JACKSON telling his daddy that it's time to farm his own place. He's waited so long that the words choke in his throat. The old man has seen this day coming, his son now with a pretty wife and two young children and dreams of his own. They shake hands—big men locked in an awkward moment. James turns away. His father, a little shorter than his son but twice his breadth, shoves his hands in his pockets and paws at the dirt with the toe of his boot. He's not sure how well things'll turn out for young farmers, what with money as scarce as rain on the Southern Plains and James renting his land to boot.

Picture James and Virah as they pack everything they own into one borrowed wagon. It's just another chore for James, and he goes at it like hell bent in a fury. Virah doesn't like the way he's handling the furniture and she tells him so. He snaps at her to either load it herself or shut up about it. He climbs up beside her and snaps the reins on his daddy's mules.

The family of four creak along until they reach Whitharral and a Spanish *labor* of leased land—a little over 177 acres. The house looks more like a barn. Virah doesn't smile until James shows her the electric icebox in the hard-used kitchen. Virah lets her kids stick their heads in the freezer to feel the cold and scrape off frost with their fingernails. "Ain't that something?" she says. "We can make ice in August."

A BROTHER AND SISTER ride the top of the ice-cream maker, a tow sack for their saddle, their skinny butts ballast to keep the whole operation from tumbling over. Papa Jackson works the crank, fairly stiff now that the ice cream starts to set up. Joaquin and Dorothy Gail slide off to let their mother toss in some diced peaches and then climb back on with a giggle. Their daddy takes a turn on the crank until it's done. He yanks out the dasher and hands it to the kids to lick off the fresh ice cream.

After supper, Virah dishes ice cream into cereal bowls that ain't near big enough for two skinny kids. The ice cream melts fast in the summer air. Joaquin drinks the last of his. Dorothy Gail copies her brother. Virah kisses off the white cream mustaches.

JAMES AND VIRAH JACKSON sit down for Sunday dinner at Papa Jackson's house with all their other kin. Mounds of fried chicken crowd an oblong dish with bowls of green beans and potatoes all adorned with corn and tomato relishes canned the year before. Joaquin tugs at the tie around his neck, standing back from the table as his father, uncle, their wives, and his grandparents hold hands as Papa Jackson speaks the blessing. When the old man's done, he looks around at his grandkids to make sure they chime in with a hearty *amen.*

Joaquin's old enough to know that the grown-ups eat first in a workingman's house. It's like this every Sunday.

VIRAH BLOWS A STRAND of errant hair out of her face as she works the iron back and forth over khakis and denim overalls. She sprinkles water out of a corked Dr. Pepper bottle. The boy hears the sizzle as the iron rides over the new drops. When Dorothy is a few years older, she'll iron, too. James expects everything he wears to be clean, starched, and creased, even when he's going to hoe a few rows of cotton or maize.

THE ENTIRE JAMES JACKSON FAMILY pulls up in a tractor and cotton trailer to the new project farm near Ropesville. Part of Roosevelt's controversial New Deal, the house and outbuildings are brand-new. The farm is James's first opportunity to own his own land. There are plenty of young families around and a community center where they gather. Churches, homes, and a school pop up like Johnson grass. Barefoot kids run everywhere. Hear Virah's steps echo through the house's four hollow rooms. "All right," she says. "So this is it. I'll make do." It belongs to her and James both, at least as long as they can make the payments.

Dorothy and Joaquin scramble up the windmill, in lieu of a climbing tree, and holler to children on neighboring farms. "Y'all come play!" A pack of them come running across the edge of a field. Their footsteps leave a little cloud of dust behind them.

It's ninety-eight degrees in the shade if you can find any, which on the Southern Plains you can't. Virah watches her husband's Adam's apple bounce as he downs a Dell Dixie pickle jar full of lemonade she brings to him in the field. The sweat on his neck and brow is matted with grit. He hands the empty jar to her, tips the brim of his dirty straw hat, and walks back to the tractor without a word. He's got his job. Her job is to help him do it.

Papa Jackson times Joaquin and Dorothy as they race around the peach orchard. The second heat is between the telephone poles that stud the Jackson farm. While they're running, Papa Jackson pulls a contraption out of the back of his Ford pickup. The kids walk back sweating and winded, eyes wide open at the sight of a crabapple red Western Flyer. "Take her for a spin, Joaquin," the old man says, "it's supposed to be able to fly."

JAMES WALKS SPRYLY to the dirt road where his friend is waiting. He comes home alone in a used 1939 Chevrolet sedan. The dents and dings don't bother him at all. It's got tires and the motor runs strong and it's his. Virah walks out when he honks the horn. James grins big and says, "Well, round up them kids and let's go for a ride." They drive off. She worries about how James spends money. Cash is a long way from easy come around here. James thinks that no matter what he does it ain't good enough for her.

James sees what the Chevy will do in third gear. The transmission hangs a little when he shifts out of second. He's drawn to a baby blue skirt flapping in the wind. A young wife hangs out her laundry. He slows a little to study the smooth cut of her legs. When he glances back at Virah, she glares at him. It ain't the first time James has eyed the pretty young ladies. Virah knows that they come looking for her handsome husband, too. She's got enough on her plate without worrying about that. Her spite festers like a splinter stuck deep in the heel of her hand.

JOAQUIN AND DOROTHY wrestle in the backseat of the Chevy, parked with a hundred other black cars and pickups outside of the Cotton Club in Lubbock. They spot other bored kids sitting in cars, but they know better than to disobey their parents and play with them. They hear fiddles hanging Western swing in the dry air, a wall of human voices interrupted only by shouting or cackling or by the crowd clapping hands at the end of a fast number.

The kids are asleep when the car door pops open. The image is fuzzy, but Virah spits out words as soon as James slides behind the wheel. The kids smell bootleg liquor on their parents' breath, sort of like the smell at a doctor's office or in the fertilizer section of the feed store. James jerks the car into gear. The kids are tossed against the door as he accelerates onto the blacktop, and he burns rubber he can't afford to replace. Virah shakes her head and makes a show of checking the kids for bruises and bumps. She looks anywhere but at James.

Virah's jaw keeps working. She grows angrier as he continues to ignore her. Joaquin looks in the mirror as the headlights of passing cars illuminate his father's narrow eyes in dying rectangles. He knows better than to fool with his dad when he looks like that.

Virah shrieks when James hauls off and slaps her, more out of outrage than pain. The blow knocks her head against the glass. In an instant, Joaquin shoots out of the backseat and wallops his dad with his fists. Dorothy stares at her brother, her eyes like big blue marbles.

Everyone except James is sobbing. Virah's horrified that her argument has now embroiled the kids. James thinks that he ought to pull over and blister the boy's backside, and maybe Virah's, too—and anyone else who crosses him tonight—but he can wait. Nobody says another word.

The lights of Lubbock fade behind them. Virah herds her children into the house. James slides out his skinny belt as he follows behind them. Dorothy winces at every stroke. Virah's face flushes bright red, and she pulls her daughter to her chest to wait it out. She makes room for Joaquin when it's over. "I'm sorry, baby," she whispers over and over into Joaquin's ear.

THE DUST SWIRLS around the farm under a sky the color of tanned leather. Stunted crops wither in the fields. James hands the keys of the Chevy to a stranger in exchange for a few worn-out bills. Every day after school Virah and Dorothy sweep up the day's dirt. Virah's deaf to all complaints about the grit in the potatoes and peas.

Virah and James dance at the community center now. Joaquin and Dorothy Gail run wild with the other children, but they can't ignore the squabbling couples. There isn't as much food at the potluck suppers as there used

Joaquin Jackson, his mother Virah, and his sister Dorothy Gail, circa 1940

to be. Fewer people laugh. Men draw hard on quarts of clear liquor and stare long at empty fields. They have that doctor's office smell when they stagger by. James stares hard at strange women, and Joaquin feels certain that his daddy knows those ladies. Every now and then, a dark-eyed woman whispers in James's ear. He gives her a tight-lipped smile.

Virah rides to town on the family tractor now. Her kids ride on either side of her. They come back the same way, only the kids hang on to sacks of groceries. Virah's little arms shimmy as she fights the steering wheel, but she can drive with one hand long enough to slap Joaquin's hand out of the sugar sack. Every now and then they pass a project farm with new boards across the windows.

THE SEASONS DRAG BY, a slow passing of long, dusty years. Joaquin and Dorothy grow strong on hard work and farm-fresh food. They're fast, too, and athletic. Every sport they play comes so easy. Papa Jackson plods along now when his family gathers. "I'd come see you play ball," he tells Joaquin, "if y'all didn't play on Sunday."

JAMES PACKS THE LAST LOAD—they've accumulated so many more possessions and pieces of farm equipment than before. Husband and wife don't say a word, with the baby Jimmie Sue squeezed between them. Driving past the sign that reads "Welcome to Smyer," Virah pales at first sight of what's supposed to pass as a farmhouse. "I've seen chickenhouses fancier than that," she says. James doesn't pay her any mind. It's the best farm he's ever owned, and the house is a woman's problem anyway.

With a grain scoop, Dorothy and Virah shovel the field dirt blown into the house. Sandstorms loom on the horizon like spring thunderheads. They hit hard enough to scour the hide off a hog. Dust blows in through every crack and cranny, and the kids hold a wet dishrag to their faces. Virah fetches the broom as often as she yanks the pull chain on the bare bulb lights. She hates the house. She hates the weather. She thinks she ought to shoot the man who brought her here.

James kicks the butane fuel open and cranks the motor that drives the rusty irrigation pump. What the farmers call butane is really liquefied natural gas, but they don't care about proper terminology. They care about the goddamn taxes on gasoline. The engine turns over in a puff of black smoke, but soon it hits its singing stride. Six-inch irrigation pipes tremble with the flow of well water. James looks up at a fuzzy horizon thick with brown dust. He doesn't care if it never rains again.

Let the summer pass. James pays a few of his less fortunate neighbors cash money by the day to haul cotton trailers to the gin. He made a quarter to a half bale of cotton to the acre in his best year on that sorry dry farm. He reaps close to two bales an acre on the new place by running the noisy, rusty irrigation pump in the long hazy days between rains. He struts through the squeaky door wearing his hat with a gangster's tilt. Pops a check in front of Virah's face. He's all winks and white teeth. "Your man can grow cotton out of a rock," he says.

FROST COATS THE STALKS on a clear winter's morning. Virah's breath vaporizes inside the house. She snatches a wool blanket that she warmed on the space heater and wraps it around her children's feet. The kids moan at how good it feels and roll over to go back to sleep. James, arms and neck dark with dirt and grit, a clear white line where his hat rests on his forehead that never sees the sun, waits for his turn in the galvanized tub. The kids and Virah bathe first. He smacks the youngest, Jimmie Sue, on her butt with a wet towel as she goes running by, then climbs into the tub while the water is still warm.

gym to watch him work out. Joaquin feels like the ticket off that farm is already between his fingers.

Joaquin stands an inch or two over six feet. He's tough as a fence post and just as thin. Sheets of gristly muscle stretched over long, limber bones. It's after school. He was up early doing his chores, and then had practice to handle after classes. They ran extra laps for missing too many foul shots in the last game. James motions for Joaquin to join him in the back yard. James crams a shovel in his son's chest and tells him to fill in the sewer ditch that James has fooled with for the better part of a hot day. Joaquin starts to toss the soil onto the new line. He thinks he'll be a pilot or a cowboy, he's not sure. He only knows that he'll never be a farmer, never end up like James.

His daddy sees him leaning on a shovel like some sorry county road worker. "I said get that goddamn ditch filled in," he barks. Joaquin throws the shovel aside and says, "Fill it in yourself." He stomps off. He gets maybe three steps away when he gets slammed to the ground. He can't breathe. He feels the heat, the swelling, and the deep ache. James stands over him with a crowbar. "You'll do what I tell you, boy, and you'll do it now!" Joaquin's shoulders throb from the blow, but he stands up and reaches for his shovel. He feels like crying but he'd never give that son of a bitch the satisfaction. He can't get away fast enough from that goddamn farm.

Virah buys little things for her home with her own money. She feels good about what she's created for her kids until her husband walks through the door. Can't paint over James Jackson. Dorothy Gail takes up house chores now that both parents work outside of the home. Joaquin cooks a little, but he's a bit of a slob. He's restless, too. Joaquin and Dorothy Gail see how James dotes over Jimmie Sue. The older kids are up before daylight and after their chores, or else. But James beams at Jimmie Sue curled up in her bed. "Let that baby girl sleep," he says. Joaquin and Dorothy resent it, but don't dare speak the words.

Joaquin practices his quick draw with the .38-40 Colt single-action revolver. He mimics the same action favored by his childhood heroes Gene Autry, Wild Bill Elliot, or Red Ryder and his redman sidekick, Little Beaver, whom he watched on the Saturday matinee at the State Theatre in Lubbock. These days he and his friends sit up in the balcony and puff on ten-cent cigars like some black-hatted villains and think maybe they were born eighty years too late. "Quicker than you can blink an eye," he brags to himself, the leather rig riding low on his hip as he squares off with a Green

Giant bean can. His thumb slips off the hammer as he draws. The pistol goes off a little quick, Joaquin notices. He feels first the burn of the bullet against his skin, and then the warmth of the blood as it soaks his jeans. Little Beaver has just shot himself through the meat of his thigh.

VIRAH SOBS against the front door after she sends Joaquin to sit for his senior picture in a simple dress shirt and tie. She can't afford a new jacket.

JOAQUIN RUNS to the mailbox every day. Finally he sees what he's been waiting for—a letter from West Texas State in Canyon. He shucks the envelope and lets it blow in the hot wind. He's got himself a scholarship. Suddenly the road in front of his house leads almost anywhere except to another farm.

When Virah comes home from work, Joaquin picks her up and twirls her around. He sets her down and shows her the letter, and she throws her arms around his neck. In a flood of tears, she tells him she always knew that he could do it. It's a different story with James. Joaquin drops the letter in his daddy's lap while James waits for Dorothy to serve smothered steak with biscuits and gravy. "Looks like I'll be heading to Canyon this fall," Joaquin says.

"I expect so," the old man says. He hands the letter back to Joaquin, pulls a pack of Camels out of his breast pocket, and cups his fist around a cigarette as he lights it.

Joaquin takes the letter back and, face beaming, walks to his room. That's the most anyone would ever get out of James Jackson after the drought was through with him.

PART III

What is there left to tell about these people, my family? My sisters and I left for lives of our own. Dorothy Gail married a classmate of mine, Jim Moring, the son of our school superintendent. Jim became a petroleum engineer. He and Dorothy eventually settled in Midland, where they raised a family and prospered. Dorothy earned her real estate license and later helped Shirley and me buy our home in Alpine. She'll skin you good on the golf course, too.

Jimmie Sue was left behind during the bitter years. James and Virah were too embroiled in their wars to be parents to her. She quit school, married, and moved away, only to lose her husband and daughter in a tragic automobile accident. True to the Jackson name, she picked herself up and went on.

She married two more times, both marriages ending in divorce. She works for a chip manufacturer in the Dallas area. We don't see Jimmie Sue nearly often enough. She reminds me so much of my mother.

My father continued to struggle with his farm. To make ends meet, he worked a succession of jobs. He went on the wheat harvest one year, migrating from field to field, state to state. He "measured cotton" to check that farmers didn't abuse government subsidy programs. He worked at the local gin, was a janitor at the local school, drove a school bus. In 1958, he finally gave up farming and moved to Levelland in 1959. The next year, my long-suffering mother kicked him out of the house.

James's divorce depleted what little initiative the drought had left him. He never thought Virah would go through with it. Stunned, he staggered off to Lubbock and worked at a Humble gas station. He later ended up in his brother's house, married to another woman, and ran a used car lot in New Deal, Texas. All three of these projects failed. He moved on to Pampa, where he worked as a school janitor until retirement age.

Always game for the ladies, James married once or twice more. One of these unions lasted only a day. In the early 1980s, he moved to Midland to be closer to Dorothy Gail's family. Even though he suffered from emphysema and arthritis, among other ailments, he continued to attend senior citizen dances in his shiny "slippers" until dementia sentenced him to a nursing home. He died in 1993. To the end, James always loved to dance.

In 1987, James made his only visit to my home in Alpine. The first thing he did was walk around with his hands behind his back, staring at the soil. He stopped dead in his tracks and looked at me.

"I'm gonna tell you something, son," he said. "This place ain't worth a damn."

"What are you talking about, Dad?" I said.

"Got too many rocks."

I reckon James Jackson died a farmer.

Virah also struggled after the divorce. Her experience in women's fashion retail got her hired on to manage the Franklin Ladies Dress Shop in Levelland, the high-water mark of her career. She married an alcoholic cook and became an alcoholic waitress. Together they served chicken fried steaks and hamburgers in broken-down greasy spoons all over West Texas, leaving a swath of broken bottles, unpaid bills, and shattered dreams behind. She cut loose one cook only to take up with another, and the next drank even more.

In 1980, after two decades of alcoholism, Virah Alice Jackson sobered up and joined AA and never touched another drop. Gradually the light returned to her eyes. She rekindled a relationship with all of her children, especially

From left to right: James Jackson, Ruby Lollis, Dorothy Gail Jackson, Virah Alice Jackson, and Joaquin, circa 1940

Dorothy Gail, over the next ten years. Virah died in 1990. In 1987 she gave me a schnoodle pup (half schnauzer and half poodle). We named her Alice after my mother. We buried Alice in 2003. They both died of bone cancer.

NO MATTER WHERE any of us failed, regardless of how they disappointed me or I them, these people are my family. I think better of them now that I'm older. Their times were so much harder than mine, their choices fewer. Their flaws were given every opportunity to take root and, in some cases, overwhelmed my loved ones until they wrought their own destruction. My sisters and I turned away from my parents' ruin until it had run its bitter course.

No one gave my parents anything. They, in turn, gave everything they had to my sisters and me. Time has washed away the anger and the hurt. After it was all said and done and so much time has passed since those drought years tainted by tears and dust, only love remains.

Love and a few sad photographs.

CHAPTER TWO

Rider through the Storm

IN FOUR PARTS

1950–1966

A BOY AND HIS GUN

I HAD THREE LOVES in my youth—sports, hunting, and the West. Each of these passions prepared me for my Ranger career. As I came of age I pursued them all.

I introduced myself to hunting on my family's Smyer farm. Like most farmers and ranchers, my dad couldn't afford the spare time to hunt and fish. Other than the preliminary orientation to shooting, handling, and maintaining a weapon, he expected me to teach myself what to do with it.

He bought me a single-shot .22 when I was about ten years old. A fifty-round box of .22 short ammunition cost a quarter. A box of .22 longs cost a dime more. I scratched up spare change doing odd jobs for my neighbors, hoeing cotton or stacking feed. Once I had a rifle and ammunition, I drilled holes through just about everything that we didn't need anymore or that didn't belong to us in the first place. Two bits and the little .22 bought me loads of entertainment.

Once I reached a reasonable level of expertise, I went after small game, mostly rabbits after the first hard autumn freeze. Times were never hard enough to mess with a nasty jackrabbit. I kept the crows at bay from my father's corn crop and policed my mother's garden from vandalizing varmints. The single-shot was like a third arm. If I could see something, I could probably shoot it.

As time wore on I got my hands on better equipment. My dad bought me a Winchester Model 62-A slide-action .22 rifle for my sixteenth birthday.

Texas Department of Public Safety
Trooper Jackson, 1957

He never liked the idea of the Model 62's exposed hammer, especially after I accidentally popped off a cap in the middle of my father's conversation with our neighbors. After my dad chewed my ass about my carelessness, he abruptly traded it for a same make hammerless Model 61.

Armed with my dad's Winchester Model 24 double-barrel 12-gauge shotgun, I jump shot ducks, geese, and sandhill cranes off the stock tanks and playa lakes. I flushed quail and cottontails from out of the fencerows and winter stubble. Each September I hunted mourning doves over milo and wheat fields. I was blessed with good hand/eye coordination, which meant that wing shooting came easily. I put a lot of meat on my mama's table.

I'm not sure, however, that a natural proficiency mattered much. Guns and I bonded to each other. I can't say that I love guns the way some people do. I simply discovered that I had an affinity for firearms. I liked them. I respected them. I was infatuated with everything about them—the design, the action. Long before I was in law enforcement, I shot thousands of rounds through all sorts of weapons. If the gun performed well in the field, I kept it. If it didn't, I traded it for another. I relied on a very subjective selection process, but I valued accuracy and reliable operation above cosmetics and price, and function over form. I'd treasure a rifle that looked like a pawnshop boat paddle if it punched a tight five-shot group at a hundred yards.

I liked the smell of gun smoke from my father's Winchester shotgun. I'd pop open the breech and pull the gun to my nose to catch the scent before the breeze whisked it away. I liked the look and feel of a slick English-style walnut stock against my cheek when I swung on autumn doves or winter pintails, the beauty of the woodgrain in the late afternoon sun, and hearing the sharp crack of a rifle at first light on a winter morning. Every now and then, when the sun was angled just right, I could watch a bullet fly to its target, or see a shot pattern spray over a flushed quail.

I felt a rightness about guns that I can't describe. But I don't go around telling people that I love them. I love my family, my God, and my country. Guns and I were good friends when I was a kid. Later, when I became a man, we became professional colleagues, working together for thirty-seven years. We get along very well.

LESSONS IN SPORTS AND POLITICS

Sports came next on my list of passions. I played football and baseball and ran track, but excelled at basketball. A kid who was nearly 6′5″ was a giant on the High Plains in the 1950s, and a little athletic ability could carry even the gawkiest fellow a long way. I received several offers to play at the college level, finally choosing West Texas State's hometown court.

I started on the freshman team and got lots of varsity playing time as a sophomore. I received a nice write-up in the *Amarillo Globe News* after spring training. Coach Gus Miller informed me that I would start the following season.

Shortly after that we were scrimmaging in preparation for a road game against our rival, Texas Western at El Paso. I guess I was a fairly aggressive player. I went up for a rebound against a teammate of mine. I was aware that this fellow was endowed with certain social and economic advantages, but like most farm boys who had come up hard, I could whip the snot out of any city dudes. He somehow came down with the ball, but he couldn't keep it for long. I snatched it away, and he swung at me with a haymaker punch. I ducked, which opened up his belly as a target. A quick combination left him groaning on the floor.

I'm not proud of how I handled this confrontation. I can only say that at the time I knew of no other way to respond. It was just another scuffle in the heat of battle, but Coach Miller seemed unusually aghast. My competitor was later hospitalized with ruptured stomach muscles. In the end, however, this altercation would do far more injury to me than him.

In the summer of 1956 this incident was the lone dark cloud on an otherwise clear horizon. Coach Miller told "Bones" Simpson and me that our futures as Fighting Buffaloes looked bright. I went home to tell my family the news of my good fortune. I then gathered my boots, hat, leggings, and spurs and headed to the Bell Ranch and my summer job as a working cowboy.

THE LAST ROUNDUP

I knew that I wasn't cut out to farm, but nothing ever reared up between me and ranching. The Kenney family out of Lubbock owned the Spade Ranch, a fabulous spread not far from my daddy's farm in Smyer. I worked out there every chance I got.

Once I established my enthusiasm as a worker and a cowhand on the Spade, other opportunities to cowboy blew my way. I'm really proud of one of these in particular.

The Spanish Crown had granted over 700,000 acres to Pablo Montoya, the original *comanchero* owner of the Bell Ranch, elder sister to the Spade, situated in the mesa country some forty-five miles northwest of Tucumcari, New Mexico. It lay east of the Canadian River basin, where the locals claimed that the wind knelt beside the prairie to pray. The shape of the Montoya grant was an exact rectangle, tilted up on its points to run almost due north and south, incorporating over 1,000 square miles.

By the time the Kenney family of Connecticut and Lubbock acquired the property in 1947, the Montoya grant had been carved into six ranches. The heart of the ranch, which contained its signature bell-shaped mesa and with it the rights to this storied brand and name, contained 130,855 acres.

Most of the Bell's twenty-two pastures lay below 4,500 feet in elevation, which meant that its country wintered better than surrounding spreads. Blue, black, and sideoat grama grasses and low-lying flats of galleta provided graze so nutritious that it never became necessary to supplement the herd with hay or other feed.

I was one of a dozen or so cowboys who worked the ranch on horseback, and one of the last to cowboy under the old chuckwagon-supported roundup system originated by Charlie Goodnight in the 1870s. I had the privilege of riding beside old-timers who had first saddled up when the cowman was king.

The Bell dodged all the social and economic bullets of the times, including the seven-year drought of the 1950s. It was one of the most innovative ranching operations in the West, even as it adhered to time-tested traditions. Crow-eyed, leather-skinned foremen ran the Bell much like their grandfathers had at the turn of the century. It wasn't the open range of 1870s Texas, but with 130,000-plus mesa-studded acres behind barbed wire, it sure felt like it, especially from the back of a horse. The experience turned out to be one hell of a ride.

George Ellis managed the Bell with a firm, but gentlemanly, hand. He kept his distance from the seasonal workers, but he was first and foremost a cowboy. Come the summer branding, George Ellis was in the saddle like the rest of us.

The cow foreman was Bill "Yaqui" Tatom. Buster Taylor was the wagon boss. Cowboys included Erlindo Alarid, Juan Maldanado, and Moses Romero. There was a white guy named Pete, who ran with a Mexican man half his age and size called "Re-Pete." I could never explain the derivation of my name to their satisfaction. They called me Sonny instead of Joaquin. I didn't mind.

The Kenneys pastured over a hundred horses, their *remuda*, on the Bell. My first day the vaqueros cut out seven for me—five drive horses to herd cattle from one pasture to another, a cutting horse used to separate cattle on their way to the appropriate working pen, and a night horse. Ellis's son, George Jr., who went by the name of Rusty, shoed two of my horses and then ordered me to shoe the other five. I hammered the square peg nails into the hoof and filed them down nice and smooth as I'd seen this other fellow do. They held just fine. I didn't quick a single animal. None of my horses threw a shoe, either, and I rode them hard for the better part of the next six weeks.

George Ellis believed in starting a little later in the morning than most outfits. Cowboys were awakened right at the break of day. As one of the horse wranglers, however, I was out of my bedroll at 4:30 A.M. The grumpy old cook woke me with a nudge of his boot. My night horse was hobbled at the ankles nearby. I grabbed a tin cup of coffee, saddled up, and rode off with Re-Pete to the horse trap where they pastured the entire *remuda*.

On the Bell even a horse trap could swallow the average Texas ranch. But if you gave your mount a loose rein, he'd generally walk right up to the rest of the loose horses. If he didn't, Re-Pete and I found the lowest ground on the western crossfence and looked back east to skylight the horses just as day broke. Such a beautiful scene was a great way to start your workday.

We drove the horses back to the rope corral—a makeshift pen that was usually attached to a hoodlum wagon. Once we had them in the rope corral, the other cowboys showed up to claim their mount for the day, and we wranglers went to see the cookie about our breakfast.

The horses in the corral were too closely quartered to rope them in the traditional manner. The old cowboys relied on the *hulahand* toss, in which they flipped a loop high in the air and let it drop down over the horse's head. The technique was akin to throwing a big washer around the neck of one particular Coke bottle in the middle of a full crate. The wranglers knew every horse's name. And they were all experts with a rope. The entire process fascinated me.

In no time at all, all twelve cowboys were fed, mounted, and riding out to the far pasture, ninety sections of rolling hills, windswept golden grama grass, and purple sage, flushing cattle out of the low draws, dead canyons, "Indian Rocks," and upland plateaus. The yearlings grazing among them had never before seen a man. Just after daylight the young horses pranced and tugged hard against the reins, wanting to run for the sheer joy of it while the day was still cool. Young cowboys like myself preferred to let them for the same reason.

The chuckwagon, pulled by a team of four dun horses named Mustard, Custard, Nip, and Tuck, rolled after us. The hoodlum wagon followed along, piled past the sideboards with gear and supplies. At the next camp, the cooks and a few cowboys stretched a tarp over the wagon hoops to fashion a tent fly for shelter from the rain and sun. The cooks had hot meals for everyone at breakfast and supper, even if they didn't have a kind word. We ate lunch with our boots in the stirrups.

Most of the men slept in tepees on the Bell. For reasons I never understood they were real particular about their support poles, too. If I didn't draw duty as the nightrider, I slept next to a dying campfire, awakened the next day before the dew soaked the grass. I loved every minute of it. And so did the rest of the men—except the cook, who hated everybody and everything.

One morning Buster Taylor picked me and one other rider to drive a herd of dry cows and bulls to pasture away from the working herd. We managed our task, returning to the chuckwagon ahead of the other cowboys. A boiling thunderhead rose over the mesas to the north. We were standing under the fly when our one-armed horse wrangler came barreling up hell-bent for leather. As a kid, he'd lost an argument with a Winchester .30-30. But you couldn't tell that he was short of a limb or two the way he rode that horse.

"The thunder's scattered those damn Clabber Hill horses," he said, Clabber Hill being an adjoining ranch. One of its cowboys had been riding with us and he'd brought along a few extra cow ponies. "Can y'all help me round 'em up?"

Hoping to beat the storm, we saddled up and lit out after the strays. We cut their trail about a quarter mile from camp. They were meandering up a path that led to the top of a mesa a thousand feet above the range. We leaned low against our mounts' necks and climbed the rocks after them.

The storm blew in fast. Heavy gray clouds with snow-white edges rolled over the top of the mesa. Stringers of thinner clouds cut loose and began to swirl. The temperature dropped twenty degrees. Gusts of wind laid the grama grass flat. The hair stood up on the back of my neck. Even the horse's mane rose a little. Then the first bolt of lightning hit.

I never saw one strike out of the continuous barrage connect earth and sky. Instead, each bolt veined out parallel to the ground in solid, cobwebbed shafts of white. Each finger struck some solid object, leaving only smoke, a sulphurous odor, and one very scared cowboy behind. The immediate thunderclap that followed nearly blew me off my mount. Old cowhands always say that horses draw lightning. I didn't want to find out for myself.

Horse and human alike couldn't get off that flat top fast enough. Nearly fifty years have passed, and I've never seen Mother Nature turn so violently against man and beast. I can't remember when I was ever that scared again.

Way too soon the summer roundup was over. My dad had a first-ever plane ticket waiting on me. I was expected at Quantico, Virginia, for Marine Officer's Candidate training. Mr. Ellis returned to ranch headquarters. The older hands settled back down with their families or whooped it up in Tucumcari.

My dad drove me home. I had a letter waiting on me from Coach Miller informing me that my scholarship had been canceled. Stunned, I called to my roommate, Bones Simpson. According to him, the fight with my teammate had cost me my scholarship.

There was an oil company executive who contributed $5,000 a year to the basketball program, a substantial sum of money in 1956. Turns out that this man's son was the one who'd thrown the haymaker. Bones officed next door to Coach Miller during the summer. He overheard the guy's dad when he threatened to terminate his financial support if I suited up for another season. Coach Miller figured he could replace me more easily than the $5,000.

I was bitterly disappointed. For years I stewed about this injustice. It was the first time I saw money talk louder than merit. The experience left such a bad taste that I never responded well to backroom politics or wealthy people trying to buy a favorable outcome. I never forgot what it felt like to have a rich man muscle me out of a college education.

I flew to Washington, D.C., and caught a train to Quantico, Virginia, where I first encountered a marine drill sergeant. Turned out that my daddy didn't know the first thing about tearing into a young man's ass. I thought the devil wore a Smokey the Bear hat. They roughed up all of us candidates, gutted what was left of our egos, and left us to stand in the rain for half the first night while our Quonset huts aired out. They were all business—the discipline and humiliation business—tearing down each individual to rebuild us as marine officers.

Quantico refined my self-discipline and knowledge of how to be an effective member of a team. I also learned more about firearms. I qualified as an "expert" and "company high rifle" with the M-1 Garand. I ran a few rounds through .30 caliber machine guns, .50-cal Brownings, while I mastered the .45 Colt 1911-A1 pistol, the same weapon, generally speaking, that I relied on as a Texas Ranger.

At some point, our drill sergeants cut us loose with weekend passes. A fellow candidate from California and I were wandering around the Coliseum in D.C. when we saw on the marquee that country singer Jimmy Dean was taping a live appearance for his national television show. I liked Jimmy Dean all right, but Patsy Cline was the real attraction. We laid out a few wrinkled dollar bills and caught ourselves a show.

Roy Clark was on the bill, too, but a young, skinny brunette girl from Oklahoma stole the show. She wore a tight green squaw dress and had brown eyes warm enough to melt cold butter in a coffee cup. When her angelic voice lit into "How Many Arms Have Held You?" she owned my heart and anything else she wanted.

All of the performers put on quite a show, but none could touch the little Okie dynamo. When we left the Coliseum to return to base I looked up at the marquee to find her name: Shirley Conder Frazier. I'd look for her again.

After marine school, I returned home to Smyer. My mother had enrolled me in Texas Tech, but without the athletic program a college education seemed of little value. I'd shot myself just above the knee practicing quick draw about this time, so there I was, limping from one course to another like *Gunsmoke*'s Chester.

I'd always wanted to be a fighter pilot, and I took the first steps toward achieving that goal by applying with the navy recruiter in Lubbock. I was already 6' 3¾", when the maximum height for a pilot was 6'4". I performed wonderfully on the written exam, but washed out because I was deaf to high-frequency sounds. Too many guns without any hearing protection. No big deal, really. In another month or two I'd have been too tall anyway. I think of my fighter pilot ambitions as a boy's dream. For me, plenty of them would still come true.

THE MAKING OF A RANGER

I went through the motions of a student for a while, reining in my restless type-A personality behind a wooden desk, listening to some professor drone on about stuff a cowboy couldn't care less about.

Mercifully, my attitude toward higher education would change, and as an adult I would successfully pursue a bachelor's degree. But in 1956, I didn't have enough cotton bolls on the bush to haul a full trailer to the gin, if you know what I'm saying. Sometimes I have to look back on the decisions I made with a sense of wonder. A sense of humor helps, too. Lord, God, what a sap!

As I was stumbling along at Texas Tech, I ran into Delmer Tuggle. I'll be damned if Delmer wasn't wearing a snappy new Texas Highway Patrol uniform. Old Delmer's background was just as dusty as my own. We were handy with a hoe and a hammer and maybe a used shotgun and that was about it.

A job's a job where knotheads like Delmer and I come from, and a steady paycheck stamped with a government insignia looked like at least a few weeks of immeasurable wealth. In Delmer's line of work you could carry a gun, too. Seemed like a perfect fit for a fellow who was born too mean to hold on to a basketball scholarship, too tall to be a fighter pilot, too dumb to be a doctor, and too damn late to be a cowboy. I may have been graced with the sophistication of a feed sack back in 1956, but I still outflanked Delmer by taking the Border Patrol exam, largely because I had heard that G-men enjoyed better benefits.

The State of Texas phoned first. (Uncle Sam called later, but by then he was too late.)

A blizzard of paperwork blew my way. I tackled a number of academic and psychological tests. I endured a rigorous physical examination. The cleanliness, maintenance, and furnishings of my parents' home, according to my investigator, were "good." My home life seemed "well adjusted," complete with a "congenial atmosphere" and a good general attitude toward our neighbors, at least the ones who didn't owe us money. The investigator visited on a lucky day for the Jackson family and their ambitious, unemployed only son. I've never been certain that this fellow hit the right house.

I skated through the personal interviews, described by the department as "well-dressed," with a "quiet, reserved" personality. Not sure they had the right applicant. After considering the "community" attributes of honesty, sobriety, industry, intelligence, integrity, dependability, personality, credit, and congeniality, the interviewer typed "very good" on the solid black line. I don't reckon I've ever scored higher except maybe when I was born naked into this world, and my mama did the evaluating then.

The department investigated my scholastic record, my credit report (which in 1957 consisted of a single account from Thompson Hardware of Canyon, Texas, paid out as agreed at the rate of $5 per month), employment history, criminal record (ran a red light in 1953—one of the first I'd ever encountered as a licensed driver, as a matter of fact; along with a ticket for speeding in Lubbock in 1955), and my character and reputation, as reported by the leading citizens of Smyer (I received excellent recommendations, the first time all three of them had ever agreed on anything).

I began courses at the Department of Public Safety Training Academy in Austin on May 14, 1957. The DPS was formerly headquartered at the old Ranger Camp Mabry, but by then had moved into its modern brick-and-mortar campus in what was then far north Austin. Rustic Camp Mabry, now a Texas National Guard base, has aged far better than the austere, factory-like North Lamar Boulevard DPS headquarters built to replace it; architectural styles change along with everything else. But the new facility was a mighty impressive place when I stepped through its glass doors in 1957.

Sergeants Edwin Dewey Pringle and Albert G. Dalton were the monitors of my class of sixty-three buzz-eared student patrolmen. Proven veterans of the force, both monitors owned pump-house builds, humorless demeanors, flattop haircuts, eyes dead to anyone under twenty-one, and weathered complexions favoring a smoked ham.

Each week Sgt. Dalton checked off a thirty-two-category evaluation form that described an applicant's every conceivable attribute. It took more than a month for the old buzzard to give me a single "above average" rating. He once remarked, "This man is critical of any order that doesn't agree with him." I don't recall which incident provoked such disparaging commentary. Sgt. Dalton was one of the meanest-looking junkyard redneck bulldog son of a bitches I'd ever seen. I can assure you that if I understood the orders coming out of his meat-grinder mouth, I was jumping out of my drawers to agree with them.

Pringle and Dalton rode us hard. Our days were filled with classroom instruction on the Texas criminal statutes and penal codes, law enforcement techniques, driving and pursuit, first aid, procedural methods, ballistics, and firearms. In between classes, we either ran or exercised in the summer sun. At night, they woke us to climb on a reject Harley motorcycle and led us up and down the interstate, or worse, out Ranch Road 2222.

Unless you've ridden a fire hydrant across the potholes of hell you have no idea how rough a 1937 flathead Harley Davidson motorcycle drives. I'd sooner lie down with a diamondback rattlesnake than pop the clutch on one of these bone-jarring iron jackasses. Ranch Road 2222 features one of the most scenic views of the Texas Hill Country as it twists its way north to Lake Travis, but it's also one of the most dangerous roads in and around Austin. Failure to negotiate its banked, 90-degree curves or its steep, roller-coaster inclines yields one of two results: a head-on collision with a limestone bluff or a three-hundred-foot plunge through a dense cedar brake into Lake Austin. Swerve left or right as you will, you're dead soon after you leave the gravel shoulder.

For a twenty-one-year-old sodbusting farm boy clinging to the rain-soaked handlebars of that jackhammer on wheels, RR 2222 was a funeral procession waiting to happen. I longed to enjoy the relative calm of a thunderstorm on a mesa.

The look of abject terror pasted on my face delighted Pringle and Dalton. They chose the worst roads on the darkest nights in the worst weather conditions. If I heard rain on the dormitory roof, I knew they were coming for us. Due to their efforts in constantly probing for human weakness, half of my class either quit or washed out that summer.

Mercifully, the State of Texas had a shiny new white 1956 Ford two-door sedan waiting for me back on the High Plains in Brownfield. Over the years, I learned to appreciate the job Dalton and Pringle had done when it came to molding patrolmen. They were damn good fellas once they saw you as a peer. But my contempt for a goddamn motorcycle has never died.

I REPORTED TO SGT. HEWEY and Sgt. Black in Brownfield, under the auspices of Lubbock Highway Patrol Captain E. L. Posey. I partnered with Amos Egen, who influenced my early law enforcement career more than any other officer. Amos was on in years, had never seen a promotion in the department, and had no ambition other than to be a capable and just servant to the people of Texas. He was also a good husband and father. He was that steady sort who quietly commands respect because of the simple and honorable way he lived.

For the first three months, I followed Amos like a puppy, learning how to tell a professional whiskey smuggler from a dumbass kid on a drinking spree, when a man was on vacation or had just skipped bail, and when to arrest a suspect or give the poor bastard another chance. Amos did all the talking. I did all the observing. Law enforcement, as Amos saw it, was about how to walk a fine line between the Criminal Code and human compassion. He knew people, and he knew when it was time to slap the cuffs on them.

One day we pulled over this fellow who had obviously been drinking. At the time, the law enforcement community—and maybe society itself—was more naïve when it came to alcohol abuse. We had none of the sophisticated blood alcohol testing and videotaping methods in use today. We also didn't fully understand how alcohol and other drugs impair people's judgment and driving skills.

Back then a "driving while intoxicated" arrest boiled down to a judgment call by the officer about the motorist's ability to drive without endangering himself or others. The officer also factored in the subject's demeanor and whether he was someone we knew deserved to be arrested. A brief but costly stay in the Crossbar Motel is the best thing to straighten out some folks.

I was waiting for Amos to decide what was right for this particular driver when he stopped talking. He stepped back from the suspect's window and looked over the top of his sunglasses at me. He cleared his throat a couple of times before I understood that he wanted me to step in. That moment marked the crossing of a threshold in my career. I was no longer some farm boy jackass who needed a job. On that lonely, godforsaken stretch of highway I represented the State of Texas. The decisions I made each day would seriously affect a number of lives beyond my own.

Amos Egen taught me to never take that responsibility lightly, especially on that day. I arrested that guy. He was too drunk to drive. It turned out that he was a local politico. Amos told me that I'd made a good arrest but would never get the guy convicted. Sure enough, the county judge walked the suspect, just like Amos predicted. It was the second time I'd seen money talk and the primary reason I've always believed that politics and law enforcement don't mix.

Amos soon transferred to Pecos for a while before he finally made sergeant. He served his last years in Stephenville. He never handled the high-profile cases that make cops famous. You won't find his picture up on the wall at headquarters in Austin. Nobody wrote a book about him. But I'll tell you this: Amos Egen was one of the best officers—and the best men—that I ever knew.

I served nine unremarkable years as a state trooper, transferring from Brownfield to Littlefield, Texas. (Never seemed to stay out of a *field.*) Early on, I was still involved in enough off-duty hell-raising to inspire a little gossip around town. I drank little and only smoked the occasional cigar. I couldn't hang out in beer joints and whatnot because no good could come from that. Most of the gossip revolved around the several pretty young ladies I attended to.

My carousing ended during an ill-fated marriage when my spouse and I were too young to understand the commitment we had undertaken. I'm proud of the daughter this marriage produced—Kellye Danette. The rest I'd prefer to forget. I took a few lumps during this painful period and I learned from them. Enough said.

One woman in the community constantly called my supervisor to complain about my activities. I drank too much, she said. I was a blowhard and a bully. I didn't pay my bills. I abused my office. These accusations flew in and out of the sergeant's ear until one day she claimed that she'd caught me helping a friend move sheets of half-inch plate glass. This was moonlighting in uniform, a clear violation of department policy, and the informant decided to alert the upper echelon of DPS officials. She somehow reached the revered director of the department, Col. Homer Garrison Jr. She claimed that I was working three days a week at the Littlefield Glass Company.

Once again my sergeant was assigned to investigate. It didn't take him long to vindicate me. He knew the woman. I knew her, too. She was my grandmother, Ruby Marlin Jones Lollis Lee, who had left behind a string of ex- or dead husbands and many, many empty Mogan David wine bottles. She was a delightful woman when she was sober. But when she drank she turned demonic. May God bless her. I hope this tormented woman found peace.

I went to the American Legion dance with my old Ropesville friend and Korean combat veteran Don Osben, his pretty wife, and his sister on New Year's Eve in 1961. Old Joaquin cut some nifty grooves on the dance floor that night, but no sparks flew between Don's sister and me. I didn't pay any attention when the bandleader announced the addition of a woman singer, but I stopped cold when she broke into her first number. I'd heard that stunning voice before. Maybe on the radio. Maybe in some honky-tonk. I couldn't place it.

The singer was the most curvaceous, gorgeous, tightly packed stick of dynamite I'd ever seen. When she sang a couple of songs with the band, the hair stood up on the back of my neck. Then I connected all those sparks ricocheting around in my head. I'd heard her perform years ago with the Jimmy Dean Band. She'd knocked me out then. She did it again this time, only now her singing had little to do with it. Shirley Conder Frazier was, quite simply, a heart-stopping knockout.

Instincts sharp, hormones pumping, Joaquin was on point. I pasted an eye on her, waiting for the opportunity to pounce. Her boyfriend left her alone to pay their dinner tab, a fatal mistake. I swept in and escorted her out to the parking lot. Before I let her go she agreed to see me on my only day off. Speeders, smugglers, burglars, and felons of all types probably slipped right under my nose as the hours ticked along. For the next six days I was the worst damn patrolman in the state. I thought of nothing but the time I would spend with that stunning Okie singer.

When Thursday rolled around, I damn near scrubbed the hide off my bones as I bathed. I shaved my chin as smooth as a baby's ass. Slicked back my hair with "a little dab'll do ya." Sprinkled plenty of Old Spice on my manly chest, dressed in my finest shirt, slacks, and sport coat, and walked up to Shirley's apartment looking like the ladykiller I always wanted to be.

I'm loath to be cruel to those who still call Lubbock home, but back then unless you were inspired by straight crop rows or a packed feedlot, the only romantic place for miles around was Buffalo Lake. With electricity sparking between us, I hooked a beeline straight for it, stopping only at a Dairy Queen for a couple of Cokes and some ice water.

We found a remote place to park. I slipped a bottle of Jack Daniel's out of its brown paper sack and splashed a little into the Cokes. I made the fascinating small talk for which I had become notorious. I swear to you that shortly thereafter a full moon rose over the middle of that sparkling lake. For all Miss Shirley knew, I'd taken her to experience Lake Tahoe from my winter chalet. Everything was perfect. The moment was right. I leaned over for a tender first kiss.

She clammed up colder than a freshwater mussel. Those long fingers that should have been stroking my temples balled into a rock-hard fist. Her shoulder and jaw muscles tightened like rawhide. My law enforcement training told me that she was fixing to wallop me good if I didn't back off.

"Take me home!" she said, just like a rifle shot and just as final. Normally, I relied on quick thinking to get me through these moments of crisis, but I didn't have a clue what had gone wrong. Whatever it was, I didn't want to be arrested for it and have the sergeant back on my case.

I slipped the transmission into gear and watched the moon sink over Buffalo Lake in my rearview mirror. I was not known for reticence, however, so I kept on with the small talk. I learned that Shirley had been dating some of the more eligible men in our area, mostly flyboys from Reese Air Force Base with college degrees and sophisticated backgrounds—and fatter paychecks than a highway patrolman.

I was still a sap back then, but gradually the picture cleared. She was accustomed to the best restaurants, exclusive nightclubs, and first-run films. I, on the other hand, hauled her straight out to the only lake in Lubbock County for some serious mugging.

I told Shirley I could remedy that with another shot at romance. What I didn't say was I wasn't about to part company until she agreed to see me again. I had made up my mind.

Gradually relations improved between us. I showed up for dates with more money and less whiskey. Like my daddy before me I was a wizard on the dance floor. I loved country music and she loved to sing it. I took her to the best places I could afford, making sure that when she wasn't around I intimidated the hell out of her rubbernecking suitors. She saw me at my Smyer, Texas, best. But for her, I swore to get better.

On October 5, 1962, we were standing before a Lutheran minister at the home of Yvonne and Bob Kahn in Weatherford. The Kahns were about to become my sister- and brother-in-law. Not a single member of my family attended and maybe that was for the best. My parents were divorced. I was, for a time, alienated from my father. My mother had taken up with a drunk. Dorothy Gail and Jimmie Sue had married and lived too far away. I felt like I was on my own. The fact is that I was ready to start my own family, and I didn't care if my parents approved of Shirley or not.

I don't think Shirley's mother was enthusiastic about our chances for a successful union. She drank for the three days leading up to our wedding. She couldn't stop sobbing. She thought Shirley could do so much better than a highway patrolman, and I guess that I did, too. Nevertheless, I slipped a ring on Shirley Conder's finger and carried her off to honeymoon in Fort Worth. We checked into the first decent hotel and picked up on the plan I'd first formulated at Buffalo Lake. This time the law was on my side.

I had three days off to forge a bond that has lasted a lifetime. Shirley is and will always be everything to me. Roughly a year later, she gave birth to our son, the first baby I ever looked at when only the word *beautiful* came to my mind. We named him Don Joaquin Jackson.

I held that boy to my chest, thinking about all the years a happy family had eluded me. Love and contentment washed over me as I held my son in

Shirley Conder Frazier Jackson

my arms. He was the best of Shirley and me. All of a sudden I was the least important member of my immediate family.

NOT TOO LONG AFTER MY MARRIAGE I transferred again, from Littlefield to Jacksboro. New surroundings, same damn job. As I patrolled the highways of Texas in the new year of 1965, traffic supervision and my chronic complaint-filing grandmother were wearing hard on me. I was happily married but unfulfilled at work. There's no question that my performance suffered, largely because I wasn't doing what I wanted to do.

I was still ranked above average for law enforcement (receiving my lowest marks, of course, for "Care and Use of State Property"—I was always hell on a car). I wrote enough tickets to keep my sergeants happy, but my heart was no longer in traffic supervision. I felt a strong pull whenever I broke a smuggling operation, jailed fugitives, and assisted local law enforcement with felony arrests. I wanted to concentrate on the investigation of serious crime, and in this state that meant becoming a Texas Ranger.

In the mid-1960s the Ranger captains still recruited their own men. I'd learned at the DPS Student Training Academy that Ranger applicants needed to be at least thirty years old with a minimum of eight years of law enforcement experience. As I neared the threshold to qualify under both conditions, I spent my only day off making personal contact with Ranger captains around the state.

I soon learned that there were no vacancies in the Dallas–Fort Worth or Midland (West Texas) companies. Disheartened, I had a chance encounter in a Midland coffee shop with Texas Ranger Alfred Allee Jr., a young, fourth-generation Ranger. He suggested that I contact his father, captain of Company D in Carrizo Springs.

Captain Allee was well known by my generation of highway troopers. During a disagreement, he had pistol-whipped one of my colleagues. I assumed that highway patrolmen would be low on the list of suitable applicants for Ranger vacancies in Company D.

"Oh, no," Alfred Jr. said. "My dad likes troopers just fine. He just didn't like that one. I'll give him a call. And then you go down and see him."

That was all the encouragement I needed. After working a full shift the following Wednesday, I drove three hundred miles to a ranch ten miles north of Carrizo Springs to visit with Captain Allee and his wife, Miss Pearl. Since I wouldn't arrive until midnight, I suggested that I get a hotel room and meet with him first thing the next morning. Captain Allee wouldn't hear of it. And there he was, stepping out on the porch to greet me, when I shut off the car engine.

We talked until three that morning. Captain Allee finally stretched and stubbed out his cigar. "Levi Duncan is retiring from my company," he said. "I'm going to ask for you to take his place."

My heart liked to bullfrog right out of my throat. Captain Allee took note of my enthusiasm. He warned me not to get my hopes up. It was true that he could recruit men, but headquarters in Austin had to approve them. He said that his last appointment had not gone smoothly. He put up his candidate, a veteran lawman named Tol Dawson. But the citizen chairman of the DPS Commission, a wealthy, influential West Texas oilman, had written a name of some other guy on his sleeve. Guess who got the job?

I spent the better part of the next day hanging out with Captain Allee. Being a man of his word, he put my name in the hat. On March 27, 1966, all the Ranger hopefuls showed up in Austin alongside the captains who had appointed them to begin the selection process under the auspices of the DPS Commission, Director Homer Garrison Jr., and Assistant Director Col. Wilson Speir.

Every patrolman and Ranger I knew worshiped Homer Garrison, the man most responsible for modernizing the department and salvaging the Texas Rangers. We likewise respected Colonel Speir, who had come up through the ranks under Garrison and set the standard for leadership and initiative. Garrison and Speir made quite a team. I placed a great deal of trust in them both.

The variable was the three business-suited citizen-commissioner appointees. For a notorious talker, I tried to keep my interview answers brief. I had

The swearing-in of young Rangers at the Department of Public Safety Director's Office, Austin, Texas, April 1, 1966. From left to right: Joaquin Jackson, Bill Gunn, DPS Director Homer P. Garrison Jr., and Charlie Neal.

everything on the line. With ten applicants competing for four vacancies, I started to sweat out the interview like some guy who had farted at a funeral.

After it was over, I went home to my family and my job. Pretty soon I got the letter. I knew my life was about to change. I was sworn in by Colonel Garrison on April 1, 1966. Shirley, Don Joaquin, and I moved everything we owned in one load to the border country of South Texas.

On April 21, the telephone rang in my new home in Uvalde. Captain Allee ordered me to rendezvous with him in Carrizo Springs for a quick tour of the thirty-nine Texas counties that formed the jurisdiction of Ranger Company D. After one hell of a wild ride, we ended up in Cuero, where a crowd of striking textile workers planned to march on the county courthouse.

There were all the makings of a riot on my first day of service. There were two Texas Rangers and one local sheriff to face off with the mob. I couldn't imagine a better way to kick off a twenty-seven-year career than the three of us—me not knowing my ass from a pistol bore—dispersing that crowd without firing a shot or even making an arrest. Close enough to the legend for me.

I knew then that I was living my dream.

CHAPTER THREE

✪ Order before Law

Then I heard the voice of the Lord saying, "Whom shall I send?
And who will go for us?" And I said, "Here am I. Send me!"

ISAIAH 6:8

To UNDERSTAND MY EXPERIENCE in the Texas Rangers, you need to know
about what went on long before my time. The ranger tradition was
over five hundred years old before it took root in Texas in 1823. Rangers were
generally understood to be members of a military force that patrolled a large,
often hostile territory. They were typically citizens, often mobile, usually
volunteers, involved in an offensive strike deep into enemy territory or retaliation against an enemy that had struck their homes and villages. They
were partisans out for blood for as long as it took to get it or die trying.

The ranger concept followed my ancestors from Scotland and Ireland to
the wilderness of the New World, which presented new hazards and threats—
largely from the Indian nations that called the eastern seaboard home. The
contest would be long and bloody, and its rules would be vastly different
from what the colonials had known in Old Europe. The Indians were more
likely to attack in quick, slashing raids than in a pitched battle. The European immigrants learned hard lessons coping with Indian tactics in an alien
terrain. Those who survived adjusted their battle strategy.

There was almost always a professional military presence in the American colonies, but volunteer forces were also active on the frontier. Colonial
farmers not only warred with their Indian neighbors, they learned from
them, and in the process they transformed themselves into pioneers, or
frontiersmen—something far different from what their European-born parents had been. Descended from a long line of border warriors, born in blood
in a contested country, hardened and brutalized by their violent, wilder-

ness environment, they bore countless worries and many fears. But they seldom ran from either.

In 1670, Captain Benjamin Church organized a company of rangers to fight against the Wampanoag chief Metocomet in a conflict known as King Philip's War. Almost a hundred years later, during the French and Indian War, Maj. Robert Rogers of New Hampshire formed an effective detachment of frontiersmen and Indian scouts loyal to the English king to fight the French and their Native American allies.

During the American Revolution, six companies of frontiersmen organized into what George Washington described as the Corps of Rangers. Congress authorized twelve companies of Rangers to pacify and protect the frontier in the War of 1812.

In between formal wars and chronic informal feuds, the pioneers pushed against the backbone of the Alleghenies, the boundary the English king had forbidden them to cross. A few trespassed anyway, and those who survived reported back about the magnificent Eden that lay just over the great ridge.

After the American Revolution, the frontiersmen, who had mastered Indian warfare, saw no obstacles between them and the West. The most independent and intrepid followed Boone through the Cumberland Gap— at first in a trickle and then in a great flood until they spilled into the Mississippi River valley. Still they looked west to the endless plains.

These people considered themselves democratic, but no government ruled them. At best, constituted authority tried to keep up with them. When it came to the frontiersmen's protection, they looked after themselves. They called up their husbands, fathers, and sons to serve as their rangers. For the hopelessly outnumbered Indians the pioneers saw squatting between them and the raw, cheap land essential for their prosperity, there would be no mercy.

Soon the settlers confronted the western borders of America. Largely economic hardships pressured them to immigrate to another country for the second time in as many generations. The Mexican province of Coahuila y Tejas beckoned in a language the pioneers could not understand. They forded the Sabine River anyway with their wives and their children, and their slaves if they owned them—everything they thought they needed to farm land the Mexicans sold to them for only a few cents an acre.

They brought their guns, too. And they brought knowledge hard won from generations of warfare with the Indian nations. They pledged allegiance to the Mexican government and promised their faith to a Catholic God, and once they eyed the horse Indians, they swore they'd soon bury those magnificent heathens beneath freshly plowed fields. They'd do it, too, but it would cost them plenty.

The young Mexican Republic welcomed our ancestors, mostly because she was desperate to pacify her northern frontier. In the eyes of the Mexicans and the Spanish before them, the warlike, nomadic horse Indians were largely to blame for the slaughter of their citizens. All attempts by Spain to subdue the plains tribes by Bible or sword over the previous two centuries had failed. After 1821, the Indians were Mexico's problem, and Mexico decided to set loose some American settlers and see what happened.

The Mexicans sanctioned the Empresario system, allowing Stephen F. Austin to settle a few hundred Americans between the Brazos and Colorado Rivers. Despite her best intentions, the young Mexican Republic was ill prepared to administer the astonishing growth of the Texas colonies, let alone protect them. Stephen Austin became acquainted with a mounted cavalry unit of Mexican soldiers, vaqueros, and horsemen who occupied a failed, crumbling mission across the river from San Antonio de Bexar.

These were rangers in the best European and American tradition, local men who were adapted to their environment and skilled in war on the plains, willing to protect their families and friends at all costs, usually by a series of preemptive strikes against the Comanche, Kiowa, and Lipan Apache deep in their sanctuary of grass, the *llano estacado*. These guerrilla fighters rode fast horses and carried lances, smoothbore shotguns, and sharp knives. They terrified the Comanche and Lipan Apaches when few men could.

In 1823, adapting the Mexican methods for his own colonists, Austin offered to "employ ten men in addition to those employed by the government to act as rangers for the common defense." In response to depredations by the Tawakonis and Wacos in 1826, Austin proposed a force of "twenty to thirty Rangers in service at all times." Austin's act of self-determination was the dawn of the Ranger tradition as Texas would transform it. Almost 150 years later, this spark of light would shine down on me.

FOR AUSTIN AND ALL ANGLO IMMIGRANTS to Texas, perpetual skirmishes with the Indians would soon turn to all-out revolt against the Mexican dictator, Santa Anna. After Sam Houston's victory at San Jacinto, Texas established herself as an independent republic, which meant she would have to fight the Mexicans and Plains Indians at the same time.

Three proud, belligerent cultures waged genocidal war against each other for one land. Blood flowed over forty years with the Comanche and Kiowa, and over a hundred in one form or another with the Mexicans. This was the era of John Coffee "Jack" Hays, who set the standard for Ranger captains. Hays rained hell upon the enemies of Anglo Texas wherever they were by relying on the best weaponry technology in the hands of the toughest, boldest men.

Texas finally entered the American Union in 1845. No other state had been admitted with so much territory left unsettled and two disputed borders to defend. In annexing Texas, the United States had most certainly annexed war. Generals James K. Polk and Winfield Scott begged Texas to put men in the field against the superbly trained Mexican army. Texas sent Jack Hays and officers he had trained in campaigns against the Comanches—men like Ben McCulloch, Rip Ford, and Samuel Walker. The Rangers showed up with their Walker Colts, big-frame .44 revolvers heavy enough to club a man who wasn't worth shooting. For the Texans, what historians termed the Mexican War was just another row with their old enemies.

The Texas Rangers proved decisive in the Mexican War. Their superb scouting and intelligence allowed Polk to pick his ground in key battles. They hunted down the bands of guerrilla fighters that harassed Scott's supply lines in his campaign from Vera Cruz to Mexico City. American soldiers had never seen fighting men that looked as mean, moved as fast, and fought as hard as the Rangers. But they were so unmerciful against their Mexican enemies that Polk and Scott washed their hands of them all.

After the Mexican War, the U.S. government soon proved ineffective in pacifying Texas's contested frontier. Texas subsequently insisted on her right to deal privately with any threat. The young state picked through the best of her young men and unleashed them against the Mexicans and Plains Indians until the matter was settled. For Texicans the mandate was clear: order before law.

Before the turn of the nineteenth century, the Anglos emerged as the masters of Texas. Native American culture was wiped off the Texas map. Mexican Americans were cowed into a segregated society, while African Americans were introduced to the unwritten laws of Jim Crow. The Ranger companies, in one form or another, were constantly in the field—except during Reconstruction, when they were replaced by state police consisting of a few freed blacks and many Yankees, all of whom were unacceptable as peace officers to the majority of white Texans.

In 1874, the state authority organized the Frontier Battalion, a handful of Ranger companies that rode against smugglers, rustlers, renegades, gunmen, organized criminals, and feuding clans. The Frontier Battalion was under the auspices of the adjutant general's office, which meant that the Rangers were still considered a military force. Maj. John B. Jones, a rigid, bureaucratic officer whose management techniques began the Ranger evolution from guerrilla fighters to law enforcement officers, commanded his men as best he could.

In the meantime, a special Ranger force under the command of Capt. Leander McNelly, a former Confederate cavalry officer and ex–divinity school student, was cut loose in deep South Texas to put an end to the chronic border depredations. McNelly tamed the "Nueces Strip" with a ruthless efficiency. He died young of tuberculosis but lived long enough to shoot his way into Ranger legend.

Despite the Texas government's continual failure to properly support the Rangers, young men considered it an honor to ride for the state, at least for a little while, until the external enemies of Texas were laid low. When that was done, the Rangers policed the criminal element within their own citizenry.

Justice was in a rudimentary stage for the Frontier Battalion. The Rangers hauled suspects in for trial when they could but hanged them sideways in the South Texas brush when they had to and when nobody was looking or really cared. A "Ranger conviction" was often adjudicated from the bore of a Colt pistol. The Rangers performed their duties just as mainstream Texas desired, but often the ethnic minorities and labor organizations suffered terribly under their thumb. During this period the mandate shifted: now it was law before justice, not order before law.

There was never enough money in the state coffers to properly train, equip, and support Rangers in the field. As the twentieth century ushered in the modern age, budget restrictions had starved the Frontier Battalion down to its bare ribs. There was no longer a frontier per se, although there was still a surplus of criminals operating on an ever-widening scale once Henry Ford's Model-T hit the market.

The border violence, which had never been snuffed out, erupted again in Pancho Villa's time. The Feds passed the Volstead Act but did next to nothing to enforce it. Smuggling across the Rio Grande reached epidemic proportions, and with it spiked violent organized crime. Some Rangers were misused by politicians. Gov. Miriam "Ma" Ferguson fired all the Rangers who didn't quit in protest and handed out Ranger badges like cheap cigars to supporters and fat cats. Texans started to question what the Rangers were all about. They wondered if the Rangers had outlived their usefulness. From a public relations standpoint it was low tide for the legend.

Meanwhile, there was work to do. During the first third of the 1900s, different configurations of state police were commissioned to stamp out riots, organized crime rings, labor agitators, and industrial saboteurs. These state policemen were still called Rangers. They maintained their independent nature. There was no set uniform, no standard issue of weapons. They carried on.

In 1935 Texas consolidated its law enforcement agencies. What was left of the hard-used Rangers was transferred from the adjutant general's office to the Department of Public Safety. Romantics saw this move as the final blow to a fabled tradition, the death of the legend. As if I came into this world with the single purpose of proving them wrong, I was born this same year.

The director of the DPS was Homer P. Garrison, a man who looked like a cross between Dwight Eisenhower and J. Edgar Hoover. Garrison had a new vision for the Rangers. Texas was fast becoming an urban, industrialized society, but there were still remote, unsettled places and vast distances between them and state authority. Sheriffs were elected officials and, as such, were often untrained, ill-equipped, and subject to the whims of the local electorate. Garrison recognized the need for professional lawmen who would never mix law enforcement with politics. The state needed men to support local authorities, officers skilled in modern enforcement and investigative techniques who were as comfortable on horseback as they were in a Buick sedan.

Homer Garrison understood that Texas had not outgrown the Rangers; they just needed a little adjusting. The DPS director salvaged the best traditions of the service—namely, its independent nature, no official uniform, and sweeping jurisdictions—while he trained the new breed of Rangers that soon set the standard for a state police force.

I was one of three of the last Rangers inducted while Garrison was at the helm, and I was the last Garrison Ranger to retire. In the nearly sixty years between Homer Garrison's tenure and my retirement in 1993, what Garrison set in motion blew past us both in a technological blur.

It would have delighted the colonel to see a Ranger in a cowboy hat receive an e-mail on his laptop confirming that the suspect's DNA material matched that recovered at the crime scene. From the saddle to the cell phone, the end is still a good arrest. Today's Texas Rangers are everything Col. Garrison hoped they would be. They're what he wanted. If you live in Texas, they're what you need. And they're what I devoted my life to.

Read the history books to celebrate what we were—Walter Prescott Webb's *The Texas Rangers*, Robert Utley's *Lone Star Justice*, and Mike Cox's *Wearing the Cinco Peso: A History of the Texas Rangers*. Getting acquainted with the men who rode right into legend is well worth the time. But there's also something magnificent about the Rangers in the last half of the twentieth century.

That's where I came in.

CHAPTER FOUR

The Ghost and the Great Bear Hunt

1967

A S IS THE CASE IN MANY MURDERS, Leopoldo Ramos Flores knew his killers. A shallow, hand-dug grave indicated little planning before the act. Flores—a Mexican national—had obviously been smothered to death, but when the lab later reported a blood alcohol level of 0.11, I had to factor in drinking. An impulse acted on. A frantic, halfhearted attempt to hide the crime. The murderers' hasty escape across the Rio Grande in the hope that Mexico would protect them.

On July 6 I got the call from Uvalde County Sheriff's Deputy Morris Barrow, who met me at the scene. My investigation soon revealed that Leopoldo Flores, along with two young boys, lived and worked on the Cecil Reagan farm, where the South Texas chaparral of mesquite and prickly pear gave way to sandy loam and lush fields of corn, maize, and cotton, all ripening under the July sun. Leopoldo had been a loyal, longtime employee and one of Cecil's favorites. Soon after each payday, most farmworkers and ranch hands bought money orders with their earnings to mail home to waiting wives and worried parents. This fellow decided to have a few beers with his young coworkers before he sent the $300 he had earned over the last month. The casual decision to enjoy pleasure before business cost Leopoldo his life.

Two days later, his bloated, blistering body shoved nearly a foot of loamy soil up from his grave. The coyotes had taken an interest. Wild hogs could not have been far behind. Two sets of footprints and one drag mark connected the burial site to the metal barn where all three men lived in an old trailer. Two sets of tracks trotted south toward the Rio Grande and Mexico.

I swabbed Mentholatum ointment inside my particle mask to ward off the stench of decomposing flesh. Morris Barrow tried to help me unearth the body, but the noxious odor sent the young deputy to wrench his guts out under a mesquite tree. Decomposing gases had formed softball-sized blisters. In some places, the skin tore loose with the lightest pressure. I began to piece together a plausible scenario of the crime—a murder of opportunity for money; young, thoughtless boys with too many bad impulses mixed with too much drink. There was little pertinent evidence found with the body, but even in its advanced state of decomposition it appeared that the victim had not surrendered his life easily.

The local justice of the peace pronounced Leopoldo Flores dead at the scene. I took numerous photographs of the victim and the surrounding area. Then we gently rolled the body into a body bag and shipped it off to San Antonio's Dr. Vincent De Mayo, one of the best pathologists of his day.

The suspects took $300, an old transistor radio, and a pair of dress shoes.

FOR CLOSE TO TWO CENTURIES the people who call the Texas-Mexico border home have relied on each other. Nations can draw whatever line they like on the map, but the Rio Grande has never separated these reluctant neighbors as much as it has bound them together to create a unique culture. Academics claim that the border is the only place in the world where a developing nation neighbors a superpower. Perhaps Mexican dictator Porfirio Díaz summed it up best: "Pity poor Mexico. So far from God. So close to the United States."

I'm not sure the local residents have paid much mind to the diplomatic situation between the two countries. The irony is that while God and the Rio Grande joined them together, the same forces have isolated them from everyone and everything else. The border people live too far north for Mexico City to bother with them, and too far in the arid Southwest for Washington to be concerned. There aren't enough voters to interest the politicians. All the native vegetation features spines or thorns, and the fauna is cursed with venom, pincers, or claws. God forgets to let it rain. The mountains are crumbling. The rivers are dying. The soil blows away in scorching winds. The people are economic or political refugees who either believe a better world lies just across the river or who just naturally love it. I was born into the latter category when I was thirty-one years old.

Skeptics will tell you that greed lies at the root of the border economy— where Texas farmers and ranchers depend upon cheap migrant (and undocumented) Mexican workers. With human beings involved, most of the time it probably does. The last few decades have witnessed the rise of the notorious corporate-sponsored maquiladora system, designed to manipulate the absence of environmental and worker-friendly legislation. Maquiladoras are the totems of greed-based economics.

But I knew from the grief and anger on Cecil Reagan's face as he stood over Leopoldo's grave that these two men had transcended what had begun as a mercenary relationship—a wealthy Anglo Texan who profited from a Mexican's labor. Cecil cared for that man and he stated in clear terms that he wanted his murderers brought to justice.

"I'm not sure I can do that, Mr. Reagan," I said. "The killers are deep into Mexico by now."

"He was killed on Texas soil," Cecil said. "Surely the Rangers can do something."

This was most likely true, but I had no idea what that *something* could be. Owing to the bloodshed and animosity between our two countries the United States has never signed an extradition treaty with Mexico. I didn't speak Spanish well enough to negotiate a local deal with the *federales*. I was unfamiliar with Mexican society in general and with the structure of its law enforcement agencies in particular. I had no earthly idea what I could do to bring these murderers to justice.

But I looked into the face of an old man nearly in tears over the rotting body of his friend. "I'll get started on it right away," I said. "I'll let you know." I meant to figure out how to hunt those bastards down. The experience took me into a whole new world.

HOMERO MORALES NIÑO. Ramiro Niño Otero. Eighteen-year-old cousins from the neighboring villages of Hermanas and Qualles, respectively, in the Mexican state of Coahuila. These young men had left their homes while they were still boys to labor for $4 a day, earning maybe thirty bucks a week—and most of this they would send to their struggling families.

They were wiry, tough boys, the larger standing only 5'2" and weighing 120 pounds. They worked hard and spent just enough money to feed and clothe themselves, and on rare occasions maybe spring for a cold beer. They were accustomed to taking chances and looking after themselves, clinging to the simple faith that in the United States hard work wrought good fortune.

Homero Niño and Ramiro Niño Otero lived off their wits and resources in a country where they did not speak the language or understand the culture. They were as suspicious of Anglos as the locals were indifferent to them. They were kids in a foreign world with no family to guide them. Given the right situation—an environment where they thought no one was watching and, more importantly, in which no one would care, they were also capable of murder.

I soon pieced together a working sketch of Ramiro—the younger and smaller cousin. After two years of education he began his career as a sheep-herder in Hermanas. He worked for his grandfather until the old man passed on, and then in Ejido de Matas Corona as a field laborer. When his cousin Homero spoke of his lucrative, freewheeling experiences in the United States, Ramiro knew he had to go.

They paid five pesos each to ride in the back of Pedro Corrales's old green truck to Sabinas, and from there they caught a bus to Piedras Negras, where they sought out a dry, shallow spot in the river. Under cover of night, they crossed into the United States, walking through the brush near highways but never on them, heading for Cecil Reagan's ranch near Knippa, where they knew they could find work. They stopped only once at an unknown ranch to beg for food and water. The journey had taken seven days.

The immigrant workers were killers now—determined to avoid all efforts to capture them. Running them down across the river was not going to be easy.

I spent a few days piecing together all the information I could about the crime. When I knew who I wanted and where they'd fled I drove down to inform my captain, who was probably hosing off the latest coat of Chicano militant José Angel Gutierrez's urine from the Ranger Company D sign. (These two political adversaries were locked into a dance of mutual scorn and confrontation that included Gutierrez's pissing on the sign to provoke Captain Allee. It usually worked.)

By then I was already mighty fond of Captain Allee. He'd lived long enough to see the world of South Texas that had spawned him reinvent itself. Toward the end of his career, he couldn't understand the changes swirling around him. Capt. Allee was sixty-two in 1967 (although no one knew for sure); however, he was still all man and in firm command of his company. After I'd spent twenty-four hours with that man, I would have followed him into hell with a hotdog. I don't know a single Ranger who served under Captain Allee and didn't respect and admire him. But me? I came to love him like the father I lost to the Depression and to the great drought of the 1950s.

I laid out the facts of the Flores murder to this veteran Ranger and then waited for his advice.

"Well, what're you planning to do, Joaquin?" Captain Allee said in that folksy manner that in an instant could contort into the most godawful interrogation.

"I'd like to haul them son of a bitches in front of a U.S. judge and quick," I said. "Who's gonna know if I just go down there and fetch 'em?"

"Not me, that's for sure," he said. "'Course the Mexicans might tend to frown on that sort of thing."

"Oh," I answered. "Didn't figure on that."

"Plus, you don't speak Spanish for shit, so how you gonna operate down there?" I heard him scratch a match before he lit his cigar. "'Course, I know a man down there that you can call for help. He'll tell you how these things are done. And when he does, you best do exactly what he says." He hesitated a moment, peeling back the blinds in his obsessive vigil for José Angel Gutiérrez, and then he added, "Do what you gotta do, but don't let me hear that you took your state-owned vehicle into Old Mexico."

"Oh, no, sir, Captain," I replied. I jotted down all the extra digits of the phone number and made a call to a Mexican national who would become one of my best friends. Pretty quick I had myself an international investigation in progress.

IT'S HOT DOWN HERE—up to 110 degrees and more in the summer. I had traded a Model 94 Winchester .30-30 carbine for the aftermarket air conditioner that was installed in my 1966 Plymouth four-door sedan. The flow of cool, clean air was more important to me than the tires. As I pulled up to the pontoon bridge that spanned the Rio Grande at Piedras Negras, I couldn't see letting all that comfort go to waste while I bounced around in some old bus with my skin stuck to a vinyl seat. I took my foot off the brake and idled on across.

Piedras Negras claimed a population of around 30,000 at the time. There were no tall bank buildings or churches, just acres of bright adobe buildings, some rising to three stories, many painted the colors of the Mexican flag. Among their many qualities, the Mexican people are staunch patriots.

My trunk carried the usual array of weapons and ammunition and emergency supplies. I unbuckled my gun belt and unpinned my badge. I was on Mexican turf, and Captain Allee had warned me that flaunting either would offend law enforcement officials south of the river. I tucked the Colt pistol inside my belt behind my back, and drove on.

Mindful of escaping air-conditioning, I cracked the window just enough to speak through it when I reached the border guards and customs officials.

"Buenos dias, señor," they said.

"Howdy," I said and lit a cigar.

"*Adónde vas?*" they asked. Where are you going?

"Esperanza," I said, a small mining town in Coahuila, home of Captain Allee's contact, a captain in the Mexican state police. "Nueva Rosita after that."

"What is the nature of your visit to Mexico?" one asked in perfect English.

"Pleasure," I said. Which was true. I derived great joy from investigating crimes and arresting their perpetrators, Mexican or otherwise. They couldn't possibly have believed that I was on a vacation, but they didn't seem inclined to belabor the point.

"Anything to declare?" the customs officer asked.

"It's mighty hot down here," I said, and I cranked up the air conditioner another notch. The Mexicans agreed and waved me through. I wondered what all the fuss was about when it came to pursuing Mexican suspects. Nice enough fellows in uniform down here. Air conditioner worked great. Crossing the border couldn't be any more convenient. Of course, I'd soon learn that getting out is a whole lot different than getting in.

LIKE THE UNITED STATES, Mexico fields layers of police with overlapping jurisdictions and specialized areas of crime. *Policía municipales* are your uniformed city cops. *Policía transito* are akin to our state highway patrol. The old Policía Federale de Camino belonged to the federal authority and enforced traffic laws on federal highways. Next is the Policía Federale Preventivos, a cross between the Border Patrol and U.S. Customs. There is also the Mexican Federale Judiciales Policía, or the MFJP, the force most closely related to our own DEA and recently celebrated by Benicio del Toro's character in the extremely realistic feature film *Traffic*. The screenwriter obviously did his homework. Last, one encounters the PJE (Policía Judiciales de Estado), state plainclothes officers who investigate serious crimes like homicide and robbery. These independent, locally bred, field-trained, street-smart professionals are the cream of the crop, the Mexican version of the Texas Rangers. I understand that there has been a reorganization of these agencies, but this was the structure I encountered in 1967.

Into this mix one has to add the Mexican army, as its portrayal in the movie *Traffic* shows. I can't explain how it all works and who steps on whom, but I know when I die I want to come back as a Mexican general. They wield more power than any other human beings I've ever seen.

Woe to the common criminal or drug smuggler, muckraking journalist, political reformer, or DEA informant who blinks on a general's radar screen. A phone rings. Inquiries are made. There's a quick check to see who's protected and who's wide open for swift and appropriate action. Once everyone understands the situation and the risk involved, things happen in the Mexican desert. And after they do, no one saw anything. No one talks.

But I didn't know any of this in the summer of 1967, when I was a young Ranger with less than a year of service under my belt. I just knew I was going to see a man who promised to help me arrest two murderers. With my blinders strapped on, I was oblivious to the potential for personal and professional disaster. At the time, seemed like everything was going pretty well.

CAPTAIN FELIPE ZAMORA supervised a detachment of state police officers who worked cattle thefts, I believe, under the PJE umbrella. Zamora was around fifty when we met. His salt-and-pepper hair lent an air of distinction to his already immaculate, solidly built frame. He walked with a sure-footed grace and spoke meticulous Spanish in a deep baritone voice. He had bright, piercing eyes that bespoke intelligence and hard-won wisdom. I liked him immediately.

Zamora and I discussed our mutual business sitting beneath portraits of the governor of Coahuila and Gustavo Díaz Ordaz, the Mexican president, and a rack of AK-47's and Remington riot guns. Zamora said that he had arranged for me to meet a colleague who would help me locate the suspects. He advised me to strap on my pistol and Ranger badge before we left, and I did so.

Like the Rangers, Zamora favored the Model 1911 Colt .45 auto with gorgeous custom grips of silver and gold, which he stuffed cocked and locked inside of his belt—and so did the smaller man who shadowed Felipe everywhere he went. The bodyguard moved slowly through the door with Felipe following. Out of habit, they both scanned the street for signs of trouble. Cops like to see those traits in other cops, so I took a good gander myself just to let them know I was on the job, too.

Liking Zamora was one thing; trusting his judgment was another. This Mexican captain quickly put me at ease. I don't know why he needed a bodyguard, but he'd found a damn good one. The guard walked in silence behind Zamora and never interacted with him. He wore a black cowboy hat, faded Levi jeans, and black boots that showed heavy spur wear. He carried a .45 Colt automatic pistol, also with grips of sterling silver, stuck into the left side of his belt so that he could pull it with either hand. A double-edged Walden knife hung in a sheath from his waist. He had ink-black hair and piercing obsidian eyes—and a demeanor that more than suggested he'd kill any man who made the first move against his captain. He was incredibly subtle and unassuming about his mission, though. After a while, it was like he wasn't there at all. I nicknamed him the Ghost.

Every once in a while, in response to Zamora's patient instructions, the Ghost grunted, "*Si, Jefe.*" And *nada mas.* Felipe and I climbed into his state-issued 1966 Dodge pickup. The Ghost crawled into the bed, his back against the cab, a Winchester rifle lying across his lap.

Zamora checked me into the local hotel, where I enjoyed excellent service. As soon as I was settled, we went and had dinner together. Felipe ordered Tecate beer and Herradura tequila for us both. I've never again seen tequila like that. It was milky white and satin smooth. I never drank in the service of Texas, but what the hell? If this was the way Mexican cops conducted an investigation, who was I to question them? Then came the sizzling steaks. To this day I prefer Mexican-raised beef grilled over coals of Mexican mesquite.

Felipe surrendered his fork and pushed back from the table. He fixed me with smiling eyes. "So," he said. "How did you ever get a name like Joaquin?"

They always ask. I always tell them about my dad's mystery University of Texas Longhorn football player and then move on.

After the meal, we drove together to Nueva Rosita, Coahuila, in search of the *comandante* of city police, Xicotencote Flores. This fella cut a striking figure. He stood over six feet tall and weighed over two hundred solid pounds. Probably the same age as Felipe. His sandy brown hair was splotched with gray. He had a peculiar ruddy complexion with bright red veins running down his pocked, weathered face, which was highlighted by intense green eyes. A country boy like me couldn't begin to speculate on his ancestry, but with a name like Xicotencote, I imagined him as the descendant of some Aztec warlord who'd once gone on an Irish vacation.

When Felipe and I arrived, Flores had three terrified young boys corralled in his office. The *comandante's* interrogation methods seemed simple but quite effective. The suspects stood at attention while he sat at his desk and read to them from a thick black book. I assumed that he was advising them of their rights, a fact I found refreshing given that Americans had only recently instituted a suspect's Miranda warnings. I learned later that Flores was making sure those boys understood that lying to him would cost them five long years in the Mexican penitentiary. Then Flores asked them the whereabouts of their relatives, the suspects Morales and Niño. Those scared little boys coughed up everything they knew in a hurry.

Flores regarded them in silence. I felt like they were telling the truth, and I guess Flores did, too. After a stern warning, he had them escorted out.

"I'll need a few days, Señor Jackson," he said.

"Take as long as you want," I said. "I can come back."

"The price," he said, "will be $300 a head."

Captain Allee had warned me of the going rate for a captured fugitive on the freelance plan, a fact I had explained in some detail to Cecil Reagan, who agreed to foot the bill.

"We're good for it," I said. We shook hands. And that was it. I told Felipe Zamora that I looked forward to our next visit and headed for the border.

Six miles shy of Piedras Negras, I came across a Mexican customs checkpoint. Its agents appeared to take a special interest in me. When they pulled their pistols and pointed them in my face, there was little doubt of that. The senior officer wove his way through the gun barrels and motioned for me to carefully roll down my window. The air conditioner was working great.

"Would you mind following me to the *comandante's* office in Piedras Negras?" he said, his beseeching tone inconsistent with the appearance of all the hardware. All of this seemed so unnecessary, since I was headed to Piedras Negras in the first place.

"What gives? Am I under arrest or what?"

"On, no, Señor Ranger. You are our guest. The *comandante* merely wants to visit with you."

"Well, sure," I said. "Guess I've got a little time."

"That's good," he said.

Our procession soon arrived at Piedras Negras, and I was unceremoniously deposited in the lobby of the police station. Some of my new friends sat around me, pistols in hand. It was hot, a stale, stifling heat, and I wasn't there long before I began to miss my air conditioner. The way those municipal cops were bird-dogging my state unit, I really felt like I was about to be literally missing my air conditioner. Minutes ticked into hours, and I asked if I could call Captain Allee back in Carrizo Springs.

"That won't be necessary, Señor. Only a few minutes more."

An hour or so later my patience gave out. This time I insisted on calling my captain. I hope to God I had a look in my eye that served as a dire warning to these bastards. Soon, the *comandante* arrived with formal but friendly greetings, apologizing for the delay, as he had many pressing matters on his hands. Mexican officials are always so goddamned polite when they jack you up that it takes a while to sink in. When I'd had enough, they decided it was time to get down to business.

This officer, far more delicate than Zamora and Flores, informed me that he had been in communication with his superiors in Monclova, the capital of Coahuila, about my unauthorized investigation. I explained that the state authorities in the jurisdiction where the suspects most likely were hiding had authorized my visit. I had followed Felipe Zamora's instructions to the letter.

The officer slowly shook his head. He understood my ignorance, but from now on they needed me to be aware of proper procedure. I was to obtain their permission before I began any sort of investigation, which would allow them the opportunity to explore how best to assist me. Who could argue with that? I apologized and assured them that we could easily avoid these types of bureaucratic misunderstandings in the future.

I was escorted to my state unit, where I was relieved to find my air conditioner still intact and operational. I got in and cranked her up. I was about to kick her into gear when one of the Mexican officers rapped his knuckles against the window.

"Pardon me, señor, but do all Texas Rangers have air-conditioned cars?" He stuck his hand in to feel the flow of cool air.

"Damn right we do." I lied to that poor bastard and flew that Plymouth across the bridge without ever looking back.

I headed to Quemada, just fifteen miles north of Eagle Pass, where Deputy Barrow lived with his mother. I wanted to bring him up to speed on the investigation, which I did over some slow-grilled, mesquite-smoked barbecue brisket. I don't know why I don't weigh three hundred pounds after twenty-seven years of similar investigative habits. Before I'd wiped my chin, I got a call on the radio from Uvalde that Comandante Flores had already rounded up one of our suspects and wanted me to return to Nueva Rosita for a positive ID.

I crossed the Eagle Pass bridge to Mexico that same night. It was too late to stop by the Piedras Negras *comandante*'s office and let them explore ways to assist me. I blew right through town and into the Mexican desert.

Turned out that Xicotencote had rounded up the wrong two guys. I headed home, reaching Piedras Negras shortly after dawn. If the local cops seemed incredulous at my reappearance at that early hour, at least they didn't invite me to be their guest. One waved me through. Another picked up the telephone. I crossed the river and headed north for Uvalde and home.

On July 27, the phone rang in my office. In his monotone voice, Xicotencote Flores informed me that he had Ramiro Niño in custody and could deliver him later that day to the International Bridge at Piedras Negras. I called Cecil Reagan, who seemed more than happy to put up the bounty money, and then "hooked 'em" over to meet Comandante Flores.

Flores was parked in his blue Chevrolet sedan in the middle of the makeshift pontoon boat. He wore khaki from head to boots and for some reason was always bareheaded. When I first laid eyes on Ramiro, I was struck by how young and innocent he looked. He was also scared. I'd have felt sorry for him if I hadn't dug up Leopoldo's festering body a few days before.

I slipped three crisp $100 bills into Flores's hand, and he promptly stuffed them into his pants pocket. "Gracias, Señor," he said, unlocking his cuffs from the suspect's wrists. I thanked Flores, slapped my cuffs on Ramiro, and loaded him into my car.

Since I had a warrant for Ramiro Niño Otero's arrest, I saw no reason to register him as an illegal alien at the American port of entry. I had him arraigned by the local magistrate in Eagle Pass and then carted him to Uvalde for a second preliminary round with the judicial system. The jailer notified the local Border Patrol agent, who processed Otero behind bars. U.S. Immigration later raised a minor stink about how I smuggled the suspect out of Mexico, but I didn't care. A murder in Texas has nothing to do with the Feds.

That same day Ramiro confessed to the whole affair. He denied, however, that this crime had anything to do with the $300, the radio, or the pair of shoes. Niño claimed that Leopoldo was a very disagreeable man. They argued almost every day, especially he and Homero, usually over who would cook the evening meal but very often because Leopoldo disapproved of the cousins' work ethic.

On July 4 Homero and Niño had worked all morning. They stopped to rest and drink a little beer. That evening Leopoldo returned to the trailer. He took off his shoes and shirt as was his custom and sat next to Homero on the sofa. Ramiro cooked their dinner.

Leopoldo didn't know that two days before Homero had proposed killing him for his money. The two men got into their customary argument over who was lazier. When Leopoldo rose to go into the back of the trailer, Homero attacked him from behind, pummeling him until Leopoldo crumpled to the floor.

Niño claimed that he was about to run to Cecil Reagan for help when Homero threatened him with Leopoldo's fate. Niño watched helplessly as Homero stiff-armed a cloth against Leopoldo's mouth and nose until he quit breathing. After that, they were on the run until they got home to Mexico.

On the last day of July 1967, I learned that a game warden had arrested Homero Morales Niño in Bandera County. I picked him up that day and took him to be arraigned in Uvalde. The cousins were tried a year later and sentenced to thirty years each. Though there were a number of conflicting statements in their respective confessions, both of these boys agreed that Leopoldo Ramos Flores had been most disagreeable.

Among Leopoldo's meager personal possessions left behind by his murderers, I found the following unmailed, handwritten letter:

May 10, 1967

Mrs. Candelaria Falcon Zertuche:

I am writing this letter in the hopes that you and your wonderful family are all fine.

I want you to do me a favor and go to the house of Uncle Chuy Apriola. Please ask him to loan me some money to pay the store where I owe. Tell him also that I have had some good luck since I came from Jimenez and that I have been living like a real king. With God's help, I intend to stay three or four months more. . . .

I am getting so fat off much meat and sausage that I eat here. At first I had not found a job, but now I am working. I want you to place a one peso candle to the Virgin of San Juan.

Also, give my best regards to Mr. Jesus Fernando and to all his family. And do me a favor and tell him to loan you twenty pesos besides the money he has already loaned me. And do me the favor of asking him if the girl from Moral, Coahuila has answered me and if she has I want you to do me the favor of sending me the letters she has answered.

Here I am smoking cigars.

And I had not written because there was no one to do it for me. I am poor at writing and here at work there is not any time to write letters only during the night. I want you to answer to this address:

Cecil Reagan; Knippa, Texas; 78870

This is all for today, with nothing I will depart.

And I want you to answer me and tell me if he loans you the money so that when I return I will have the money to repay him.

Respectfully yours,

Leopoldo Ramos Flores.

Does he sound disagreeable to you?

A strange thing happened to me whenever I conducted a murder investigation. I tended to find myself standing in the shoes of the victims. I tried to understand the life they lived, maybe even get a feel for how they viewed the world. Leopoldo's murder, like many others, made me angry. He could not avenge himself. In my jurisdiction he had been "living like a king." I felt like there could be no peace for him or for me until his killers were brought to justice. Maybe Felipe Zamora and Xicotencote Flores were motivated by these same emotions, this nagging sense of loss for people they never knew. I worked homicide for twenty-seven years. It never got any easier.

ABOUT A YEAR AFTER THIS CASE I got a call from Comandante Xicotencote Flores. He wondered if I knew where he could buy a Thompson submachine gun. The sheriff of Medina County was in the process of upgrading his arsenal and was selling his collection of Thompsons for around $300 apiece. While I assured Xicotencote that I was comfortable brokering the sale, there was no way I could cross the border with the weapon. I told him he'd have to come to the United States and pick it up himself.

"I'm afraid that's not possible," he said in a tone more morose than usual. Turns out that he was in the hospital with a bullet wound in the leg.

The *comandante* of Piedras Negras was well aware that I had returned to Mexico without his permission and that Xicotencote had delivered the prisoner to me for a fee in the *comandante*'s jurisdiction. I don't know how the Mexican law reads in matters like this, but neither Felipe Zamora nor Xicotencote Flores seemed much hampered by it when it came to supplementing their salaries with American bounty money. From the beginning, I saw Felipe Zamora as an extremely professional friend. Xicotencote, however, was a colleague, a highly skilled bounty hunter, a mercenary for hire, but of the highest integrity. He was good for his word, and that's what mattered most to me. But he wasn't worth a damn at allowing the Piedras Negras jefe to explore ways to assist him.

When it came to the bounty earned by *comandantes* of rival districts, there was the matter of *la mordida*, "the bite," those occasions when a percentage of one's cash needs to be slipped into the right hand to grease any transaction along. For better or for worse, it was a time-honored custom in Mexico. Americans are appalled by what they view as base corruption. The Mexicans see it as a fact of life, just another method to spread the wealth, and as a way to ensure that people who rise to prominence get their tribute.

Xicotencote Flores routinely passed through Piedras Negras to deliver his fugitives and claim his fee. The act itself was probably no big deal, but refusing to offer up *la mordida* to his Piedras Negras counterpart for the right to trespass on his turf was a serious breach of Mexican custom.

The entire reason I was detained while they explored ways to assist me was to send a message to Xicotencote. I don't think my colleague cared what they did. He felt like bounty money belonged to him and that's where he left it.

Xicotencote was delivering a U.S. citizen to the FBI to claim $1,000 (Feds always pay better) when a number of local Piedras Negras cops confronted him. Their long-festering disagreement quickly escalated into violence. For my part, I'd rather slap the devil than tangle with Xicotencote Flores. The fugitive was killed at the scene, along with two or three police officers. Several others were wounded, including Xicotencote, who managed to cross back into his jurisdiction of Allende, Coahuila, in his bullet-riddled vehicle.

While still on the operating table, he placed that phone call to me, looking for the Thompson. The *comandante* of Piedras Negras had no idea who he was fooling with. But a second confrontation in the feud never materialized. Xicotencote never arranged to buy the Medina County sheriff's machine gun. His heart gave out before he recuperated, and as far as I could tell that was the end of the police turf wars. I can tell you for certain that when Xicotencote Flores died, an era passed with him. You won't find cops like him anymore on either side of this troubled border.

Had he lived a little longer, however, I have no doubt that the blood would have run in the streets of Piedras Negras. Xicotencote was born with muscle, courage, heart, and honor. He was not the kind to walk away from a fight. He'd formulated a detailed plan for revenge. It included a used Thompson machine gun, a hundred-round drum magazine, and a short trip to a hot, dusty border town.

FELIPE ZAMORA AND I maintained our friendship over the years. I continued to visit his home in Esperanza, Coahuila, often accompanied by Shirley. On warm days, we enjoyed Felipe's favorite swimming hole, where a clear mountain river cut a bank into the foothills around Musquez. We'd flop down on a blanket under a cottonwood and sip ice-cold Tecate beer and a squeeze of lime and watch the other Mexican families play together in the river.

Felipe and his wife also shared our home in Uvalde. Generosity emerged foremost among his many admirable Mexican traits when he presented me with a gold, seventeen-jewel Illinois brand pocket watch, and, most stunning of all, a set of silver-and-gold pistol grips for my Model 1911 Colt Commander—similar to those that adorned his pistols and the Ghost's. He gave the equivalent of $35 in Mexican money for these unique treasures, which were handcrafted and engraved by a prisoner in the Mexican prison system. I still carry this weapon.

I reciprocated as best I could on a Ranger's salary by slipping into Uvalde's Slades Western Wear to let Felipe pick out a fine Stetson hat. He wore it every time we got together. I hope he still does.

Most of my adventures with Felipe enriched my life beyond measure. One particular expedition, however, has always haunted me. I've always appreciated the great beauty of the desert mountains of northern Mexico, *la frontera,* that I knew as a young Ranger. I've always sensed the warmth and joy of the people who made that hard land their home. But one as affectionate for the Mexican land and culture as I am also has to come to terms with cruel and tragic circumstances. It seems to be a feature of this unusual world. I've seen some bad things in my life. With time, most of them fade. This one never has.

In the fall of 1967, Felipe Zamora invited me and a few close friends to hunt black bear on his ranch in the Carmen Sierras. Except for respected rancher and gun dealer Wesley "Bubba" Kyle, the American guests were all South Texas lawmen—Vance Chisum, Uvalde chief of police, Uvalde County Sheriff Kenneth Kelley, "Little Alfred" Allee, son of my captain, also a Ranger stationed in Ozona, Texas, and Ben Salinas, a rough old rodeo hand who got himself elected as sheriff of Maverick County.

We had all grown up in the Big Country living and working on ranches, listening to the stories of old cowboys. But times were changing fast in 1960s Texas, even in our brush country ranch jurisdictions. We knew we could cross the border into Old Mexico, drive through the busy cities along the Rio Grande, enter the desert and the blue mountains that lay shrouded on the horizon, and journey back a hundred years to the West our grandfathers had known. What young man could pass that up? Plus, it was a bear hunt. I'm a lifelong hunter, and I'd never hunted black bear.

We gathered at the home of a general in Piedras Negras. A good friend of Zamora's, the general presented us with handwritten permits for our handguns and rifles. We later slipped the papers to incredulous customs officers who said, "*Pasale, pasale,*" and waved us through. We bounced along pockmarked highways in two pickups, their beds stuffed with worn saddles and bright tack, boxes of groceries, and ice chests full of Pabst Blue Ribbon beer. It feels great to be with good friends with a hunt ahead of you.

We rendezvoused with Felipe Zamora and an attorney friend of his who was part owner of the ranch. As always, the Ghost shadowed Felipe wherever he went. I started to take a real interest in this saturnine man. I planned to find out how good he was at his job.

Ninety miles due west of Musquez stood the Carmen Sierras, a 6,000–8,000-foot-high range of bald faces, sharp slopes studded with piñon and juniper, and thicket ravines and foothills choked with white oak and pine trees. The range reminded me of the Davis Mountains—an area of rare beauty in West Texas.

Our group relished the ranch's spartan accommodations. The permanent staff consisted of a few families headed by vaqueros who spent their entire lives living in grass *jacales*. One of the mothers drew water from the *olla*, the large clay reservoir near the well. She entered the house with a worried look on her face. I could hear her speaking in soft tones to someone. I thought I heard a child moan. The rest of the staff seemed genuinely glad to see us, constantly flashing their bone-white teeth as they helped us settle in.

The ranch headquarters was little more than a large, tin-roofed adobe barn with a fireplace and a long dining table. We slept together on a dirt floor in an area that opened to the cool mountain air. Felipe threw his bedroll down on a cot. The Ghost rolled out a blanket beside his *jefe*.

The vaqueros rounded up the rancher's *remuda*—the horse herd—and drove the mounts into the mesquite-walled pen. Felipe and his partners owned many fine horses—small Spanish ponies, quarterhorses, and even a few thoroughbreds. A muscular 15 1/2-hand paint gelding caught my eye, and one of the vaqueros motioned that when the time came I could throw my saddle over his back.

I looked over those grand surroundings. In late afternoon, the clouds cast gray creeping shadows on the slopes. The rest of that country seemed to throb with green and gold, all growing brighter as the sun sank. I couldn't wait for dawn to strike off while the mountain air was still cool and the peaks were shrouded in mist. I could probably ride for a week and never hit barbed wire. I planned to find out for sure. I didn't care if I never saw a bear.

We saw to our gear, tack, and weapons while the vaqueros slit the throat of a young Spanish nanny goat, careful to catch every drop of blood in an old pewter pot. They dressed the animal with sharp knives, and dumped the viscera into a bucket. All the organs—the intestines, heart, kidneys, liver, etc.—were carefully separated, washed in well water, and set aside for later use. Then they peeled back the goat's hide, quartered it, stuffed the parts, the head included, into separate wet burlap sacks. They buried all of it in a hole several feet deep, layered with mesquite coals and sheets of tin.

The aroma of the goat filled the night air as we slept, with only the mountains between us and the stars.

Except for the Ghost, who did not sleep at all.

He sat on his blanket next to Felipe's cot with arms around his knees and his back against the cool adobe wall. Across his lap lay a .30-30 Winchester rifle. His Model 1911 Colt .45 automatic sat on his holster, cocked and locked, ready for God knows what. Even after the long journey, a few shots of fine tequila, and the cool mountain air breeze gently rattling the roof, I did not sleep well. Perhaps it was the strange surroundings. Perhaps my senses were overwhelmed because of the strange, exotic place. Regardless, I awoke at roughly two-hour intervals all night long. Each time, I looked for the Ghost to see if I could catch him napping. I never did. He stared back at me with eyes darker than wet, week-old coals. The Ghost was one of the few people my size and professional demeanor could not intimidate. He left it to me to break eye contact and roll over.

BEFORE DAWN, HOSTS AND GUESTS sat down to breakfast, prepared by the wives of the vaqueros, who must have been up for two hours. I never heard them smack a spatula against the slick iron metate as they grilled hand-rolled flour and corn tortillas.

Felipe's attorney friend sat at the head of our table as the women dished out scrambled eggs and *chili macho*. He motioned for us Texans to dig in. Soon the vaqueros entered. The ranch hands presented the Spanish goat to their jefe. They seemed proudest of the skull arranged in the center with a clean machete gash splitting it in two. Always the gracious host, the attorney went down the line offering us first dibs on the brains. The tequila from the night before roiled in my stomach. With regret, I passed and tore into a warm tortilla. The other Anglos followed my lead.

The attorney didn't seem too disappointed. He skewered the eyeballs first and popped them into his mouth. I nearly spewed just watching him. He was about to tear into the brains when I rose from the table. I took slow, deep breaths of fresh mountain air and threw my saddle on the paint.

The others joined me after breakfast. I filled my canteen with fresh water from the well, packed a few tortillas in my saddlebags, strapped on my leggings, lit a cigar, and cast an eye to the high country. God, what scenery! And I saw it all from the back of a fine paint horse.

I HEARD THE SHOT late in the afternoon on the second day. The vaqueros had the bear hung up by its hind legs as Sheriff Kelley watched. Kelley talked a little trash to us about his success, as boys sometimes do. I watched them skin the beast—a series of quick, busy knife strokes as they stripped the fur from the flesh. The carcass looked human when they were done. I'd seen a few bears, but I couldn't get a clean shot. Looking at Kelley's bear, I wasn't sure if I'd pull the trigger even if I got the chance. Probably would, though. I didn't think twice about sport killing when I was young. I do now. Without prompting, Sheriff Kelley gave the bear's meat and hide to the vaqueros and their families. After the goat incident, we knew none of the bear would be wasted. I tipped back a shot of tequila to honor his generosity.

We were beat after hunting all day and drinking much of the night. Most of us had wives and children waiting for us. There was the job waiting for us, too. Under cloudy skies, we packed our gear. Nobody said much. A quiet gloom replaced our celebrations.

One of the vaqueros approached us with his sombrero across his chest. All the days I'd spent with these gracious and hardy men, I'd never seen such a supplicating demeanor. I'll never forget the humble tone of his voice.

"Señors," he said. "Would you mind terribly if I asked you for a favor?"

"*Por supuesto*," I said. "Of course. We're friends."

"Would it be too much trouble for you to give my son a ride into Musquez? I promise you that he won't be any trouble."

"*Seguro que si*," I said. "Damn right, we will. We've got room. Tell him to come on."

The vaquero spent the next few minutes expressing his gratitude. My Spanish isn't what it should be, and I wondered if I'd told him that we'd rather just give him the truck.

We were tying down our load when the man reappeared carrying a boy about ten years old. I didn't need my DPS first aid training to know that this kid was really sick. His face was the color of schoolroom chalk. Sweat beaded up on his forehead. His leg and ankle were horribly swollen. On closer examination, I noticed a red line up the back of his neck.

"What's wrong with him?" I asked.

"He stepped on a rusty nail the other day. First there was the swelling. And then the fever came." The vaquero looked at us again with apologetic eyes. "I'm sorry to trouble you so," he said. "His mother is worried."

"I'd be worried, too," I said. "We're glad to do this thing for you. It's no trouble at all."

The vaquero looked around for a bare spot in the truck bed. Sheriff Kelley popped the passenger door open. "We'd prefer for him to ride up front," Kelley said.

The vaquero seemed reluctant to take him up on it. We all insisted until the boy sat on the bench with a blanket wrapped around him. I pulled a Coke from the bottom of the ice chest and handed it to him. He smiled like any kid would, only we all felt like this kid was dying. If we were slack about getting that truck on the road before, we made up for it now. Within minutes, we were hurtling the ninety miles to Musquez, stopping only to fetch that kid another drink from the cooler. Sometimes, we just pressed the can against his brow.

Neither one of his parents made the trip with him. I couldn't figure that out, along with all the rest.

With the Ghost by his side, Felipe Zamora led the procession to the hospital in Musquez. We all milled around the truck while Felipe briefed the doctors on the kid's condition. I wanted to do more for the boy, but didn't see how it was my place. When Felipe came out he wasn't smiling.

"They say he'll be all right," he said in Spanish.

Our concern pretty much wasted what was left of our energy. We passed through Mexican customs, flashing our passes from the general and getting the same officious reaction from underlings. All favor ended as soon as we encountered U.S. Customs. Some battle-axe pounced on Alfred Allee and me about wearing our guns and badges in her "area" because it was Federal property or some such. After the deal with the kid I was in no mood. That Fed saw the worst of this Ranger, but Alfred and I kept our guns on. I've never dealt with any Mexican officer that was half as rude. Welcome home.

Just a few days with the boys were plenty. I hungered to be back with my family. The Texas criminal justice system seemed to get along fine without me, but things started popping as soon as I turned on the radio. In the time it takes to scuff a boot, I was back after crooks.

But then a quiet moment rolled around and my thoughts turned back to the boy. I called Felipe to see how soon the little vaquero would be back in the saddle again. Felipe didn't seem like his jovial self. There was only this quiet on the other end of my phone.

"I'm afraid the boy died, Joaquin," he said.

I don't really remember how I responded to the news. I just felt as empty as I can get. Only a few tragedies have devastated me like that, and those occurred in my family.

Almost thirty-five years have passed and I still think about that kid. I grew up with farmers every bit as poor as those vaquero families, yet we all knew about the relationship between nails and tetanus. I believe the family knew what was happening to their child. But why didn't they do anything about it? And did they come to Felipe Zamora and the attorney only

Loaded for bear, Sierra de Sangre Mountains, Coahuila, Mexico, November 1967. From left to right: Alfred Allee Jr.; Wesley "Bubba" Kyle; Uvalde Chief of Police Vance Chisum; Uvalde County Sheriff Kenneth Kelley; Maverick County Sheriff "Bean" Salinas; unnamed ranch co-owner; Joaquin Jackson; and unnamed Mexican vaquero.

to be turned away because, as our hosts, they couldn't be bothered? Had it been my child, I would have stolen the truck to get my kid to a doctor and worked everything else out later. I don't know why this horrible thing happened like it did.

Two images stay with me: the vaquero begging us with his hat in his hands to take his son into Musquez. And that dying little boy drinking those sodas as fast as we could pour them down him. In two days he'd be dead. But for us, he only smiled. So handsome, so brave.

That little boy had some of the whitest teeth I'd ever seen. What a beautiful angel he must have made.

CHAPTER FIVE

The Reconquest of Aztlan

AN ANGEL ON MY ASS

1972

WHAT I REMEMBER MOST about that warm November evening is the shouting. I hear angry voices threatening me and every other law enforcement and voting official ensconced in the Zavala County courthouse. A mass of Mexican Americans—most on foot, but a few idling in battered Chevrolet Impalas and Ford Falcons and a '50s-vintage Dodge pickup—swirls around us. People who used to be migrant workers have turned into militants. White-haired women, the wind tugging at the scarves around their heads, offer fresh *frijoles* wrapped in homemade tortillas to their friends to stave off the chill. A few cowboy hats dot the heads of *viejos*, but I see far more bandanas and baseball caps in that mass of T-shirts and unbuttoned flannels. Beneath their Mexican wedding shirts, some of the young, hard-eyed men have pistols stuffed into their jeans waistbands. If things don't go right tonight, lots of folks are going to get hurt.

Inside the courthouse, Anglos thump their #2 pencil erasers against tally pages as they stare at padlocked precinct boxes. Camel cigarettes burn down. Smoke hangs heavy in the air and black coffee cools in untouched Styrofoam cups. The election officials, along with the entire Mexican American community of Zavala County, know those boxes are crammed full with ballots marked in favor of La Raza Unida Party candidates.

I watch the anguished expressions of the Anglo election judges, county commissioners, sheriff, police chiefs, and politicos as they deliberate the dilemma before them in silence. They're wondering if they can do what they've always done. Maybe the storm outside will blow over. Or maybe this is the moment when nearly 150 years of unchallenged Anglo rule of South Texas crumbles. None of us in authority knows how we got here. We all understand very well, however, that we have just stepped into unknown territory, the cusp of change. Staring at those ballot boxes and all those troubled expressions, I understand that we have to make the right decision or many innocent and not-so-innocent people could die together on the segregated streets of Crystal City. We need to do the right thing. I'm not sure that we're capable of doing that.

Now I hear the amplified voice of one handsome, gifted, resourceful, intensely motivated, and very angry man—José Angel Gutierrez. I don't know him. We met for the first time this morning soon after the precincts opened. But he's fairly certain he knows me. To him, I am *el Rinche*, Mexican slang for a Texas Ranger ever since the war of 1848, the embodiment of Anglo oppression, a man authorized to crack his head wide open if he doesn't obey the law. In fact, Gutierrez not only knows that I'm mentally and physically able and thoroughly trained to gain compliance by whatever means necessary, he expects me to shove the law aside whenever it suits me and enforce the status quo.

For this young Chicano militant, obeying Anglo law lies at the root of his people's problems. The law is the means by which the American system has excluded an entire ethnic group of citizens. He and his organizers have gone to some trouble to qualify Mexican American candidates for this fall's ballot and then register thousands of Mexican Americans to vote for them. In other words, they are using the democratic system to gain a voice in how they are governed.

But should that effort fail tonight and yet another election be stolen from them, I know their frustration will escalate into outrage, and then violence. The pistols tucked into their pants are just the beginning. There are shotguns and rifles stowed in their vehicles. They are ready to confront violence with violence. This demonstration is not the end of a contested, highly emotional election. It is a gathering of kindling awaiting the first spark of civil war—the Texas outbreak of the racial bloodshed we've seen in Chicago, Watts, and Montgomery, and throughout the deep South after Martin Luther King's assassination. Tonight the battle for civil rights in America has clawed its way to my home.

The protestors wave banners that read *No hay nada que Dios no pueda realizar* ("There is nothing that God can't make happen") and *Viva La Raza.* They march and shout slogans as they idle in their cars, waiting for us to announce the election's outcome. And so there I stand, the man who's always said that politics and law enforcement don't mix, between the Mexican American people of my jurisdiction, whom I've sworn to protect, and their Anglo authorities, whom I've sworn to support but who are, the sheriff included, likely about to be voted out of office. Tonight they're at each other's throats.

The city police officers, who have no riot training, are so outnumbered that it wouldn't matter if they had mastered crowd control. The sheriff's deputies suffer from the same limitations, only their situation is further complicated because they are loyal to a boss who's going to need a new job. Due to numerous escalating confrontations between city and county authorities and the Chicano population of Crystal City, much bad blood flows between them. Many of the Mexican American police officers and sheriff's deputies are more loyal to their families and their neighbors than to the badge. There is only one neutral law enforcement official—only one Ranger.

Before this protest escalates into a violent confrontation, I'm going to surprise Gutierrez and every disenfranchised Mexican American Texan he represents. I'm going to expect him and everyone else in this county to abide by the law. Gutierrez didn't see that coming. No one else did, either. It's a simple issue, really. And it will change life in this brushy part of the world forever.

As with most of the broader events that occurred when I was a Ranger, the cause of this clamor reaches back into history. To understand what was happening in 1972, you have to consider the social structure of South Texas that evolved after San Jacinto.

IT'S NO SECRET that the settlement of Texas involved cultures in perpetual conflict. It seems that neither the Anglos nor Mexican (Tejano) people were blessed with a tolerance of the other's traits and reputations. Even their table manners appalled one another. Furthermore, open-mindedness was a worthless virtue when it came to survival on the northern Mexican frontier. Resourcefulness and blind determination offered more utility in an era when the daily struggle for survival granted little time for reflecting on the cultural assimilation already in progress around them. Hard lives; tough, aggressive people. Narrow minds.

The Anglo pioneers were notorious for setting aside their Protestant teachings when it came to their relationships with people of darker skin. They saw no reason to alter their convictions and prejudices as they crossed the Sabine River into the Mexican state of Coahuila y Tejas. Ignoring the mixed nature of their own ancestry, they quietly subordinated the mesti-zos upon first encounter. The thousands of Anglos who entered Mexico during the Empresario era without the proper documentation, by the way, were known derisively as "wetbacks."

If nothing else, however, the land ultimately bound these reluctant neighbors to one another. Although there were conflicts and misunderstandings, the first Anglo settlers in Texas lived amicably with the Mexican *norteños, los Tejanos*. Until the Texas Revolt of 1836, the social scheme was working peacefully, especially as Anglos discovered that they had little choice but to adopt time-proven Mexican methods of land use and animal husbandry, and their aggressive self-protection against the Plains Indian tribes.

Anglo and Tejano fought and died together in the joint revolt against the dictator Santa Anna, who had usurped the Mexican Constitution of 1824. On the other hand, many Texas Anglos (especially those who had lived in Texas the longest and had the most to lose) supported Santa Anna's regime during the Texas revolution. The Texas War for Independence was a complex, multicultural, regional struggle against an oppressive regime, a remote theater of the civil war already raging between the centralist and federalist factions in Mexico.

After San Jacinto the infant Republic of Texas lured thousands of Anglo settlers in search of cheap land and unbounded opportunity. These people, who had no idea about the value of Mexican culture and no inclination whatsoever to experience it, viewed Tejanos—and all Mexicans—as a vanquished and inferior race, a shiftless breed entirely capable of what they considered to be the massacres at the Alamo and Goliad. The hard lines thus drawn, Tejanos who had lived in this country for a century or more found themselves excluded from the nation that they had helped to build.

This tragic occurrence was compounded after the Mexican War of 1848, when thousands of Mexicans were stranded behind the borders of a new nation that wanted little to do with them. The Mexican Americans of Texas were never slaves, but the social structure forced upon them by the Anglo majority rendered them little more than serfs—the condition that had first propelled millions of the Americas' European immigrants to the New World. Tejanos were politically, socially, and economically sterilized because Anglo Texas society believed they deserved it. Even more arrogant was the prevailing notion that Mexican Americans were better off in segregated Texas than in Mexico.

This wound festered for decades. Anglo and Mexican American alike were born into such a system and generally accepted it. Anglo landowners, farmers, ranchers, professionals, and businessmen who created unchallenged feudal estates in the fertile farm and lush ranch country of South Texas were keen to maintain the status quo.

But the Mexican Americans were reduced to poverty, humiliation, institutionalized ignorance, and government-sanctioned apathy. Today, we recognize this as *racism*. A decade ago, it was known as *apartheid*. For generations of South Texans, however, it was just the way it was. Lots of folks probably didn't think twice about it. Those of us with a conscience knew it wasn't right. But none of us knew what to do about it.

In the early 1960s José Angel Gutierrez emerged from the barrios of Crystal City with a vision for his people. He told them that the American Southwest had once been *Aztlán*, the original homeland of the Mesheeca—the warrior nation misnamed by the Spanish as the Aztecs. Today geographers and cartographers believe the heart of the Mesheeca's earliest empire ranged from beyond Texas to somewhere in Utah. Gutierrez's general concept, however, reminded Mexican Americans that their ancestors had been the masters of their domain. He looked around and realized that they didn't need guns or armies to win this inevitable battle. The secret to reconquering Aztlan lay in the democratic power to vote.

I've never come close to agreeing with Gutierrez's controversial politics, but I can tell you that he's one of the most interesting men I've ever met. I'll probably argue with him until my last breath, but I'll always admire him.

José Angel Gutierrez's father rode with Pancho Villa. The story goes that José Gutierrez was a young medical student at the outbreak of the Mexican Revolution. Villa basically impressed into service an entire class of reluctant medical students as physicians for his troops.

While I couldn't speculate on medical student José Gutierrez's political convictions, it appears that he gradually fell under Villa's spell and fought against the Mexican government for close to twenty years. He lived through several battles and several wives, rose in the military and political arenas, and was appointed *comandante* of Torreon, Coahuila. He earned the trust of Torreon's citizens, who ultimately elected him as their mayor. At last Villa was murdered, and in 1929 young Dr. Gutierrez was exiled north of the Rio Bravo for the rest of his life.

Dr. Gutierrez took his fifth wife, Concepcíon Fuentes, and opened a medical practice in Crystal City. A gifted and passionate speaker, he traveled the Rio Grande valley cities lecturing on such topics as "The Price of Honor" and "The Art of Love." Among the Mexican American community he so often inspired, Dr. Gutierrez was depicted in the flyers that advertised his appearances as *"el pico de oro,"* the mouth of gold.

Dr. Gutierrez's interests, passions, and loyalty lay across the river in Mexico. Well advanced in age when his fifth wife gave birth to her first and only son, he passed away before the boy reached his thirteenth birthday. "Make sure they bury me in Mexico," would be among his last words to his child.

José Angel Gutierrez had enjoyed a privileged life as long as his father lived. The community Dr. Gutierrez cared for showed their appreciation in daily gestures—a few pesos here, fresh tamales there, *gracias a su padre* heard everywhere. The boy was welcomed in Anglo-owned stores and restaurants where no other Mexican American dared set foot. He could even bill his purchases to his father's account.

Young José Angel was sent, as a learning experience, to wash dishes for twenty cents an hour in the bleak *bracero* camp operated by the California Packing Corp., which later evolved into Del Monte. He rode the truck to the fields with the migrant workers at four in the morning, seven days a week, observing the bare conditions of the laborers' clapboard barracks and outdoor privies, the American diet forced on people who detested it, the dismally low wages, and the transience of their mean employment. The workers were not even welcome at the local Catholic mass. After his father passed on, José Angel Gutierrez was not simply exposed to this life of segregation, he was sentenced, along with all of his kind, to live it.

The Jim Crow social structure of Crystal City was typical of its time. The Mexican American community faced three basic employment options: the Del Monte cannery, local ranches, or seasonal work on farms up north. All paid a low hourly wage. Close to a thousand households earned less than $3,000 annually, the poverty level for a family of four at the time. More than half the Chicano families did not have a toilet, and a third had no indoor plumbing. One section of town had no access to city water or sewage. The streets of Anglo neighborhoods were meticulously maintained while the barrio roads were left unpaved. There were Anglo-only days at the public swimming pool—when the water was freshest.

Those of Gutierrez's community who wanted to vote for candidates promising change, up until 1966, first had to pay a $1.75 poll tax. For most, the privilege to vote for Anglo Democrats was hardly worth the effort or the expense. This was the "separate but equal" world that bred José Angel Gutierrez.

The Texas public school system would not allow him to speak his parents' native language. The history and social studies curriculum ignored his ancestors' contributions. Mexican American kids were excluded from sports teams and cheerleading squads and "most beautiful" elections. José Angel Gutierrez, son of a revolutionary, had his nose rubbed in all of this. When he came of age, it became his turn to rebel.

Gutierrez possessed a number of attributes that served him well when it came time to confront Anglo authority. He radiated cunning, resourcefulness, intelligence, and charisma. A tireless worker and a gifted, passionate speaker, he was further armed with the conviction that he was right.

José Angel quickly established himself among Mexican Americans and Anglos alike as a leader *con huevos*, a force to be reckoned with—and, for some, to be feared. Among whites he was considered a militant and even a communist; for Mexican Americans he was a hero. I knew all about him, including the fact that circumstances would inevitably hurl José Angel Gutierrez and me into one another.

EVERYONE SENSED THE TENSION. Before daylight, I was cruising between my home in Uvalde and Crystal City, the epicenter of the burgeoning La Raza Unida Party and the most likely scene of violence in the 1972 county elections. Upon arrival I idled around each of the six or so voting precincts in Zavala County to make sure everything was in order and that there was no improper electioneering in progress.

Things seemed quiet as I made small talk with the chain-smoking election judges and their clerks. They were anxious about how the day would go. It was rumored that some La Raza Unida activists were prepared to shoot it out, but officials remained hopeful that the voting process would run smoothly. As day broke I felt there was a good chance things would. I left for Sheriff Lewis Sweeten's office to share a cup of coffee and get his impression of the situation.

I'd had a sip or two of coffee when the call came in from the election judge of Precinct 5 informing us that he had encountered serious problems. Precinct 5 was the Zavala County road administrator's office, which sat on the west side of Crystal City on Highway 83.

Texas bestows election judges with the same powers held by district justices on election day only. Generally speaking, when one of these daylong despots cries foul, droves of law enforcement officers come running. On this day they summoned me.

Once I'd connected Gutierrez's agenda with the incident location, I pretty much got the picture before I ever set foot on the scene. That particular precinct's election judge's distinguished appearance would soon prove illusory. I knew this bird, and in my opinion he was an arrogant, loud-mouthed, obnoxious all-service carpet lawyer, businessman, rancher, and renowned redneck. If Gutierrez's people were worried about election corruption, they had probably stormed the right precinct. I knew enough about both Gutierrez and this jackass election judge to assume that we had the makings of a full-blown riot on our hands.

My suspicions weren't far off base. Across the highway were hundreds of banner-waving protestors, most of whom were shouting *Viva La Raza!* At the front door of the precinct, a bilingual brawl was spilling onto the front porch. The Anglo judge was directing his clerks and sheriff's deputies to carry the still-seated Chicano poll watchers out the door. Gutierrez and his group, including the wellhead-sized bodyguards who were always with him in those days, were shoving them back inside. The poll watchers, knuckles white and faces damned determined, clung to their chairs like bare-bronc riders.

No place but South Texas could a county election get as rowdy as this. I love everything about my home state, but politics almost always disintegrates into an ugly, mud-slinging shouting match. Pour racism into the pot and contested elections take on all the characteristics of a blood feud.

I don't remember exactly how I did it—probably set off a bomb or something—but the first step was to get the brawlers' attention and shut down all that clawing and caterwauling. This was more or less accomplished, except for the hundreds of folks across the street. They kept on protesting, but they weren't the immediate problem.

The acrimony gave way to an eerie moment as quiet as a mouse pissing on a piece of cotton. As soon as Sheriff Sweeten and I restored order, the election judge began to throw his weight around. He said the poll watchers —Richard Díaz, Richard Gatica, Rebecca Perez (whose husband Rey was a fine police officer and would one day be elected district judge), and Luz Gutierrez (wife of José Angel)—would have to go. He claimed that Precinct 5 was too damn small to accommodate *any* poll watchers of any inclination and still allow people room to vote, which was sort of true.

These four La Raza Unida activists would rather nail their feet to the floor than break eye contact with the ballot box. The framers of Texas election law probably envisioned a fair and impartial election judge overseeing the process. Whoever nominated this *Hee-Haw* henchman hadn't come close to the ideal. He didn't just resent Mexican American poll watchers at his precinct; he wanted them hauled off in chains.

I could see that the election official was distraught that the word "arrest" didn't come out of my mouth. The expressions of the Mexican American activists darkened also, mainly because I think the presence of a Texas Ranger signaled foreboding and doom. (Especially here, in Zavala County, where in 1963 a Chicano political movement was violently oppressed old-school-style by the Rangers. Things were different now, but local residents didn't understand that yet.) I didn't give that crowd the confrontation they wanted either. I'd disappointed everyone right off the bat. Not a good start. When the poll watchers didn't twitch the first muscle fiber toward getting out of those seats, I began sorting through my options. None of them was any good.

I was thinking about ordering everybody to give me enough peace to sort through this mess when out of the pack came José Angel Gutierrez waving a book, which in his hands is a far more deadly weapon than any other.

"Ranger, can I just show you something?" he asked with the book already open to the appropriate passage.

"Sure," I said, and soon my eyes were following a few sentences in the *Texas Election Code*. Basically, the law provided for two poll watchers to be present at any precinct for each candidate on the ballot. I think close to thirty offices were up for election that year.

I looked at the election judge. "Are you aware of this?" I asked him. "According to the law, they're entitled to have maybe sixty people sit over the poll, which would be ridiculous here. But they're only asking for four."

José Angel said nothing while I pursued this line of questioning. It was a rare occasion when the modern, Americanized version of the "Mouth of Gold" would let others talk.

"I'm aware of the law," the judge snapped. I sensed a haughty tone, but I can be more definite when describing the man himself. He was an asshole. "I'm the election judge. This is my precinct. I don't want 'em in here and that's the end of it."

South Texas has long been notorious for its dubious elections, especially when Lyndon Johnson and Coke Stevenson squared off for the Senate seat back in 1948. Many historians agree that the election was stolen from Stevenson in Duval County, where dead people not only took a surprising interest in politics, they also voted in alphabetical order.

I'd like to think that this sort of thing didn't go on in Zavala County, but the election judge's behavior did little to support my hopes. Years later when Gutierrez and I sat together with a couple of college professors and discussed these events, he stated that when La Raza Unida Party members posted poll watchers at the precincts, La Raza candidates won their elections. When they didn't, La Raza candidates lost. Readers can draw their own conclusions.

"These four people have a right to be here," I said to the judge. "Are you gonna let them sit over that box or not?"

More stubborn than he was thick, the election judge shook his head. His refusal was a complete abuse of his ephemeral powers, but what are you going to do? I felt like the next move was an end run around him.

I looked at José Angel and said, "I tell you what. Let's go talk to a real judge and see what he's got to say about all this." I hoped that District Judge Jack Woodley could override the election judge, or at least talk some sense into him.

Gutierrez seemed shocked by my suggestion, but he quickly climbed on board, with one caveat. "We've gotta go in my car," he said. He pointed to the mob. "If I go with you, they'll think that you arrested me and all hell will break loose."

I told the election judge to sit tight and suspend voting long enough for us to return with a final determination. Confident that things would go his way, he seemed happy with that plan.

Before much else happened, José Angel stuck a La Raza Unida pin on my shirt. You don't ever want to put your hands on a uniformed officer, and I've never let anyone touch me without serious repercussions. But this was an act of political symbolism rather than a threat, and I had to admire the man's gumption. The crowd erupted in victory as I crawled into the passenger seat of his car. *El Rinche* has been subdued by *la raza*. Okay.

About then Gutierrez looked at my Ranger badge, noticed my name, and then, as his expression clouded, took in all six foot five of my hopelessly Scotch-Irish features. "How did you ever get a name like *Joaquin?*" he asked me. They always ask. I always tell them.

At Sheriff Sweeten's office we placed a call to District Judge Woodley in Sabinal, whom I quickly apprised of the delicate situation at Precinct 5. Judge Woodley informed me (and later Gutierrez) that he had no authority to override the election judge's decision—a determination I question to this day. He nevertheless informed us both that there were civil remedies available to La Raza Unida *after* the election, an expensive proposition for a grassroots workers' movement and a long time to wait for a prize legally won. His best advice was to work out some sort of compromise with the election judge. Gutierrez and I climbed back into his car with the unspoken intention to do just that.

When we returned to Precinct 5, the mob reignited. Sheriff Sweeten was visiting with the election judge and that party ended, too. I advised the election official that the district judge strongly suggested that we avoid a lot of hassle (not to mention media scrutiny) by allowing the La Raza Unida Party to post just four of the sixty watchers they were entitled to inside his absurd shack. He refused.

Two of the four poll watchers were women, and there were a number of students and young children with the mob across the street. I'd have to sit tight on this situation or somebody was going to get hurt. But I could at least try and bluff the son of a bitch.

"Okay," I said. I pointed across the street at six hundred armed and angry protestors. "You're on your own." I waved for Sheriff Sweeten and his deputies to follow me, and we all started for the door.

"Wait a minute, Ranger," the election judge said. I took a deep breath and spun on my heel. "You can tell *them* they can put two poll watchers in here," he said. "Can't have four."

"Are you sure about that?" I asked him. "Can't have four but they can have two?" He nodded. Good enough.

I went outside and informed Gutierrez that the election judge had relented, sort of, and I suggested to the activist that he learn in a hurry to like it. José Angel seemed happy enough and immediately sent in Luz and Rebecca, who were still clamped into their chairs. They dragged themselves inside the precinct for the long vigil.

We all knew that the main event would unfold later, when the local officials tallied the election results. But La Raza Unida had won the first and most important round. It seemed to me like a minor episode, yet its repercussions have lasted to this day.

FOR ANGLO OFFICEHOLDERS, the writing was on the wall.

Later that same night, results were phoned in to the district clerk at the Zavala County courthouse, where absentee votes had been counted during the day. Outside stood a big chalkboard with both candidates' names along with a changing tally of votes.

After the election judges count their ballots, the boxes are sealed and padlocked. If there's a court order in place, a Ranger arrives to pick up the box. I don't recall if this was the case in 1972. The precinct ballot boxes began to arrive at the courthouse for a second tally and the final figure.

La Raza Unida activists hung around. Gutierrez and others, megaphones in hand, blared angry speeches in Spanish. They wanted to see the numbers go up on the board, and I remember thinking God help us if they aren't what they ought to be.

Inside the courthouse all was quiet. Somber-faced election judges and their clerks started to drift in. I knew that Sheriff Sweeten had poked around about the opening for a feedlot manager for Chapparosa Ranch. Other officials would be checking the employment listings in the Uvalde and San Antonio newspapers next Sunday. José Angel Gutierrez had just orchestrated the conquest of Aztlan—the part of it that he was born in anyway. Politically speaking, Zavala County belonged to La Raza Unida. The last thing the party members demanded was to have the Anglo authorities come out and tell them so to their faces.

They hadn't done that and the crowd was growing increasingly agitated. That's when I wondered if these officials were thinking about fudging the numbers. I didn't hear a single person in the courthouse suggest that they do anything of the sort, but they weren't in a hurry to report the election results either. Every now and then one of them would stare at me as if to evaluate my expression. I hope it sent the right message. I hope I urged them to tell the truth.

All the election officials needed to do was take a good look at my badge and consider what that silver cinco peso stands for. Every day of my Ranger career that badge compelled me to reach for the ideal. I expected the same of them. Regardless of their personal opinions and prejudices they didn't disappoint me. They rose to the occasion and reported the true tally of the votes, knowing that the results would cost them their jobs. I was as proud of them as I was of the underdog Mexican Americans who had just won back their county.

After midnight, morose clerks posted the final numbers, and angry demonstrations soon gave way to jubilation. Conservative Texas Democrats were buried alive in a Raza Unida landslide. Chalking the tally on that green board seemed like a small thing, a perfunctory duty. For the Mexican American community of Zavala County, however, it was like the Berlin Wall crashing down.

On his way home, José Angel Gutierrez sauntered up with a grin that I would come to know all too well and invited me over for a drink. I declined, but I don't think he was disappointed.

I would have liked to have had that drink with him. He probably noticed that I was on duty that night. The invitation stands.

LA RAZA UNIDA'S REIGN in Zavala County and throughout South Texas proved short-lived. The reasons are complex and maybe beyond a Ranger's grasp. I suspect that differences arose within the party, fracturing what in 1972 was a solid, unified movement as La Raza Unida battled a common foe. Things dramatically changed. Alliances unraveled; the Democrats regrouped. Anglo candidates, however, did not recover their hold on South Texas. Mexican American candidates began to run as Democrats and ultimately, strange as it may seem, as Republicans.

More Mexican Americans became educated. With education, many moved into the large Texas cities, which funneled them directly into the American middle class and beyond. They changed America and America changed them.

There's an old racist statement in Texas that went something like this: You rarely find a rich Mexican in Texas. As soon as a Mexican makes lots of money, he becomes *Spanish.* That's not true anymore. There are many powerful, wealthy, and influential Mexican Americans throughout Texas. An affluent Laredo banker and businessman was the Democratic candidate for governor in 2002, while a schoolteacher named Victor Morales ran in 1996 and 2002 for the U.S. Senate. It was inconceivable that any Mexican American could launch viable campaigns for such high offices when I became a Ranger in 1966.

We now celebrate Cinco de Mayo and Diez y Seis. Our children are taught in school about the Mexican contribution to our state. South Texas politicians, authorities, business owners, and law enforcement officials are overwhelmingly Hispanic. Year by year the playing field in Texas becomes more level. But Aztlan belongs again to La Raza.

Mexicans served with the Texas Rangers back in frontier days. The first Mexican American inducted into the modern Ranger service, however, was a friend of mine from Uvalde, named Arturo Rodriguez. Many more would walk in Arturo's boots. In 2002, almost a quarter of the Rangers are Hispanic. That's a long way to travel in thirty years, my friends.

I can't wait to see where we are in another three decades. Even José Angel Gutierrez will be surprised. It's beyond me to speculate, too. But I can guarantee you two things: we're all going there together, and it's going to be something to see.

CHAPTER SIX

The Things I Carried
(WITH APOLOGIES TO TIM O'BRIEN)
1966–1993

I EXPERIENCED MY FIRST real firefight during a 1969 jailbreak in Carrizo Springs. A group of hardcore felons with nothing to lose seized control of the county jail. They ransacked the armory, securing plenty of guns and ammunition, and, once they realized that they could not escape, barricaded themselves behind the walls. The Rangers were called to the scene, and veteran Captain Alfred Allee assumed command. Using a megaphone, he informed the inmates that he would give them until the count of ten to surrender. He had counted to three when he popped off a magazine full of .30-30 rounds from his Winchester rifle.

I was surprised that events had taken such an abrupt turn. "Captain," I said, "I thought you told 'em you'd give 'em till ten."

"Ah, them sonofabitches can't count no way," he said, and the shooting between us and them became indiscriminate. Back then, I carried a Springfield Armory .30 M-2 fully automatic carbine, and as the prisoners made it clear that they preferred a pitched battle to capitulation, we answered violence with violence. My bullets ricocheted off the prison bars, sparking like fireflies on a summer night. I'll never forget the sound of bullets popping past my head, of lead slamming into the cars around me. I'd been shot at before, but never like that.

We stormed the prison in the exact manner you'd expect of the Texas Rangers, and before it was all over we'd taken it back. But the violent experience left an impression on me, along with the image of the fireflies— a brief, brilliant flash and then only darkness.

Soon after the prison break the nightmares started. The faces changed, but the circumstances were always the same. I'm alone, shooting it out with two or three suspects. I've got them pinned down pretty damn good, but I can't get the clear shot I need to put an end to it. One of them makes a move and I draw a tight bead on him. I lead him just a little, and when I know he's mine I pull the trigger. Nothing happens.

I know I'm out of ammo, and so do they. My hand slaps my gun belt, but I don't have the extra clips I always carry. I'm too far from my vehicle, where I always keep plenty of extra rounds. I look back at my enemies. They're coming for me, grim smiles on their faces. They didn't expect this opportunity and they're glad to get it. Helpless, I watch as they level their gun barrels in my direction. All I can see is the dark hole at the end of the bore, and then they pull the triggers.

I always wake up at that moment. Lying in the dark beside my wife, I go over my inventory of weapons and ammunition, just to make sure the nightmare doesn't become a reality. I can't go back to sleep. There's nothing to do but go over my supply of guns and ammo again. I want to make damn sure nobody ever catches me unprepared.

The list of firearms in my arsenal is substantial and, perhaps for some readers, shocking. I've been a lifelong hunter, and it's certainly true that I appreciate the look and feel of a fine weapon. But I'm no gun nut. I am a craftsman who appreciates the finest tools of my trade. I mastered them to perform a beneficial service—my defense and the defense of others against the criminal element. I own the guns, but they have never owned me.

In 1966, when I first made Ranger, Texas DPS issued me a Smith & Wesson Model 19 .357 caliber revolver. This was a fine and accurate workhorse pistol. For precision shooting, I always relied on the Smith & Wesson.

But most Rangers carried some version of the Colt 1911 model .45 semi-automatic pistol. It was better for general work, featured tremendous knockdown power, held a few more rounds, and could be rapidly reloaded. My particular choice was a lightweight Colt Commander. Along the way I made a few adjustments. I replaced the stock trigger with another one from an older model 1911 Colt, which extends farther from the frame, giving the shooter a better feel on the trigger pull, which I adjusted to exactly three pounds. Not a "hair" trigger setting, but it still meant business.

When it comes to handgun ammunition, the name of the game is hydrostatic shock. Placement is important, penetration certainly matters, but tissue damage carries the day, and the .45 autos pack a punch like a sledgehammer.

I didn't care for the way the Colt Commander's factory grip safety wore blisters on the skin between my thumb and forefinger. The solution was to increase its surface area with a beaver-tailed grip safety. The factory wood grips won't do for a Texas Ranger. Grips of heavily lacquered wood or ivory can become slick with perspiration or human grease; they were just plain dangerous. And only pimps and whores carried grips of mother of pearl. I prefer the custom grips made of engraved silver and gold that Felipe Zamora gave me. I've never seen any that were more beautiful, but they are intensely practical, too.

Once I had customized the Colt Commander, it hung from a gun belt designed and crafted by my friend Joe Peña, a saddlemaker from Uvalde. The holster was handmade by another Ranger, Tolliver "Tol" Dawson, the only supplier I knew who fashioned holsters for .45 autos on the old Brille design. The Brille holster has never been surpassed in efficiency, utility, and beauty. And no leatherworker before or since has made holsters more beautiful than Tol Dawson. Tol has gone on now, and Brille sold out long before Tol, but I still have the holsters. Every now and then I take them out, hold them in my hand, and admire them. They remind me of my good friend Tol.

Peña designed his gun belt to carry two clips of seven 230-grain .45 caliber rounds. In case penetration became an issue at some inopportune moment, I generally alternated one round of ball ammunition with one hollow point. I carried four more loaded clips in my vehicle and quite a bit more department-issued ammunition in my car trunk. I usually packed another Colt Model 1911 .45 with a 5" barrel in the car. In bad situations, I would stick the extra .45 in my belt opposite my holstered Commander.

Both .45s, of course, always carried a full clip of ammunition, with one round in the chamber, cocked and locked, military-style. "Isn't that kind of dangerous?" some fellow once asked a Ranger friend of mine. "I wouldn't carry the son of a bitch if it wasn't dangerous," the Ranger said. I couldn't have said it any better.

When I first made Ranger, the department sent me out with a Remington Model 8 .30 caliber semiautomatic rifle that had once been carried by Ranger Levi Duncan. I couldn't see how this weapon was going to work for me. As soon as I could afford it, I replaced the Remington with a lever-action Model 94 Winchester .30-30, manufactured in 1957 during Winchester's heyday.

I commissioned Utopia gunsmith Lem Sinclair to cut the 20" barrel down to a nifty 16¼" just to make sure I could get it pointed in the appropriate direction from inside my car. (I have a friend who shot the passenger mirror off his pickup in a similar situation. I don't believe he was acquainted with Lem Sinclair.) Lem further plated the rifle with a brushed chrome finish, practically impervious to rust. Plus, there was no chance that a glint off the blue would catch a crook's eye.

I kept the stubby Winchester in a worn saddle scabbard at my feet in my state unit. When I retired a quarter century later, it was still there, always gorged with five rounds of 150-grain flat-nosed silvertips in the tubular magazine and one in the chamber. That rifle became a part of me. Aiming that customized Winchester was like pointing my finger, and woe to those who found themselves facing its business end.

I stowed a bandolier with forty more rounds of .30-30 ammunition in tight leather loops. And, of course, I carried a few hundred rounds with me at all times in the trunk of my car.

The Department of Public Safety issued me a Remington Model 11 12-gauge semiautomatic shotgun. It had beaded sights and an 18″ barrel that I felt was better suited for shooting quail. I swapped it for a Remington Model 1100 semiauto 12-gauge with rifle sights and a 21″ barrel, a riot gun with far more pointability and one that would sweep the streets pretty clean when loaded with .000 buckshot. I stashed plenty of .00 and .000 buckshot loads in my trunk. Seeing as how I had rifle sights, I kept quite a few 600-grain slugs on hand, as well. Slugs were exceedingly accurate out to a hundred yards and could kill a man out to three times that distance.

I usually carried a succession of concealed weapons in case things got really rough or I got separated from my trunk. I started with a Smith & Wesson .38 Chief Special snub-nosed revolver that I shoved into my boot. But it was too damn bulky and occasionally slid too deep for me to easily get to it. Plus, it was hell to run with a snub-nosed revolver under your arch. I decided to go with an American .380 semiauto that squeezed into my belt and under my shirt.

I had another .22 magnum Smith & Wesson snub-nosed revolver on my body somewhere, too. Some people don't respect the .22 rimfires, but the magnum is more deadly than the .38 special when used at close range with .40-grain hollow-point ammunition. Plus, these smaller pistols required ammunition that didn't take up too much room in my trunk.

On horseback, I holstered a .44 magnum Smith & Wesson Model 29 revolver. The .44-caliber performs like a combination rifle and pistol. Tom Three Persons designed a custom holster and belt rig for the .44 that featured twenty-four loops for spare ammo. Kept a few boxes of extra ammunition, just in case, in the trunk.

Nothing commands a crook's attention like automatic gunfire. A three- or four-round burst seems to capture the moment and makes him think twice about pointing some pawnshop pistol in my direction. A few years back, the FBI was seriously outgunned in a shootout with drug smugglers in Florida. And police in Los Angeles learned a valuable lesson when they came up against some heavily armed bank robbers. Both of these tragic incidents resulted in a needless loss of life and forced officers and agents nationwide to reconsider the weapons required in the modern war on crime.

The Texas Rangers have never needed such a painful initiation. Our jurisdictions are so large and usually so rural that it is a matter of fact that there is no backup if we get into a tight situation—at least not soon enough to make a difference. Most firearm exchanges occur in a matter of seconds. Since the days of Jack Hays, the Rangers have always sampled the best in available small arms and put them into immediate use in the field. Automatic weapons have been a Ranger mainstay since the introduction of the Thompson machine gun and the Browning BAR. We always let the criminals worry about what we carried, not the other way around.

That said, automatic weapons were best used in psychological warfare—great for barricade situations or to encourage the bad guys to keep their heads down. Automatic rifles issue an effective statement, and when they do the problem is usually solved.

I began my automatic weapon experience with a Springfield Armory M-2 .30 carbine with one thirty-round clip installed—the very same weapon I used in the Carrizo Springs jailbreak. I generally stashed two more fifteen-round clips in the trunk. I kept plenty of boxed ammo close by. This was a dependable, workhorse machine gun and it never failed me.

But when it came to weapons I was cursed with a wandering eye, and after experimenting with M-14's, Thompsons, and Colt M-16's and many others circulating around Austin, I ultimately decided on an Armarlite AR-18 assault rifle. Chambered for the nifty 5.56 NATO (known as .223 Remington caliber by the girls I go with), the AR-18 is a gas-operated, magazine-fed, air-cooled, selective fire, reliable, American-made little metal maelstrom. I found the weapon superior in performance to the Colt M-16 and the AK-47.

I appreciated several of the AR-18's no-nonsense features, including the short piston stroke of its smooth gas action, rotating bolt, simple ergonomic design, L-shaped flip-up diopter rear sights (protected by "dog-ears"), muzzle-fitted recoil reducer and flash arrester, and rugged, space-age components. The Armalite is, quite simply, a very bad boy. I always had at least four thirty-round-capacity magazines nearby, usually in my trunk. I stocked cases of .223 ammunition around, too.

Other weapons flitted in and out of my life—usually stashed in my trunk. I feel about them like one feels about old girlfriends—they caught my eye but never my devotion. We had a little fun while it lasted, but I don't feel the need to see them again. The department issued us Remington 742 auto-loading .30-06 caliber rifles. I love Remington products, especially their extremely accurate bolt-action rifles, but this particular weapon couldn't place three shots in a Volkswagen at a hundred yards. Not good enough.

Ruger Mini-14 .223's had their day in the Ranger service, and I liked mine all right until the Armalite came around. I was married after that, and as long as the AR-18 kept the faith, so did I.

Sig Sauer and Glock large-frame semiauto pistols in .40 or .45 calibers enjoy immense popularity throughout the law enforcement community—and I had a Sig in the trunk as a backup—but Rangers have always been fond of Samuel Colt's products. Jack Hays gave the Comanches a good spanking with the first Colt revolver ever produced, a Patterson five-shot pistol. After a lengthy personal consultation with Texas Ranger John Walker, Colt produced the Walker Colt. Rangers carried this heavy, large-frame, big-caliber six-shot revolver throughout the Mexican War.

Later improvements resulted in the Colt "Peacemaker," one of the premiere weapons of the American West. Once the Model 1911 .45 auto appeared on the market, the Texas Rangers assumed it had been designed especially for us. A citizen once asked why I carried only the .45 (he wasn't aware of my concealed pistols or the contents of my trunk). "Because they don't make a .46," I said.

On any given day, I carried my Shrade-Walden two-blade knife. Its scabbard fit nicely on Señor Peña's gun belt. A couple of sets of Peerless handcuffs kept detainees quiet and respectful. I had a military-issue nightstick made out of composite plastic. In the trunk I usually had four or five tear gas grenades and two gas masks. Generally speaking, I felt prepared.

The rest of my getup was as follows:

I wore a Resistol hat, buckskin color. The DPS usually issued 10x felt rejects to state troopers, but for some reason the Rangers didn't rate. We received a clothing allowance and spread it as far as we could. I generally bought Resistols that had some kind of flaw and were sold at a preacher's discount. I grew fond of the Cattleman's Crown with a four-inch brim. I wore a coral snake hatband until I met an old vaquero down at La Pryor who had once worked for the King Ranch. He made me one of braided horsehair and I still wear it. (Incidentally, I carried a half-dozen or so plastic tie-downs in the inside of my hat. Damn fine handcuffs in a pinch.)

I wore Justin boots until my feet revolted against me. I switched to footwear crafted by hand in the Rio Grande valley by Reyes Boots. Later I hooked up with T. O. Stanley, a bootmaker in El Paso, and together we devised what I consider to be the ultimate in Ranger footwear: top-grain leather, semi-riding heel, square toe, and eighteen-inch tops for protection from snakes and short criminals.

For spurs, I always chose Crocketts. I had to have long shanks to accommodate my long legs and a medium-size rowel to keep my horse—usually borrowed from an aggrieved rancher—motivated but friendly.

What most people today call chaps were always known as leggings on the Texas and New Mexico ranches I worked on. The ones that I wore in the Ranger service were made by my old friend Joe Peña. Our neighbor, Bubba Kyle of Slade Saddlemakers, outfitted me with my saddle. Like any South Texas vaquero, I asked for *tapaderos* for stirrups, also known as "toe fenders" by gringos, to protect my feet in heavy brush.

At heart, the Mexicans are a generous people. I hooked the solid gold, crystal-faced Illinois trigger-set watch that Felipe Zamora gave me to a gold watch chain that hung from the button of my all-cotton Western-cut shirts. Dangling in the middle was an 1858 one-dollar gold piece. I lost the coin during a horseback pursuit, but the watch and chain are still with me. The only other jewelry I've ever worn is the ring that signifies my bond to Shirley. I wore Levi or Wrangler Western-cut slacks and a tie every day on the job, which pretty much completes my uniform except for one last item.

The DPS issued my first Ranger badge. It wasn't at all what I had in mind. Ranger tradition dictated that Ranger badges were cut from Mexican coins. The 1947 and 1948 Mexican cinco peso is 99.9 percent pure silver, and so I chose one of these coins for my badge. I sent the coin to a Houston-area silversmith to shape and cut it into the five-point Lone Star. He inscribed it with *Joaquin Jackson* at the top of the circle, *Texas* in the center, *Ranger* at the bottom. This particular configuration suited me just fine and completed my uniform.

There was a little room left in my trunk for the C rations I carried for stakeouts or manhunts or for whenever I was marooned in some godforsaken corner of Texas. "Beans with Pork" was my favorite, and I had plenty of occasions to choose. In the 1970s the military produced a new generation of compact meals, the MRE. These left C rations literally in the dust. I also kept an old-time, campfire-smudged coffeepot with me at all times.

I've seldom envied the Feds for anything, but I did grow fond of the Border Patrol's fancy half-gallon canteens. I finagled me one somewhere along the way, and it rode with me wherever I went in that dry, dusty country.

I carried a first-aid kit. I carried a bedroll that was more akin to what a cowboy might use on a cattle drive—basically a blanket rolled up with a canvas tarp. I slept in this many a night with a jacket for my pillow. (No self-respecting Texas Ranger in my day would show up for an extended manhunt or stakeout with his pillow under his arm. It just doesn't send the right message.)

I carried a DPS investigator's kit, complete with fingerprint technology, laboratory containers, tweezers, latex gloves, magnifying glass, and film canisters for evidence. The department also outfitted me with a Canon 35-millimeter single-lens reflex camera. I had to hire a Japanese technician to teach me how to use the damn thing. When it came to law enforcement I planned to take my shots with something other than the Canon, but no one can say that it wasn't a damn fine camera. I kept it deep in my trunk.

I think that's about it.

WHEN I HAD THE OPPORTUNITY to meet with José Angel Gutierrez years after the showdown on election night in Zavala County, it was at a university symposium dedicated to those troubled times. I really enjoyed seeing Dr. Gutierrez and was proud to take part in teaching a new generation about the struggle for civil rights in Texas. At one point, I mentioned that day back in 1972 when my instincts told me that the shooting was about to start. "What was your strategy?" I asked Gutierrez. I waited while he pondered the question.

"Well," he said, "I don't remember having a real *strategy*. I just instructed my bodyguards that if shooting broke out, they were to make damn sure Joaquin Jackson didn't get to his trunk."

Sounded like a damn good strategy to me.

THAT A RANGER MUST RELY ON so many weapons in the course of his daily duties is no laughing matter. Yes, I had many guns with me, but I tried my best to keep from using them. I guess I walked softly and carried a full trunk. I served Texas for thirty-six years and I'm proud that I never had to kill anyone. I came damn close. I've certainly shot people. Although I was never wounded, bullets flew my way more often than I'd like.

Winston Churchill once said that he found nothing more exhilarating than being shot at and missed. Maybe so. But I never once celebrated after a shoot-out. In the wake of intense violence and bloodshed, I'd always wander away from the buzz of investigators and coroners and desperate men either dead or in chains, and find me a rock or stump to sit on. I'd think the situation through—what I did wrong, what I did right. Most of all, I learned to be grateful for what God had given me. I'd think about my wife, Shirley, and our two sons, Don Joaquin and Lance, and be glad that I was going home to my family. You just find yourself a quiet place and let everything simmer back down. Then, God willing, you go home.

CHAPTER SEVEN

For Love and Horses

THE MANHUNT FOR THE "SEE MORE KID"

1967

ASK HILL COUNTRY PEOPLE who know anything about those times and they'll tell you that Texas will never see another criminal like him. Charles Brogdon is the product of the lean life and rawboned times that bred him—one part Oklahoma Choctaw, two parts Irish, one part left wild to roam wherever he wanted, the law be damned. I believe a bit of the horse whisperer stirred within him, too.

There was some native intelligence at work in Brogdon's case, even genius maybe, the homespun cunning that evolves out of adversity and cuts its peculiar channel according to its time and place. He was drawn to what high, lonesome places were left, to the Texas Hill Country mostly, where he'd spent the only happy years of his life. Only the Comanche knew the hills better. When Brogdon quit those parts, he left a legend behind.

Brogdon was a career horse thief and burglar. I was a Texas Ranger. Despite our conflicting professions, we got along just fine once we made formal introductions and put away the guns we had pointed at each other. I locked him up after a ten-day manhunt in 1966. I saw him again thirty-six years later on a ranch outside of Oakwood, Texas, on March 15, 2003. We hugged each other like old lost friends. And then we talked.

I can only tell a part of how our disparate lives touched one another nearly forty years ago. Someday Charlie will have to sit down and tell the rest.

CHARLES SANDERSON BROGDON JR. was born in San Antonio in November 1933 to a traveling salesman who peddled the family's recipe for de-

worming chickens and cattle and even for sobering up drunks, and his half-Choctaw-blooded wife, Myrtle Francis.

When Charlie was four, Myrtle would slip from this earth during a complication in childbirth. Young Charlie lost more than his mother. He would not know unconditional love again until 1974, when he married a pretty Baptist girl from Jacksonville who wanted nothing to do with a man of his reputation and notoriety until her friends shoved her inside of the Dolphin Night Club and she laid eyes on him.

Between losing his mother and finding his wife, Charlie singlehandedly waged a personal war against any semblance of authority in Texas. Before the bars slammed shut on him in the Huntsville prison and he served his final stretch of time, Brogdon racked up Texas's most extraordinary non-violent criminal record—a one-man crime wave launched by a kid who broke into a few hundred houses in his relentless search for a home. The "See More Kid," to be exact.

After his mother's death, Charlie's dad shuffled him down to the Rio Grande valley town of Mission to live with his grandparents. Charles Sr. was busy peddling Brogdon's Wormer, a concoction worthy of a U.S. patent despite the fact that it was sold in used wine bottles. The old man was on the road most of the time, hawking his only ware to feed stores, veterinary clinics, and flea markets, except for a forced hiatus when some car thieves and murderers by the name of Clyde Barrow and Bonnie Parker swiped his

1934 Ford. He arranged a posse of family members to take out after the notorious robbers before he thought better of it and went on about his business. And that's pretty much the last point of interest Brogdon Sr. has to offer any of us, his only son included.

By the age of six, Charlie came to understand that he could expect little in the way of guidance from his grandparents. He ran the streets with Mexican and Anglo kids who, like him, had no one to care about them. Before long, Charlie was smoking cigarettes he'd lifted from five and dime stores. He pinched moon pies and orange soda waters from cafés and gas stations. Even if he stayed out all night on the river, no one seemed to give a damn.

Charlie's daddy sent him, at the age of eight or nine, to Bowle's Orphanage near Greenville. The administration seemed earnest enough, but it was a working farm that required plenty of chores and discipline. Charlie didn't adjust well to either. He didn't belong in an orphanage anyway. He had kinfolks somewhere. All he could think about was getting back to Mission and the freedom he had known there. He wanted to get back to his family, to his own kind. He figured finding his uncle in Dallas would be a good first step.

Charlie followed the railroad tracks due east toward Dallas. If anyone came near him, he hauled it into the nearest woods. When he couldn't fend off his hunger, he approached a produce truck hauling fresh vegetables. The driver fed him and listened to him and took him into Dallas to find his uncle. And when that search didn't pan out, the man offered to take him home to his wife.

Charlie refused the offer with thanks and headed south. Terrified of being returned to the orphanage, he stayed off the roads and slept in cornfields during the day. He rode his thumb through Waxahachie, Waco, and Austin, and finally hooked up with a Mexican family who took him all the way to San Antonio. He lived with them for five days until he got his strength back. Then he headed south again for the Rio Grande valley.

Back on the familiar streets of Mission, he walked through the old neighborhoods greeting his former cohorts. He thought he'd slip into the backyard of his grandparents' house and surprise them with his return after his Homeric journey.

Instead, he heard his father conferring with his grandparents on the back porch, telling them that he'd heard from the orphanage that young Charlie was on the lam.

"Well," his grandfather said, "we don't want him back down here."

"I don't want him neither," Charles Sr. said.

They might as well have beaten that kid senseless with a two-by-four.

But Charlie got the message. He hit the streets, heartbroken but determined to go it alone.

He and his gang gravitated toward the citrus farms outside Mission for day work and a decent meal, and all the fruit they could cram in their mouths while the foreman wasn't watching. Their range widened until they found their way to rancheros in the South Texas chaparral. Charlie took to the cowboys like a bird kicked out of the nest when it's time to fly. He also discovered that he had a way with animals, especially the horses that ran practically wild along the Nueces River.

He spent his days in the saddle, riding other people's horses on other people's land for the joy of it, anytime the mood struck him, for as far as he wanted to go. When he came across a horse he liked better, he swapped and rode that one for a while.

Charlie finally broke into a stable on a Nueces River ranch to see what kind of horses were worth their own house. Much to his delight, he confronted the finest animal his young eyes had ever seen. He had to have it, and a saddle to go with it, and then he and his new horse had to put a little brush country between them and that place. He rode through an endless ocean of chaparral, winding up at the Norias Section of the famed King Ranch, where he worked for a cowboy's wages on the back of that magnificent horse.

It soon occurred to Charlie that such a fine animal would be worth far more with a fine brand.

His river-riding horse bore the mark of the King Ranch when Charlie rode it for four straight days to Falfurrias just to see what the hell was going on in a different part of the world. The local sheriff had never seen the kid before, but he knew the horse all right. And the fresh King Ranch brand on its hip didn't fool him.

The Gatesville reform school's rigidity was the least of its faults as far as Charlie Brogdon was concerned. The staff worked him to the bone for cold biscuits and watered-down gravy. Discipline took precedence over book learning, and punishment came hard and fast at the frayed end of a leather strap. Charlie had seen horses with better roofs over their heads.

They sent him to pick blackberries on the banks of the Leon River when Charlie made his first run. The law set the dogs loose on him. He made it to Evant before he gave out. Sentenced to fourteen months of kitchen duty, Charlie decided to run again the next chance he got. Soldiers from Fort Hood ran down his stolen horse in a Willy's jeep. Charlie would have lost them if he'd made it to rough country, but the horse gave out and back he went.

Soon enough, the folks at the reform school gave out, too. Charlie had no idea where to go except back to the streets of Mission.

Neighbors of Charlie's grandparents who knew all about his situation put his family in touch with a childless Hill Country couple. Eve and Lenny Kaffel ranched in the Medina Lake area near Bee Bluff and desperately wanted a boy in their lives.

The land Charlie Brogdon encountered in Medina County nearly stopped his heart. He handled his chores, ranch work, and schooling to the satisfaction of the Kaffels, but every chance he had over the next two years he explored the rolling hills, stark canyons, and emerald cedar brakes. After only a few months it was like he'd lived there all his life.

When Mrs. Kaffel's affections for Charlie slipped the bounds of motherly love, the sixteen-year-old found himself on the run again. He was sprinting down a country road when a local school bus driver rescued him from an armed, irate ex–surrogate father.

At least he was one of the lucky ones who, during an awkward age when boys become attracted to women, discover that women are also strongly attracted to them. From then on, women gave horses a strong run for Charlie's affections.

Brogdon landed next on the famed Y. O. Ranch near Kerrville, working with Roy and Bonita Huffacre. There he was exposed to the techniques employed by a top-notch horse trainer, the man who in 1961 claimed the world champion cutting horse Joseuno.

The Huffacres were fine people, but they couldn't scratch Charlie Brogdon's chronic itch to roam. Brogdon headed west to New Mexico, cowboying on one dusty spread after another. Mostly he worked the Cleaves Ranch, which leased grassland on the Mescalero Apache Reservation. Charlie felt his blood stir again after a few months. He saddled a bay quarterhorse to ride for the day's work and then he just kept on riding. He crossed seventy miles of some of the harshest country in New Mexico, the desert badlands northwest of White Sands. He broke through to Ruidoso, New Mexico, but his remarkable journey had turned a borrowed horse into a stolen one.

Charlie hightailed it out of state. If his father's family didn't care anything for him, he wagered that his mother's clan still would. Now seventeen, he rode the rails to Oklahoma City in search of his uncle, Eddie Eskew. Uncle Eddie took to his wild-eyed nephew right away and hooked him up with ready employment at Pauline's Bait House, a wholesale supplier to the local tackle shops with a dandy beer joint in the back. The old-timers broke out the fiddles worn smooth where their whiskered chins rested against them and sawed as close as they could get to Bob Wills Western swing.

Pauline's sat right on Lake Overholser, whose windswept waves lapped against old U.S. 66. The old girl kept order with a flyswatter she wielded like a petty officer's baton. Charlie fell in with central Oklahoma's most flamboyant characters, and at Pauline's there was always room for one more.

Charlie seined wild red horse minnows that he chummed with day-old bread before he expanded his operation into the South Canadian River. Eventually he worked his way to several private creeks shimmering with shad, where he could catch most anything except a cold. It felt good to be near blood kin who cared about him, and he liked the feel of new dollar bills on his hip, but catching minnows was no job for a cowboy. Charlie felt the tug to work from a saddle again in the Texas hills. He served his notice, bought himself a new hat and a shiny set of spurs, and hooked 'em to Texas in the first car he ever owned.

He found work in predominantly German-settled Gillespie County. Old man Dudderstadt owned a ranch not too far from Lyndon Johnson's spread near Stonewall. Dudderstadt had played football at the University of Texas. He feared no man and one woman. His hands hung to his side like the bricks that walled the Gillespie County courthouse. The old German expected Charlie to mind his business, tend to the cattle, and put in an honest day's work for a fair day's pay. Beyond that, Charlie was free to do what he wanted.

Word got out to the locals that Charlie had a way with horses, and soon thoroughbred breeders that ran the racetrack in Fredericksburg came to him to break their colts. Charlie made lots of friends, but he ran with the jockeys mostly. He was with one of his favorites at the Seven Mile Whorehouse one Saturday night when they got drunk and wild and took the place over after they'd blown all their cash. They scared the girls and spooked the regulars, and that was no good for anyone.

The Gillespie County sheriff called on the Duderstadt home to see if the old rancher could control his cowboy. Duderstadt admitted that he could do no such thing but claimed that a boy who broke horses like Charlie Brogdon deserved a little latitude, and what rancher liked to hire tame cowboys besides?

Charlie loved that old man. He stayed with him for better than a year. Out of respect, Charlie just walked away on foot instead of stealing one of his horses. The difference this time was that Charlie didn't have a destination in mind. He planned to roam the hills, sleeping where the night caught him. When he needed a hot meal or fresh clothing, he'd break into an old ranch house or hunter's cabin and take what he needed. He cooked himself whatever they had on hand and then cleaned up, making every effort to leave the place like he found it before he disappeared back into the cedar brakes.

The year was 1953. Charlie Brogdon was a twenty-year-old petty criminal and drifter, beholden to no one, living off whitetail deer and Rio Grande turkeys in the roughest, most beautiful country he'd ever seen. He liked the arrangement just fine.

Even back then the Hill Country was so checkerboarded with little ranches and so many crossfenced pastures that stealing horses made no sense at all. Instead, Charlie partnered with somebody's border collie and hoofed it across all of the Hill Country counties—Kendall, Comal, Blanco, Gillespie, Mason, Kimble, Bandera, Real, Kerr, Uvalde, Kinney, Edwards, and, of course, his beloved Medina County. They were known collectively as the Land of Eleven Hundred Springs, and Charlie Brogdon probably sipped from them all. If he wanted whiskey, on the other hand, well, he'd have had to steal that.

Free from unnatural odors, he no longer spooked wild animals. Deer walked right up to him as long as he stayed still. Once in the canyon country, he fell into a hidden cave. When his eyes adjusted he saw Indian art on the walls, neat bundles of arrow shafts and flint tips at his feet, and clay vessels full of precious foodstuffs. The cave was either a hunter's cache or a warrior's grave, but it had remained unspoiled for maybe a thousand years. During those long months in the bush, Charlie claimed to have been hounded by ghosts and harassed by a UFO. The alien lights particularly spooked the dog, which cut out for the next county. Charlie went on alone.

His crime spree went unpunished. His willingness to wash dishes, mop the floor, and lock the door behind him set him apart from other burglars. By the spring of 1953, however, the law wanted Charles Brogdon for some forty residential burglaries (not including the more subtle break-ins or the cases where the victims figured that Brogdon needed their canned beans and Vienna sausages worse than they did), two stolen horses, six cut fences, and a pilfered jeep. He wrecked the jeep. He'd never had that much experience driving.

As time went on, Charlie added one more technique to his modus operandi. When he knew the law was bearing down on him, Charlie climbed high on a bluff or a hilltop and watched his pursuers with some amusement. He already had an escape route mapped out on the rare occasions when they came close. Often he'd stay put when everyone else was moving and let them blow right on by. He might have been lying on his stomach in the thickest stand of cedars; or he might have been up a tree. He began leaving notes at the crime scenes to taunt the investigators, like "The See More Kid sees more and does less." Few people referred to him as Charlie Brogdon after that.

Local law enforcement's desire to jail the See More Kid rose with his ability to elude them. When the local sheriffs couldn't run him down, they called in the Texas Rangers.

Jurisdiction fell to veteran L. Hardy Purvis, an old-school Ranger who didn't have to worry about winning the respect of his citizens. He rounded up a pack of dogs and some good saddle horses and the posse he needed to heel his man. He waited for the See More Kid to make his move.

Camp Mystic is a summer resort for the daughters of well-to-do urban Texans. The camp featured unmatched facilities in one of the most scenic bends of the Guadalupe River. Unfortunately, the See More Kid was also fond of the area, especially at night, when he'd slip into camp to dally with camp counselors he'd met God knows where. Somebody with better sense than those teenaged girls had seen See More cut a glancing path under a streetlight and picked up the phone.

Ranger Purvis swooped in. When he crossed See More's boot tracks, he cut the dogs loose. See More could hear their yelps echoing through the canyons. He understood the ways of dogs second only to those of horses and altered his escape route accordingly. When the entire pack limped back to Camp Mystic with their tongues hanging out, Hardy Purvis scratched his head. He went home, made a phone call, and waited for another day.

Two months later, a rancher spotted See More near Wallace Canyon. This time, Purvis showed up with a regular posse, a Piper Cub search plane, and another pack of dogs. He didn't rely on local coonhounds this go-around. These were professional manhunters from Huntsville, home to the most famous prison in the state.

Officers broke into a lonely cabin to discover a stunned but freshly bathed and smartly dressed See More Kid munching on a sandwich. Somebody started shooting. See More somehow made it out of the house and into the woods, and the hunt was on.

See More couldn't help but notice the plane zooming through the air and the settling dust of scrambling trucks, horse trailers, and state vehicles that had piled into the canyon. The barking dogs nipped at his heels. Pressured like this, See More was out of his element. The usual tricks failed to throw off the dogs, and he began to understand that much better animals were after him today.

In desperation, See More dove off the bluff of Wallace Canyon into the canopy of a great oak tree, whose smaller limbs broke his fall. The dogs could not immediately follow, but they still picked their way down to the canyon's floor and took up his trail again. Purvis and the horsemen didn't have it so easy. There was no way down for them.

That left the relentless hounds bearing tooth and paw on See More's sweating back after eight or nine miles of desperate scrambling. Clear of the posse but totally spent, See More reluctantly pulled a .22 Colt Woodsmen semiauto pistol out of his pants, turned on the hounds, got himself a good rest, and head shot them one by one until four of them lay balled up on the stony ground.

Purvis and the others heard the gunshots, followed by the eerie silence. They knew. And See More kept running. Purvis set more dogs loose and kept after him.

Sixteen miles from Wallace Canyon, See More hit a cabin. A couple soon arrived with their grandchild. The man knocked the screen door off its hinges before he splashed through the creek, screaming for help. See More explained to the woman that he wasn't the kind to hurt another human being. She didn't know to ask about the dogs.

She cooked him supper before he ran on. He heard later that the woman divorced her husband for abandoning her and the child like that. I don't know if that's true, but she should have.

Purvis stayed after See More for better than a week, following him for more than sixty miles, enduring See More's taunting notes left in pillaged ranch houses and cabins. See More no longer had time to wash dishes and mop the floors. Texas newspapers picked up the story. He was becoming a legend, while Purvis became the butt of local jokes. But the old Ranger knew See More would make a fatal mistake if the law kept the heat on.

See More walked into Rocksprings and checked into a hotel under the name of Charles Brogdon. Exhausted, every muscle in his body aching, he collapsed on the bed and slept. A twelve-year-old boy recognized him from all the hoopla and let the sheriff know that See More was in town.

See More was jailed in Kerrville and arraigned on eleven counts of burglary. When a woman See More didn't recognize posted his cash bail, the cops hunted up some additional charges and raised his bond. There were some angry officers anxious to settle with See More—including the man from Huntsville who had buried four fine dogs. But Purvis kept them all at bay even after See More slipped in and out of his cell at will. In the end, See More pulled a five-year sentence to be served in the Darrington Unit, near the humid coastal town of Freeport.

B. B. Bullard was the stereotypical prison warden who, among other things, was proud of the cattle operation he had initiated on his farm. See More's cowboy talents did not escape the warden's eye, but neither did his reputation as an escape artist. Bullard offered See More the preferential job of a stock boy, but warned that if the Kid ran and made an ass out of him, Bullard would personally hunt him down—no right-thinking convict wanted B. B. Bullard after his ass. The owner of the dead dogs dropped in on him every now and then, too, just to let See More know that he had not forgotten.

He served thirty-six months. With no place to call home, See More decided to return to the country he liked best. He kicked dust around the streets of Kerrville until he came across Ranger Purvis, who helped him get a job with Charles Schriener III on the famed Y. O. Ranch. See More broke horses for the Y. O. and nearby spreads and sipped his Busch beer quietly in the local honky-tonks. Things seemed to be working out fine.

Charles Schriener III had a visionary plan for his vast holdings. He considered bringing back the Texas Longhorn cattle breed and importing hunting game from all over the world. He would accomplish both dreams on a scale so grand that his vision influenced many Texas ranch owners. But it wasn't interesting enough to keep See More around.

He drifted to the Four Sixes Ranch around Wichita Falls and later to the Waggoner Ranch in Wilbarger County. When he wasn't working he made the amateur rodeo circuit, where more times than not he placed in the money. He was riding fences for Tommy Hazelwood when he lost interest in the largest working ranches in the state. The simmering restlessness finally boiled over, and he slipped behind the wheel of Hazelwood's 1958 Pontiac Star Chief and didn't stop until he hit the Montana Rockies.

The north country suited him, at least for a while. He cowboyed for Montana outfits out of Butte, Bozeman, Gallatin, and Livingston, and also near Cody, Wyoming. He drove the Star Chief so long that he came to think of it as his own. A pilot car guiding traffic through road construction ultimately spooked him. Charlie drew suspicion when for no good reason he gunned the Pontiac and lit out. Charlie ditched the stolen car and headed out on foot again. By then the local law had run the plates and discovered why See More was so damn jumpy.

To make a long story short, See More amazed the Montana cops with the wilderness skills he had perfected in Texas. He rustled a bushy-coated mountain quarterhorse, a saddle, and a set of shiny spurs, all conveniently waiting for him in somebody else's barn, and led his pursuers through more than a hundred miles of Montana's most isolated, rugged lands. Of course, they caught him, but only after he was on foot. It's tough to hide in the mountain thickets, and then there were those fire towers overlooking every square mile. The Rockies weren't anything like the Texas Hill Country when it came to the abundance of caves, nooks, and crannies.

See More did time at the Deer Lodge prison on the grand theft auto charge. The bleak facility, the roughest See More would ever know, had once been an old frontier fort. See More worked as a cook, brewing a popular alcoholic concoction out of the local plums before they threw him in the "dungeon"— a place which justified its name.

See More was in the hole there for fighting when the inmates rioted. He found it hard to ignore the warden's brutal retaliation. Bullets flew all around him. An army artillery unit shelled the prison. They excavated See More after a couple of days from a pile of rubble, at which time he began to seriously reconsider his life of crime.

All told, See More spent about a year in the Montana penal system and was ready to be an honest man before two U.S. Marshals showed up with some outstanding charges filed by victims with long memories. See More was shuffled from one federal lockup to the next, Leavenworth included, until 1962.

Back in Texas, a veterinarian contracted to the Segerville prison became acquainted with See More when they both worked the facility's three-hundred-head cattle herd. With the vet's recommendation, he was paroled to the vet's farming operation in the Dallas area. It didn't suit him for long.

See More hooked it out of state for Arizona, where he briefly resumed his burglary career before the cops checked him into the local Crossbar Motel for a short stint. Once again, federal marshals showed up, this time for parole violations in Texas. See More served his time working in the dairy operation in the Anthony Unit outside of El Paso.

His mother's brother, a resident of Tishemengo, Oklahoma, came to call on his jailbird nephew in 1964. Uncle Woody Eskew was a city marshal for Ardmore, Oklahoma. He had also served thirty years of hard time for robbing a Wells Fargo payroll delivery. As an ex-con himself, Uncle Woody understood the prison system well. He also knew about redemption and that it was never too late for any con to walk a straight road. Good-hearted men had surfaced in Uncle Woody's struggle to see the light. He assumed that he could return the favor and shepherd his wayward nephew toward the glow of respectability.

For a while, See More responded. He worked an honest job at the auction barn, ran ranches and pecan picking operations, and did just about anything agrarian-related that would put a few clean bucks in his soiled pocket. He even bought himself a 1961 Plymouth Fury, the one with the push-button transmission. He drove it to Kerrville to see his dad, who was now a cook in the Veterans Administration hospital after the market dried up for Brogdon's Wormer. The years hadn't softened the old man much when it came to family relations. See More found his father cordial enough, but he still felt like the old buzzard could take him or leave him, which despite these hard, eventful years confounded him.

See More decided to try his hand in the oilfield—the undoing of many a cowboy. For three months he roughnecked near Aspermont, drinking Busch beer that he bought at Pinky's for $3.50 a case and shacking up with the comely Hispanic carhop at the Anson drive-in.

In a drunken stupor, See More ransacked his hotel room for no good reason that he remembers. He loaded the television set and everything else he wanted into the Plymouth and swerved on down the road, a doomed getaway after a senseless crime. They jailed him at Anson, and once they got a look at his lengthy rap sheet, they planned to keep him for a good while.

A group of disgruntled inmates overpowered a guard and broke out. Once free of the jail, See More wanted nothing to do with the other crooks and splintered off to fend for himself. Relying on the skills that made him infamous, See More acquired clothing, food, shelter, and a Ford pickup parked in a warehouse owned by an oil company that See More burglarized the day before payday. Once again he headed west for California with vague ambitions of what he would do once the stolen cash ran out.

It took a few months for that to happen. By then, See More had ditched the truck in Yuma, decided nothing about California interested him, and ridden the rails back east to Texas. It was 1965 when he hit San Antonio and simply walked toward the Medina Lake country that he still loved best. He picked up his burglary career where he left off. Nothing had changed as far as See More was concerned. He hid out in the woods and stole what he couldn't catch or shoot.

As 1965 bled into the summer of 1966, however, Ranger L. H. Purvis had been transferred to Del Rio. The State of Texas and Ranger Captain Alfred A. Allee had stationed H. Joaquin Jackson in Uvalde in place of retiring veteran Levi Duncan. Hence, the See More Kid's return to his home haunts became my problem.

BY THIS POINT in See More's career, he was accustomed to having his run of everybody's ranch house and vacation cabin. He knew where the softest beds were, where to catch the tastiest catfish, who kept a gallon of Blue Bell ice cream around, who had clothes that might fit him, and where he could watch a good cowboy movie on a color TV. Then he'd pop a little popcorn, knock back a strawberry soda or sip a snifter of Jack Daniel's, and call it a night. It wasn't a bad life.

See More was always suspicious that vengeful ranchers were plotting to poison him if he rummaged through their pantry, or at least planning to goose the whiskey with enough croton oil to make him deathly ill. Accordingly, he insisted on eating and drinking out of unopened tins and sealed bottles. He learned to swirl a fifth of bourbon whiskey in front of a light to see if it settled right.

The morning of September 12, 1966, was like any other for See More. Just before the crack of daylight, he abandoned the plundered Wylesta Ranch that sat on the bank of the Sabinal River near Utopia. He slept during the heat of the day in the cedar brakes near the river.

Well after sundown, he was on the move again. He crossed the Sabinal and entered the Pittman Ranch home through a bathroom window. He pried open the locked closet door of the middle bedroom with the blade of an axe, grabbed a clean pillowcase, and stuffed it with canned food items. He had a little room left, so he pinched a Zenith transistor radio and record player. His clothes were wet from the river, so he swapped them for some new ones. He came across a pickle jar stuffed with close to $60 in change and small bills, which proved quite a boon to a man who lived off the land and others' leavings.

Now a rich man by his own measure, the Kid loaded his booty into the Pittmans' 1959 jeep. Always meticulous, he checked the oil level and discovered the jeep was a quart low. He gassed up at the handy fuel tank near the barn and motored down the highway toward Utopia.

See More had previously mapped out several places of interest, awaiting the day when he'd come across suitable wheels and feel like driving for a little while. There was a fine saddle, for instance, that he'd seen a few days back in a vacant house south of Utopia. He needed a blanket and bridle to complete his tack, and he knew where to purloin them. He soon filled the jeep with another saddle, two rifles, and four or five antique pistols. It turned out to be quite a haul.

See More drove to Highway 83 on his way southwest through Uvalde, rolling into the thriving border community of Del Rio just before dawn, where he checked in to Western Motel's room #2.

He felt his blood rise after sunset, a sharpening of his senses and his irresistible urge to satisfy any impulse. See More's thought process during this era speaks for itself. He refused to risk his ill-gotten property in Mexico, so he parked the jeep stuffed full with his booty and walked across the international bridge to Ciudad Acuña. He partied with the professional girls at Acuña's La Zona Rosa just outside of town. He hooked up with one special and economical woman and later that night checked in with her at Los Alpes Hotel. He returned after noon on the following day to find his jeep and its contents intact—a thief's luck.

See More was calmly motoring down the dusty streets of Del Rio when a city policeman, Reynaldo Z. Andrade, spotted an odd jeep crammed full with saddles and guns. Officer Andrade ran the plates and arrested the See More Kid.

This is where I entered the story, strolling through the Del Rio jail with Captain Allee. The old Ranger captain puffed on his cigar as he regarded the man in custody. "You boys caught yourself a bigger fish than you thought," he announced. "This man here's the See More Kid."

I took note of the drawn, wafer-thin, disheveled character. Most remarkable were his coal-black eyes. They had the most unusual glow, like the sparkle reflecting off of a moonlit lake on a still night. See More seemed so polite, so warm and likeable, so utterly harmless. There was something about this notorious felon that made us feel like we'd made a big mistake in arresting him. I warmed to See More right off the bat. But I still slapped the cuffs on him and hauled his habitual criminal ass to Medina County jail to await trial. As it turned out, See More's day in court didn't come fast enough.

A few weeks later, I received a telephone call at my Uvalde office.

"Joaquin?" See More said. "You've got to get me out of this Medina County jail!"

"Why's that?" I said.

"I like beans as much as the next guy, but these sons of bitches down here feed beans, beans, beans, every goddamn meal. Three times a day—beans!"

Sometimes crooks are blind to the concept of jail as a deterrent to crime. Did See More really think that I would be willing to review menu items with the jailhouse chef? Maybe drop off a few fresh fruits and vegetables for those misunderstood boys in stripes? The adage among South Texas lawmen is don't do anything mean if you can't stomach the beans.

"Well, I can't bring you to Uvalde, See More," I said. "Captain Allee wants you out of our hair." And he wasn't alone. Anyone who owned real estate in the Texas Hill Country wanted the See More Kid shipped up north where he could terrorize Yankees for a while. The Medina County jail in Hondo was just the beginning of See More's extended stay as a guest of the state's more professional facilities.

"You tell him I'm gonna knock a hole in this wall if they bring me any more of them beans!"

"I'll sure tell him, See More," I said. "Crooks," I thought to myself as I attacked the stack of paperwork that was always building on my desk.

What I didn't understand was that determination and strength of will were foremost among See More's unique array of talents. Once he'd made up his mind that he'd had enough of the beans, powerful forces went to work. He stopped eating beans and everything else. Naturally lanky, he starved himself down until he was as poor as a snake, shedding thirty pounds in less than a month. Always amicable, he got himself appointed as a trustee, which gave him access to the runaround area outside his cell. I don't know what moron signed off on See More's trustee status. If See More had stayed longer in Hondo, he probably would have talked them into running him for mayor.

As a trustee See More gained access to rudimentary tools, always dangerous for a creative mind. He picked out a casement window that overlooked an alley from the second story of the Hondo jail. With a makeshift iron bar and blocks of wood, he pried an eight-inch gap between the bars. He'd likewise done a little grocery shopping for his fellow inmates, choosing the economy size of hair pomade for a Hispanic colleague.

When the time was right, See More stripped down to his birthday suit, greased himself from head to foot with the pomade, pitched his clothes out the window to the alley below, and began to work his way through the bars and casement window. As soon as his head was out, he noticed a young couple making love in the alley, a mixed blessing for an inmate, I'm sure. He enjoyed the show, but the timing was all wrong. Turned out that lover boy was an endurance performer. What could See More do, wedged with his head stuck out on one side of the bars and his greased, pomaded ass hanging out the other, but wait him out? I wish I owned a photograph of that.

After close to a half hour the young couple's breathing returned to normal. They smoothed their rumpled clothes and went on about their business. See More inched forth with more determination than ever now that the blood supply to the lower half of his body had been cut off for twenty-five minutes. He hung up for a time at his solar plexus, which was almost crushed as he forced his way out. But he didn't intend to be around when they served the breakfast beans. He worked the last of his appendages through the bars, shimmied down the bedsheets he'd tied together until they ran out, and dropped his greased, naked ass sixteen feet to the alley, spraining his ankle in the leap to freedom. He quickly dressed and limped out of town.

Since trustees were given the run of the jail, no one noticed that the See More Kid was not in his cell. Sometime in the afternoon, at least twelve hours after his escape, it occurred to someone that something was wrong.

By the time I was notified, the See More Kid had walked north twenty-one miles on a sprained ankle to burglarize a ranch house near Medina. He'd scrambled himself a dozen fresh eggs, which he washed down with at least one bottle of Lone Star beer. Afterward he munched on some cracked pecans and drank close to half a quart of Seagram's VO Canadian whiskey—which didn't sit well with him judging from the vomit we later found in the sink. Jail had blunted See More's love for good housekeeping.

Knowing I would be on his trail, he then outfitted himself with items that bore testament to his years in the hills. He swiped a Ray-O-Vac flashlight with extra batteries, two cans of sardines and a roll of Ritz crackers, three more bottles of Lone Star beer, one pair of size 8 leather house shoes, a ladies' tweed coat with a hood, one sheathed hunting knife and one pocket knife, and an old brown straw hat to keep the sun off his face because at his age it was likely to cause freckles.

See More would have appeared to be out on a hike if he hadn't also taken a .22 caliber Winchester pump rifle and a .30 caliber M-1 military carbine and close to four hundred rounds of ammunition. The .22 he could use to feed himself, but the theft of the carbine troubled me greatly. During the whole of his criminal career, See More had never hurt anyone. We knew he was a crack shot with a rifle, and his exceptional knowledge of the Hill Country would make him a deadly sniper. He faced completion of his seven-year sentence in Anson and was awaiting trial as a habitual offender in both Medina and Uvalde Counties. No one had to tell a convict with See More's extensive jailhouse experience that he faced two life sentences.

Once those prison doors slammed they were not likely to open up again in his lifetime. He had walked over twenty miles on a sprained ankle, which told me that after learning that jail was no place for him, he felt the weight of the law bearing down on his shoulders.

I didn't like the way the crime scene evidence added up either. See More left no silly, taunting messages on the wall. He didn't resort to his signature mischief or hijinks. He made no effort to clean up his kitchen mess. He used little care at the point of entry. He covered many a mile in rough country each day. I no longer believed that he broke jail because of the beans. The See More Kid was now a desperate felon. I had to wonder if he was likely, once he felt the heat of a posse breathing down his neck, to shoot us down like he'd done those tracking dogs. I stared at the emerald hills surrounding Alfred Brown's violated cabin, complete with the vomit in the sink, knowing that See More would be watching us long before we'd ever get a glimpse of him.

He knew what I looked like, and also that the responsibility to hunt him down would fall first to me. As I spread out my bedroll for yet another night away from Shirley and the boys, an empty can of cold C rations lying next to my .30-30 Winchester carbine, I knew that sooner or later the See More Kid would have me in his sights. What I didn't know was if he'd pull the trigger.

WITH DAYLIGHT I began to poke around for some sign. See More's prints were headed north-northeast into the heart of the Hill Country. My posse and I tracked him into the higher elevations, where the terrain turned rocky with dense cedar and live-oak thickets. Soon I lost his trail. I was aware, however, that See More was blessed with an excellent sense of direction and, being on foot, would head straight for his chosen destination if at all possible.

I asked the local ranchers and cowboys if they knew of possible hideouts that lay in See More's path. We rode up to a cave they all suggested, but it hadn't been inhabited in some time. I spent the night at another cabin about five miles from Alfred Brown's place waiting for him. See More didn't show. Three days in the bush with a cold trail, I put a call in to Henry Timmerman. Henry kept a pack of bloodhounds down on the King Ranch.

While we waited for the arrival of Timmerman's dogs, we were alerted to another ravaged cabin in See More's widening angle of escape. This jailbird was eating and sleeping a lot better than I was. We tracked him deeper into the cedar brakes until it became obvious that he was heading directly for the Nine Canyons, the same area where years before he'd shot the bloodhounds and lost Hardy Purvis's posse.

The locals advised me that there was only one cabin in that general area where See More could go for food and shelter. Timmerman's dogs showed up that same night. I gathered my posse of state and local officers, hauled a dozen saddle horses to the scene, and waited for daybreak. Hungry, dirty, cold, and homesick, I slept another night on the ground.

We were up early drinking coffee, feeding the dogs, and saddling the horses. We were all mounted and ready when I noticed that this reserve sheriff's deputy slipped a shiny new Weatherby bolt-action rifle out of its case.

"What you packin' there, fella?" I said.

".300 Weatherby," he said matter-of-factly. Lord, God. Talk about too much gun! We'd be toting See More back to jail in so many Tupperware containers if this deputy caught him in his crosshairs.

"Son, that ain't a polar bear in that cabin," I said. He smirked as he began shoving bright brass cartridges the size of a mortar round into the magazine. I should have told him that he didn't need to be loading that rifle just yet and when he did to make sure to stay in front of me. I checked on the preparedness of the posse instead. Day was just breaking on a clear spring morning. Even with the stir in camp, it was so deathly quiet. Then somebody's gun went off. A big, booming roar that echoed into the next county.

What a mess. We had howling dogs, spooked horses, spilled coffee, a stray bullet, and a deaf Ranger. Old Big Gun Barney just stood there, face glowing red with wonder and embarrassment, gawking at his rifle like this fiasco was all Roy Weatherby's fault.

I don't have to tell you what See More did after that shot shook every rock in Nine Canyons.

We ran on the cabin anyway. All the Kid left was a bad memory and enough scent on the ground to give the dogs a thrill. His trail still led us north-northeast, deeper into the canyons where the horses could not safely follow. I was afraid that See More would shoot the dogs again if we set them loose without us close behind. Last, I really wanted to corner the son of a bitch in somebody's cabin to effect a surrender. Popping off Weatherby rifles twenty minutes before we hit a place was going to make that tough.

We broke off our pursuit and settled in for lunch. Deputy Fife claimed he was off to see his local gunsmith. He needed to find out what was wrong with his rifle. I could have told him. An idiot owned it.

Later that afternoon, someone caught sight of See More near the Kelly cabin on Elm Creek, four miles south of Medina. My friend Texas Ranger Ed Gooding and a few other officers teamed up with me the next morning for another daylight strike. Things went better this time, except that See More had once again been and gone. This manhunt had to carry on for at least another day. I know I sometimes talk too much, but on this particular occasion I was tired, saddle sore, and grumpy from living rough and constantly orchestrating the movements of so many cops. See More was beginning to exact a personal toll. I turned to Ranger Gooding and said, "I'm getting tired of tracking and hunting this son of a bitch. If we catch him, I think I'll just shoot 'em and be done with it."

I didn't mean it literally, of course. Not once in thirty-seven years of law enforcement did I shoot a man in cold blood. But those few words I spoke off the cuff to another Ranger ultimately influenced how this manhunt played out.

I tracked See More on foot for another three to four miles when he changed direction. Looked to me like the Kyle Ranch lay next in his path. I walked back to my state unit and drove over to the Kyle. For close to a day and a half, I poked my head in places where a scorpion wouldn't go, cutting for See More's stale sign, catching only spotted ticks and a pesky rash.

About the time I figured out that he'd turned back north again, I got a call from Medina County Sheriff Miller, informing me that See More had hit a cabin miles from where I was. His MO was the usual. He'd scrambled up a dozen eggs, rustled a bottle of whiskey, pilfered $65 in change, and vamoosed into the cedar brakes toward Kerrville.

Sheriff Miller and I decided to rendezvous in Bandera for the first hot meal I'd had in days. We compared notes. I asked for the name of the next cabin that lay in See More's path, thinking that this time we'd hit See More after sunset, during egg-scrambling, whiskey-drinking time rather than dawn.

"I'd try Dr. Meyer's house," Sheriff Miller said between bites of his chicken-fried steak at the O.S.T. Café on the square in Bandera.

"Mighty fine," I said, gathering my plate to go back through the line. Thought it'd be a good idea to double up on mashed potatoes.

Sheriff Miller, Deputy Welch, Chief Deputy Williams, and I drove out to Dr. Meyer's place in Sheriff Miller's car. We stopped at the ranch gate and walked quietly on the wet ground toward the cabin some five hundred yards away. After a cool, cloudy day, the weather had turned cold. Sheriff Miller knew the Meyer cabin had a front door and one window each on its east and west faces. There wasn't a back door unless See More decided to make one—which, in a pinch, he could probably do.

I was juggling excitement, worry, and doubt as we approached the cabin. All available signs told us that See More was most likely holed up in this place. But what if he heard us coming? Did any of us think that a hunter who'd headshot four bloodhounds on a dead run would have any trouble drilling a round through one of us? See More had picked his ground. There was nothing for us to do but confront him and play it out.

We drifted toward the house. It was pitch black, and as we inched closer I couldn't get a sense of the place as Sheriff Miller had described it to me. I flicked on a flashlight to get my bearings. The Meyers had recently remodeled their porch with bright galvanized screen mesh. I might as well have shined that light into a mirror. I was briefly blinded, but Deputy Williams saw just fine.

"Look out!" he yelled. "He's in there and he's got a gun on you!"

I killed the light and scrambled behind the trunk of an oak tree. As soon as things settled, I went to talking to him.

"See More," I said. "This is Joaquin Jackson. You're in there. I know that."

"Yah, so what!" he said.

"I got two men out here. You better give yourself up."

"I ain't gonna do it, Joaquin," he said.

It's nice to be on a first-name basis with the criminal element, I guess, but it's nicer when they do what I tell them.

"Now look here, See More," I said. "You come on out with your hands up before somebody gets hurt." This sounds a little like a bad Western movie, I know, but it's okay when the script fits the situation.

"Well, I ain't gonna do it!" See More said.

I scratched my head with the pistol barrel. "Why not?"

"You're just going to gun me down if I do."

I cringed hearing that. I wondered where I'd gotten such a ruthless reputation. "No, I won't."

"You said you would."

"No, I didn't," I said. It crossed my mind that he was buying enough time to tunnel out or put the finishing touches on a pipe bomb. You never knew with See More.

"Yes, you did," he said. "I heard you myself when you were talking to that other Ranger back there on Elm Creek."

I then remembered my unfortunate conversation with Ed Gooding.

"Oh," I said. "You heard that?"

"I damn sure did."

"Okay, well, maybe I did say that," I said, backpedaling in a hurry. "But I didn't mean it."

"I don't want to find out the hard way that you did," he said.

Everything went quiet. I took a breath and exhaled loudly. I'd been a Ranger for exactly a year. They didn't train me back in Austin about what to do when you trip over your own boots. Clearly, the See More Kid had been close enough to hear me say something to Ranger Gooding. Nevertheless, if he were a killer, he would have shot me down days ago. He was now trapped just like I'd wanted. A peaceful resolution to this manhunt was hung up on a credibility issue because I'd run my mouth. Who knew that See More was so damn sneaky and that words traveled so damn far in the Nine Canyons? I had to do what I could to repair our personal relationship.

"I give you my word as a Ranger," I began. "You put your gun down, put your hands behind your head, and walk over to the window on the east side where that deputy can see you. You do that and nobody gets hurt."

"You swear?" he said.

"Yeah," I said, rolling my eyes. It'd been a while since I'd had a juvenile conversation like this. No way could I as a professional lawman tack on *cross my heart and hope to die.* "I swear."

Two or three minutes passed. I had to think about what I was going to do if he didn't come out. I didn't want to hurt the See More Kid, and I didn't want any of the other officers to get shot, either. I didn't think a warning shot would help us. I didn't have any tear gas. The radio was a quarter mile away in Sheriff Miller's unit. I also didn't want to come out from behind that tree and expose myself to See More's fire. I wasn't sure what my next step should be.

"He's at the window with his hands behind his head!" Deputy Williams said. I was never so glad to hear those words.

I entered the cabin. The M-1 carbine was on the floor. The .22 lay on the bed. See More was standing in front of the window just like I told him to do. I slipped the cuffs around his skinny wrists. As I started to pat him down, he said, "Talk like that scares a feller, Joaquin. Makes it hard to do the right thing."

"I know," I said. "I'm sorry, See More."

And I was. But you know me. A man once told me that I ought to save us all some time and write a damn book. I thought about doing it, too. But I don't see where it would save all that much time.

A moment later, See More said, "I was serious about them goddamn beans, Joaquin."

"I know it," I said. "But I can't do nothin' 'bout the beans, See More. It just ain't my line of work."

"They'll have better grub in a real prison, don't you think?"

"I expect so," I said, and led him out to the car.

IT TOOK RIGHT AT TEN DAYS to catch the See More Kid on his last run. He drew twelve years in the Huntsville penitentiary, which in and of itself is a miracle. See More dodged a conviction as a habitual offender on a legal technicality. Otherwise, he would have been behind bars for the rest of his life. I hate those legal loopholes, but maybe it was right that See More got a little break. By some measures, he'd led the most charmed of lives, and all of it had been in search of love and wild horses. See More was thirty-three years old when they slammed the bars shut on him in Huntsville.

What happened after that is a story that belongs to Charles Sanderson Brogdon. I can tell you that prison was no picnic. Among other horrible experiences, Charlie was once stabbed forty times by a group of inmates who killed his friend in the same attack. It took better than a year for his lungs and liver to heal. When they finally did, Brogdon placed second in the overall point standings at the prison rodeo. He was thirty-nine years old at the time.

While he was recuperating in the hospital, he befriended his physician. Like many of the father figures who entered his chaotic life, See More's doctor wanted to help him. "You don't belong in prison, Charlie," the doctor told him. "I've got plenty of cash money and a yacht moored offshore."

It was a tempting offer, but Charlie was through running from the law. And what business did a cowboy have sailing the Caribbean anyway? As Charlie neared parole, the prison stock supervisor had another plan in mind. He owned a ranch of Charolais cattle near Buffalo, Texas. Charlie could run it. At forty-four, he had a notion to go straight and ranching and burglary were all he knew.

Thirty years have passed. A man who had been most everywhere and done everything has worked on three ranches in three decades. Charlie married and fathered five children. At last count, there were eleven kids who called him "Papa."

He's on the back side of seventy now. Like all real cowboys, he's stove up a little in his gait. But he still puts in a full week of work on a ranch. Only three years ago he broke his last bronc, which told me that there was plenty of spit and vinegar left in this remarkable man.

I'm glad to see it.

I HAVE A PHOTOGRAPH taken one night back in March 1967. There're three men standing on a tile floor with their backs to the wall in the Medina County sheriff's office. Chief Sheriff's Deputy Floyd Williams, the oldest and shortest, stands with his arms dangling. Like many modest men, Deputy Williams is not all that comfortable in his pose. He wants to get it over with. He wants things to get back to normal. He wants to hear the jail door slam on the See More Kid.

See More and I stand close together, our boots still wet from wading through the Klein grass in the misting rain. We are maybe three years apart in age. I went on to be a much better criminal investigator and hopefully a better person in general, but in this photograph See More is at the pinnacle of his remarkable career, and maybe, as a man, so was I.

My thumbs are wedged behind the gun belt that rides low on my waist, my hips cocked just so like maybe I think a Texas Ranger ought to stand. I admittedly walked with a swagger in those days. I posed with pride. I'd gone after a man and ten days later I'd brought him in.

See More digs his hands deep in his pockets. The sparkle of his eyes has burned down to an ember's glow. He's weary from his days of deprivation, of being hunted. For as long as he can remember he's been on the run. He's never really understood how his criminal career started. All he knows is that he's tired of looking over his shoulder, of stealing food that might be poisoned, of sleeping light in somebody else's cabin, listening to the night for the sounds that don't belong—the crack of a cedar twig or the cock of a lawman's gun.

We are both so young in the photograph, and so tired. Other than that you can't read our expressions. There are few clues to who we are. You can't see that one man is going to prison and the other man is going home. You can't see that a moment just an hour before, when my flashlight flickered in the darkness of a misty night, I pointed a .44 Smith & Wesson pistol at him, and he, crouching in a corner, had a loaded M-1 carbine trained on me. Had I seen him make one move toward me I would have shot him dead. Very likely, he would in turn have pulled the trigger on me. One or both of us could have been on the ground, watching our blood drain onto the damp, rocky soil. Our eyes wild and rolling as we endured the last pain we would ever feel. We were both ready to kill each other, but neither one of us was really ready to die.

In April 2003, we sat together on Charlie's swing, while the breeze was still cool, and talked. I could see the light in his eyes that was absent on the night in the 1967 photograph. Family did that for him. And mine for me. We're lucky men, See More and I.

"Would you like a cold beer, Joaquin?" Charlie says with a wry smile.

"It's early yet for me, See More," I say.

He cocks his head, studying me. "A little whiskey, then?"

"I don't believe."

My cowriter works out research and documentation details with Charlie's wife. He's a younger man, a city man, always in a hurry, always sticking to the job at hand. He's got calls to make and bills to pay and work always waiting for him back in Austin. I tell him all that stuff is like wiping your ass on a wagon wheel—it never ends. He laughs, but he don't listen. He scribbles notes fast and talks faster, all the while walking toward his truck. He likes to knock out one job and pounce on the next one. He likes movement. He likes to go. I was once like that.

Joaquin and Charlie Brogdon near Oakwood, Texas, March 2003

I watch the writer as I sit with Charlie and sway in the swing. Charlie studies him, too, the same way he looks over a horse he's never seen. Pretty soon old Charlie knows what kind of animal he's dealing with, and I'm pretty sure that this writer's whirlwind feels a little too spooky for him. Every now and then Charlie looks over at me and grins. God only knows what's rattling around in that old man's head, but I think he's thinking that I've got my hands full with this younger fella kicking up the dust of the past. And I do. Sometimes it hurts to think about my life. Sometimes, like today, it's a hell of a lot of fun.

It's nice to see each other after all these years. I've often wondered what became of See More. Now I know he's done all right. It's nice to be here on this beautiful ranch in East Texas. It's nice to sit on that porch on a cool spring morning and just swing. Me and See More, well, we had this coming.

The writer's just going to have to wait.

CHAPTER EIGHT

Earth, Fire, Water, and Blood: I

(OCKHAM'S RAZOR AND THE DEVIL'S SWING)

The Colorado Canyon Shootings
1988

A border is always a temptation.

LARRY MCMURTRY, *In a Narrow Grave*

HE STONES YOU KICK out of your path on any trail in the Big Bend may date back as much as 520 million years, some of the oldest on earth. The Big Bend is stunning in its stark beauty, but for a trained and creative mind the region's rock formations evoke images of the violent forces that created every place on this planet. If you want to understand the history of the earth, study the stones. And if you want to encounter magnificent stones, come to the Big Bend.

Read any good book on geology and you'll understand that the land-masses we call continents were born to wander. Between 520 and 300 million years ago, what is now the Big Bend lay beneath a primeval ocean at the southern edge of the drifting North American continent. During the collision of North and South America, sediments two miles thick that lay between them were compressed, folded, and thrust-faulted northward until they formed a high range of easterly trending mountains, the youngest and westernmost of the Appalachian chain. Over the next 125 million years erosion wore down the mountains to low hills, the remnants of which can be seen along Highway 359 south of Marathon, Texas, some fifty miles north of Colorado Canyon.

In geologic time, the mountain-making collision was only a dalliance. After their brief dance together, North and South America sheared apart 100 million years ago. In their wake spilled in a young, warm, shallow sea that deposited several thousand feet of limestone, sand, and shale on the older rocks. A lush tropical Cretaceous jungle contained flowering trees and plants in the age of the great dinosaurs and flying reptiles. Long before the dawn of humanity, the Big Bend was a beautiful and dangerous paradise. Like every geologic, climatic, and environmental condition on the earth, however, it would not last.

When two great tectonic plates smash headlong into each other, one must yield. Fifty million years ago, the Farallon plate, on which rides the Pacific Ocean, plunged beneath the North American plate, igniting some of the most explosive volcanic activity on the western face of the planet. The volcanic activity in the Big Bend area that began 47 million years ago soon became inactive, followed by an 11-million-year hiatus before its fury resumed for another 18 million years.

During these unstable periods volcanic domes—a few as large as Mexican states—rose like boils, spewing lava and ash throughout the Sierra Rica region of Chihuahua, Mexico, and the Bofecillos Mountains in the heart of the Big Bend, covering all that lay between them in basalt or rhyolite lava and tuffs—deposits of volcanic ash along with great volumes of poisonous gases—and destroying the lush American Eden. Thirty-two million years ago the volcanic activity reached its crescendo with a catastrophic eruption in the Chinati Mountains a thousand times more powerful than that at Mount St. Helens in 1980. Everything living in the area died.

For some time afterward, sand, shale, soil, and gravel eroded from the mountain ranges, dumping fill into the newly formed closed basins. Basalts and volcanic ash tumbled with them. Then, about 18 million years ago, all volcanic activity ceased in the Big Bend.

Meanwhile, rain runoff and snowmelt from the Rocky Mountain ranges pooled fresh water on the plains and playa lakes of what would become West Texas, seeking the lowest elevations on their downhill journey to the sea. This pattern spawned all the major southeastern-flowing rivers in Texas—the southernmost being the Rio Grande, which reached the Colorado Canyon area about 2 million years ago.

During times of high-volume flow and flooding, the young river began to wash out whatever loose fill lay in its path until the sheets of volcanic or sedimentary rock lay bare. With each rain, the Rio Grande cut its channel deeper into the porous formations, until the process had carved Mariscal, Boquillas, Santa Elena, and Colorado Canyons into as much as 1,500 feet of volcanic basalt and tuff and sedimentary rock.

As furious and magnificent as the Rio Grande was, the river has not aged well. Droughts and the demands of two desert nations for irrigation water have left her but a trickle. Still she flows with a modest grace, quietly cutting herself deeper into the red rock of Colorado Canyon. Above her, the once volcanic mountains bare their slopes to the winds and sleep. Most days it's quiet and peaceful in the canyon—a real treat for the tourists. But any geologist will tell you that the way Colorado Canyon is now is one hell of a change from the violent storms that created it. It's still a rough, remote place.

As human beings inherited the world, we also inherited, at least in part, its potential for violence. In times past the harshness of the Big Bend may have intensified this trait in the local character. I don't believe the desert dwellers ever looked for trouble; but they saw plenty of it.

For twelve thousand years a succession of Pueblo Indian–type cultures peacefully farmed the fertile basins of the upper Rio Grande. Archaeologists and historians describe them as gentle, industrious, and resourceful people. Yet the Spanish, who failed to conquer them, lumped them into one classification of savage barbarian warriors—the Chichimecas. It's never been a good idea to shove the locals around.

For over two centuries in modern times, the people of Mexico and the United States have glared at each other across Colorado Canyon. Occasionally, even when they weren't at war, they killed one another if the opportunity presented itself.

The border drug trade, the rise of criminal cartels, and the dominance of cocaine as the main, incredibly addictive illegal substance of choice have threatened a centuries-old culture that stretched the boundaries of family and convention. In the mid-to-late 1980s, the frequency of dope-related shootings in Ojinaga's main plaza stunned even the most jaded DEA and U.S. Customs agents. The vast majority of honest, hardworking villagers found themselves caught in the crossfire between sophisticated, well-armed dopers and the incredible array of U.S. law enforcement agencies ordered to crush them. Suddenly, every dark-skinned resident of border villages and towns was a suspect. This tragic situation did little to improve relations between the people on both banks of the little river.

Today, good-hearted, family-oriented people who have lived on the Rio Grande for generations must battle the stereotypes along with the harsh environment, a bleak economy, and everything else. They have grown weary of this unwanted burden. And then there are a few Mexicans who, for whatever reasons (and there are plenty of them), have never warmed to their northern neighbors. Americans have only recently learned that prejudice works both ways.

Like the geologic storms that shaped the Big Bend, the human violence waxes and wanes, but it never ends. For so much splendor, there has been so much blood. The Mexican and Native American people indigenous to the area maintained no illusions about the region's potential for disaster. The confluence of the Rio Grande and Conchos River that Texans romantically think of as part of the Big Bend is known south of the Rio Bravo as El Columpio del Diablo, the Devil's Swing.

The river is ancient, the human feuds and man-made storms relatively new. These powerful currents swept up the lives of three innocent people on a beautiful, sunny day in November 1988. Two of them will never be free of the experience. One did not survive it.

EVERYONE FROM AROUND THAT PART of Indiana said that Mike Heffley could fix anything. When the automatic transmission of Jamie Sue Aliano's blue 1970 Camaro tended to stick in a high gear, she knew to take it to her friend's big brother, Mike. Maybe it was the no-nonsense demeanor of a young teenager who had grown up with plenty of responsibilities on her family's corn and soybean farm that first caught Mike Heffley's eye. A quarryman's daughter, Jamie knew how to work. Growing up with four brothers, the gangling teen also felt surprisingly at ease around men. She was smart, too, a member of the student council and National Honor Society. More than likely, however, at this first encounter it was the way her shoulder-length auburn hair swept across her shoulders in the slightest breeze. The graceful way her long legs uncoiled from beneath the bucket seat of that Chevrolet sportster. Jamie was a Midwestern beauty—unspoiled, unpretentious, respectful, deeply religious, but also quietly cocksure of herself. She knew how to talk to people. She carried herself very well.

Mike Heffley snapped out of his trance to diagnose the Camaro's transmission. Then he fixed it. Jamie thanked him and asked what she owed him. "Not a thing," Mike said. She paid him instead with a warm smile, and kept eye contact with him a little longer than necessary, and then folded those legs beneath her steering wheel and drove off. Before Jamie was out of sight, Mike turned to his little sister and said, "You tell that girl I'm going to marry her."

Mike's prospector father had towed him all over the United States—California, Florida, Colorado, and finally to the limestone quarry region of Indiana. Mike didn't know what it was like to really belong to a place. He saw that Jamie had this connectedness, and maybe he was charmed by that, too.

But there was a war on then. Mike enlisted to do his part and saw combat in Vietnam and then served a few years beyond that. He came home to Bloomington having seen all the evils that war has to offer young men. But none of that dimmed the light in his eyes or his zest for life. He still loved to go to exotic places and meet interesting people. His sense of adventure and curiosity could not be snuffed out even by war.

Mike Heffley was home with his future before him in January 1975 when he ran into his younger sister's friend, the bright-eyed, long-legged teenager with the faulty transmission. The image of her at this brief reunion nearly stopped his heart. Jamie had just turned eighteen. She wasn't the gangly young girl he remembered. She had grown into a stunning young woman who held down a job as a data processor, all of which meant to the returning combat veteran that Jamie was old enough and independent enough to be fair game.

Mike didn't waste any time letting her know he was interested. Jamie mirrored his attraction. They married three whirlwind months later in April 1975. If the nine years' difference in their ages stirred up a little gossip in Bloomington, none of it mattered to Jamie and Mike Heffley. As far as they were concerned, they were soul mates. Once they belonged to one another, they set out to carve their niche in the world. They planned to have a little fun along the way, too.

MIKE SOON GREW WEARY of teaching weapons systems to new recruits at the air force base in Kokomo, Indiana. When a friend of his called from Oklahoma to offer him a job in the oilfield and refinery pipe inspection business, Mike jumped at the chance. With Jamie in tow, he moved to Oklahoma and plunged into a new world.

Mike was good at just about everything he tried, but he excelled in mastering the pipe inspection process, managing employees, and drumming up new business for the company. His talents caught the eye of a competitor who made him an offer he couldn't ignore. So Mike and Jamie relocated once again, this time to Eastland, Texas, a ranching and roughneck town on the I-20 corridor between Fort Worth and Abilene.

Mike knew the business. Rural, north-central Texas was the variable now, and much to Jamie's delight her husband loved their adopted state. Soon, he was wearing Western shirts and cowboy boots and looking very much like one of the locals. He was blessed with the charm and charisma to pull it off, too.

But Mike couldn't hide his disappointment in the new company, and he wasn't the kind to take a step back, either. Instead, Mike launched his own

inspection firm, Tex-Ray, and dedicated himself to the exhausting sched-
ule it takes to make a success of any small business.

Jamie nailed down a position as a legal secretary for a local law firm to
earn some extra money for the struggling family and also to do something
with her free time. The couple worked hard for the next nine years until
Mike received an offer to sell Tex-Ray and manage it at the same time.
They invested some of the profits in a gift shop for Jamie, until they let
that go to work together on an old house. Mike continued to manage his
friend's company, but he didn't really enjoy working for someone else, and
he felt this pull toward Dallas. To pave the way for a future move, Jamie
found a job with a Dallas law firm while Mike worked on his exit strategy
from the Eastland operation.

During most of the week, husband and wife lived alone and belonged
only to their jobs. Come the weekend and any free time during the week,
however, they were with each other.

A weekend marriage didn't really suit the Heffleys, not after fourteen
years together. Still, Mike probably sensed that they were in danger of drifting apart. His idea was to take an extended second honeymoon with Jamie
and reestablish their bond to each other. Almost immediately, Mike thought
of his most recent motorcycle tour with the boys, his first trip to Texas's
Big Bend.

"You just have to see it, Jamie," he said, his eyes bright with enthusiasm. During the Terlingua chili cook-off in October 1988, he'd first brushed
against the quirky locals. He'd steeped himself in the irresistible rugged
beauty of the land. And he was hell-bent and determined to share both
with his wife.

Mike nearly stabbed her with a Far Flung Adventures brochure. According to the intelligence he'd gathered at the chili cook-off, the best way to
experience the Big Bend was to float the Rio Grande through the magnificent
canyons. Jamie had weathered her husband's whitewater fantasies before and
had always managed to point his nose toward the beaches of Hawaii or Florida.
This time Mike dug in his heels, explaining that there were plenty of experienced guides, large rafts, and fine hotels nearby when they tired of roughing
it—and he was already loading up the jeep with brand-new camping equipment. Besides, there wasn't too much whitewater on the Rio Grande.

The Big Bend would be their next great adventure together as a couple,
ten days exploring a magnificent desert world that was alien to both of
them before they immersed themselves into the syncopated rhythm of the
Dallas Metroplex and the pressures of a new business, when their lives

would change forever. Jamie didn't see how she could disappoint him in this one final exotic expedition, her husband's last chance to be a boy.

"Of course I'll go," she said.

MIKE AND JAMIE ARRIVED at Study Butte's Big Bend Motor Inn at eight P.M. on November 18. All Jamie saw of the Big Country south of Fort Stockton was what she caught in the headlights. The next morning, she awoke to the splendor of a beautiful autumn day in the Chihuahuan desert. By nine A.M. they'd made final arrangements at Terlingua's Far Flung Adventures and introduced themselves to river guide James Wayne Burr, a local from the fabled mining ghost town.

A native of Houston, Jim Burr had long ago answered the siren call. He owned a rugged, wiry build with a mustache thick as a whiskbroom and the easygoing manner of a man who loved what he did for a living. Burr had once worked the tugboats on the Mississippi River. Guiding the Rio Grande, by comparison, was like taking a warm bath. After four years on the river with Far Flung Adventures, Burr exuded the confidence of a guide who knew his country and the water that on those rare rainy occasions fed it. Guiding was foremost a people business, and Jim Burr naturally liked people.

Jamie and Mike Heffley warmed to Jim, but Jamie's misgivings lingered. She reread her dog-eared copy of the outfitter's brochure. It clearly stated that all rafting trips contain an element of risk. Jamie couldn't shake the feeling that the trip was ill-advised.

She grilled Far Flung's staff before she reluctantly signed their standard disclaimer. Mike expressed no concern whatsoever. He glanced briefly at the boilerplate before he scribbled his name in an exuberant hand. Then, they waited for the arrival of the other couples who were booked to join them.

A wave of nausea, Jamie's second warning, swept over her as she waited anxiously. Mike pitied his young wife enough to subdue his enthusiasm and quietly announced, "Let's just don't go."

Jamie didn't care if her husband might soon regret his halfhearted gesture. She jumped on it and herded him back to their jeep. About that time, the river guide reemerged from the office to report that the other guests had canceled.

Surprised by the Heffleys' change of heart, Jim Burr campaigned for them to stay the course. He pointed to the raft and river gear already strapped down on Far Flung's trailer, a hard-used Igloo cooler full of iced drinks and provisions, and last to the cobalt sky overhead. It was a perfect day to be on a beautiful, legendary river. Jim Burr urged them not to waste it, and reminded them that regardless of the other cancellations the $110 price quoted the Heffleys for this excursion would remain the same. The river guide's enthusiasm soon won Mike over, and Jamie once again deferred to her husband's wish.

Burr shuttled the Heffleys southeast on County Road 170 through Lajitas, Spanish for "little flat rocks," a reference to the Boquillas flagstone common to the area. Lajitas overlooks the San Carlos ford of the old Comanche Trail, the best natural river crossing between El Paso and Del Rio. Ranching and mining interests and later a thriving candelilla wax business (the Lajitas Wax Company) swelled the population of what had begun as a backwater trading post. Gen. John J. "Black-Jack" Pershing later established a cavalry camp there as a base for his campaign against Pancho Villa. For a while Lajitas was a jumping little town.

The army abandoned Lajitas for the European front in World War I. The mines at Terlingua played out soon afterward. One by one the businesses dried up and blew away. By midcentury, the community could boast only four stubborn residents.

Charmed by Lajitas's history and mystique, a succession of wealthy developers dumped fortunes into renovating the town over the next thirty years. By the time the Heffleys drove through in November 1988, Lajitas was a full-blown resort—complete with a golf course, airstrip, three motels, a museum, and an RV park. And they're still at it, too.

Once through Lajitas, CR 170 bends back west-northwest to mirror the river, featuring some fifty twisting, lonely miles that lie between Lajitas and Presidio. Jim Burr pulled off 170 at Rancho Rios, called Camp Nine by the locals, and maneuvered through a congested grove of salt cedars to back the trailer onto the cement launch. As Burr loaded the gear, snapped the oars in their locks, and doled out the life vests, he talked about routine safety measures they would be adopting for the journey ahead.

Safety is always a concern with river outfitters. Depending on capricious weather and upcountry snowmelt and rainfall, Colorado Canyon's rapids (featuring nicknames like Panther, Guacamole, and Quartermile) can be a tricky stretch. Most outdoor professionals, however, consider Colorado Canyon to be a mild to moderate challenge in the overall scheme of the whitewater world. That particular day, every variable ranked in the excellent range as far as Jim Burr could determine.

By eleven A.M. they were paddling through fast water with the wind in their hair. The Rio Grande was running steady and strong, but well below the flood stage levels recorded overhead by the gouges into the porous basalt canyon walls created by driftwood and rock. Everything was quiet and peaceful in the canyon. The sun highlighted its rusty walls and cast a golden light over its thriving flora. Native carrizo, or reed grass, lined the banks of the bronze river. Between the reeds and the rock base stretched tufts of emerald Bermuda.

Native varieties like palo verde or green limb, seed willows, retama, ocotillo, or "Devil's walking stick," and honey mesquite fight a losing battle with the foreign salt cedars (introduced by the Civilian Conservation Corps in the 1930s), but they hold their own in Colorado Canyon.

The Heffleys noticed the broad, green leaves of the tree tobacco plant sprouting from the inhospitable rock fissures. Jim Burr may have told them that in the spring the Indians dried their young, tender leaves and smoked them. Slowly the Heffleys understood that even with winter close upon the desert Southwest, the Big Bend is a vibrant land rich with color and golden light.

Spotted sandpipers and black phoebes flitted above the water, catching flies. Jamie caught the orange tint of the male Mexican duck's bill as they scrambled to get out of the raft's path. Common black hawks, zone tails, and red-tailed hawks constantly prowl the canyon. Every now and then a golden eagle joins the hunt. It is a magnificent flyer whose wingspan has been known to reach six feet. The Mojave rattlers lay unseen in the shadows. They have the ability to choose their venom to suit their victim, owning both neurotoxins akin to those of the cobra and the tissue-destroying compound ejected from the diamondback's fangs. Above them, coiled on the crags and ledges of the rock faces, waited the chameleon rock rattlers. River turtles, the native red-eared sliders, plopped off of their driftwood roosts whenever the raft swept dangerously near.

Mike pointed across the river at the rock face climbing hundreds of feet into the Chihuahuan desert sky. "That," he said gamely to his wife, "is Mexico."

Jamie's first impulsive thought—an extension of the premonitions she'd been experiencing all along—escaped her lips. "Are we safe here?"

"Just wave and act friendly if we see someone," Burr said casually. Most likely, he continued, they wouldn't see anyone at all, and even if they did, there wouldn't be enough of them to disrupt Colorado Canyon's serenity.

It never occurred to Jim Burr to mention that in recent months there had been at least three reports of random shootings in the general area. No injuries, no blood. But people had definitely been shot at for no good reason. Nor did he advise the Heffleys that once they entered the full eleven miles of Colorado Canyon, there were only two or three drainages on the Mexican side to hike out of and only one on the U.S. side—Panther Arroyo, which cut into the river some six or seven miles downriver from Camp Nine. On the Mexican side loomed the Sierra el Matadero, the "Killer Mountain," and beyond it the Sierra Rica range, the northernmost boundary of the Chihuahuan desert.

Locals take great caution whenever they venture out into the Big Bend. I carry at least a gallon of drinking water in my vehicle at all times, along with food rations, blankets, first aid gear, and lots and lots of ammunition.

Once inside Colorado Canyon you are more or less trapped by it. There is one safe way in and one way out—in the outfitter's van that brought you, parked at the downriver end. And even for those with the knowledge and gumption to escape the red gorge by climbing out the arroyos, there's still the desert to contend with. The Big Bend is not a playground for the unprepared. The Heffleys had been wise to hire a man of Jim Burr's experience.

As one of the locals, Jim Burr also knew of the violence associated with the rise of drug lords like Pablo Acosto and those who followed him after Pablo was shot down. But Burr assumed that the Mexican traffickers, like the American gangsters in New York, Las Vegas, Kansas City, and Chicago, rarely targeted civilians. Dopers kill dopers. Or maybe an informant or even a cop if a smuggler is unfortunate enough to confront one. Those of us in law enforcement come across mutilated bodies in the river—a warning to drug traffickers who might consider holding out a few dirty dollars from the bosses upstream. We find the remains of some low-level smuggler in the desert with a single bullet hole in his bleached skull. He may have been whacked by a competitor or by his best friend simply because he was seen chatting with the wrong person.

Drug runners play a rough, dangerous, and faithless game, chasing easy money all the way to either a jail cell or a shallow grave, but most of it plays out in shadows or in the dead of night. They never learn. The allure of drug money is too great for such poor people.

And the game never ends. A "mule" makes one trip across the river or he makes fifty. Suddenly he's got more cash in his hand than he ever dreamed possible. His future looks bright. He sleeps late as the honest saps of his generation drag themselves off to menial jobs. Young boys look up to him as he struts in expensive boots and fancy clothes and gold jewelry hanging from his neck. But trust me on this: his inevitably short career always ends either in blood or behind bars.

Violence had never touched Jim Burr or anyone he knew in his four years on the river. Why should he have thought to warn the Heffleys that it was even within the realm of possibility? The threat of violence seemed as remote to him as Colorado Canyon itself.

They were all three embraced by the beauty of the Big Bend, and for a while they let go of everything else. The current swept them around a red rock pillar, the crest of the river's bend, where the first waves of icy water spilled into the raft. The shock of it nearly took Jamie's breath, and she thought that she'd absolutely hate it if the raft overturned and she had to swim in that frigid water. And then the boat guide and his two clients confronted the billows of black smoke boiling upward into the blue sky.

JIM BURR SET HIS JAW at the prospect of having to row through such thick smoke as quickly as possible. Mexican farmers had long tended to garden plots along the river wherever they could burn off a little cane and remove woody-stemmed weeds.

With the rise of the marijuana trade, the new breed of farmer preferred the remoteness of places like Colorado Canyon for the year's quick cash crop, leaving a curtain of honey mesquite, retama, palo verde, and salt cedar between the dope and the rafting gringo *turistas* and letting nature take its course.

Sometimes these fires were the result of a dope plot's discovery by law enforcement officials or rival smugglers. And on rare occasions poverty-stricken pyromaniacs torched the cane simply to watch it burn. In any event, there was nothing all that unusual about the fire until it rose high enough to catch the breeze. It struck Jim Burr as a nuisance mostly, and he dug his oars deep into the water to drive the raft through it.

Neither Mike nor Jamie Heffley liked the cracking sound they heard downriver. At first they thought it was the fire consuming green wood, but soon enough Mike, the Vietnam veteran, knew damn well what sort of activity was going on.

"Why would someone be shooting down here?" Mike asked his guide. Jim Burr explained that it was normal for hunters to be out this time of year. Jamie couldn't buy that. She felt threatened, but she knew it was impossible to paddle upriver to Camp Nine. At the edge of the smoke, Jim saw two saddle horses and a small-footed mule tethered to honey mesquite limbs.

Then another chute of whitewater inhaled the raft and hurled them toward the thickest plume of smoke. The rubber craft pitched one way and then the other, finally dipping deep enough into an eddy to splash winter-chilled water over the Heffleys. The couple shook off the stun of the bitter cold while Burr struggled to right the raft. The boat was careening down the Rio Grande with its pudgy nose pointed directly at the American bank. They had not yet reached the smoke when they heard another crack—this one much louder than the rest.

The sharp clap startled all three rafters, but the path of the bullet didn't register. How could it above the wind and water and the grunts of a guide heaving several hundred pounds of people and equipment through whitewater and black smoke? Then there was a splash at the front of the raft, and for all three river riders the moment froze.

During the seconds between the first two bullets to whiz by her ear, Jamie understood that they were in serious trouble. One glance into Mike's eyes told her that he knew it, too.

The second shot missed Jamie's head by inches and pounded into the ice chest, shattering the ice and cans inside. The largest chunk of lead embedded in a dented can opener lying at the bottom of the Igloo, where the projectile stayed until forensics found it. Mike Heffley discerned the characteristic crack of .22 caliber rimfire, from a rifle more suited for plinking and sniping varmints than anything else. But he knew that weapons in the .30 caliber range and maybe larger were also being fired. Besides, even a .22 can kill a man.

The number and frequency of shots escalated until bullets fell like fat summer raindrops on the river around them. Some shots ricocheted off the rocks and, humming loudly, slammed against the canyon walls to the north. At least one shot pierced the raft, and the Heffleys and Jim Burr heard the hissing of escaping air. After a big booming round shattered Burr's oar handle their situation became clear. Someone—someone they had never met—was serious about killing them.

Jamie rose on wobbly legs in preparation to bail.

"Jump out!" Mike yelled. Jim was pounding what was left of his oars against the river, pumping the raft toward the presumed safety of the American bank. During one of the craft's many surges, Jamie fell forward into the rushing water. Mike yanked her out and dragged her over the side and back into the raft.

When Burr was close enough to the bank they all clawed their way up the loose rock and stubby brush along the steep base of the cliffs. Bullets pelted the stone around them. They were scrambling so fast that they couldn't determine where the shots were coming from.

"If they're from the U.S. side," Mike Heffley screamed, "we're dead! They're too close." But they had to know in order to hide, and so they peeked out from behind their scant cover. That's when they saw the faceless silhouettes walking down the high bluffs across the river. Four men, each either shouldering a weapon or furiously working the action to reload it, keeping pace with the terrified rafters, peering at them down long, black barrels.

Mike Heffley, the combat veteran, usurped the guiding duties from then on. He led his wife and Burr through the thorns and sharp brush. In the frantic scramble they ripped their clothing, tore their flesh, and grated the skin from their knees, shins, and elbows on the coarse basalt canyon walls. Fresh blood streamed down sweating ankles. They struggled for breath and stared at each other in disbelief. And then they sprinted again to the next tree or boulder to wipe the blood and the sweat from their eyes and figure out where to run next.

Jamie couldn't help but notice that most of the bullets were aimed at her even as she threaded her way through the thickest brush. She realized then that she was still wearing the yellow life vest and a bright red jacket. She ducked behind a boulder with bullets nipping at her knees and shucked off both. The next round of fire sounded like two full plastic milk cartons being slammed together. This time there was no ricochet.

"I'm hit!" Jim Burr yelled. The Heffleys saw him clamp his hands around his upper thigh.

"Can you still walk?" Mike hollered. Burr answered that under the circumstances he damn sure could. They ran again.

The fire slacked off when Jamie reached the boulder where her husband waited for her. Mike checked on Burr's condition and then he figured he had nothing to lose. He climbed on a rock in plain view of the shooters, clasped his hands together in prayer, and screamed, "No mas! No mas!" Jim Burr did the same, only he added that there were plenty of Yankee dollars back in the raft. The answer came first in the form of muffled laughter and next in another volley of lead.

Jim and Mike slipped back down behind the boulder. "Has this ever happened to you before?" Jamie asked Jim Burr.

"No," he answered, massaging his wounded thigh. "And I don't know what to do!"

Jamie shook her head in disappointment. She felt the rise of her anger for ignoring her own warnings, for not being more insistent with her husband, for allowing them to be lured to a place where people were shot for fun.

Mike raced for the next rock and waved for her to follow him. They scrambled like this for close to a half-hour before they reached a rock outcropping, offering them no cover and no passage. Jim was now in his river shorts, and Mike and Jamie were still in their torn jeans and ragged flannel shirts. They peeled the shoes from their feet and plunged into the November river. Not a shot was fired as they swam around the canyon wall to where the skinny northern bank took up again.

They crawled out of the river like alligators and into the thick brush. Mike and Jim beat down the path with their hands and feet. By now the fear, and the cold, and the struggle to escape the shooters had worn the runners down to near exhaustion. They stopped to catch their breath and noticed that the shooting had stopped. Protected by the tall, thick cane, Jim and Mike discussed the next move.

It was impossible to scale the cliff because of the steep incline. Camp Nine was the closest access out of the canyon, but none of them had the energy to swim upstream for five miles. They knew they had to stay the course and pick their way along the bank as best they could, swimming only when they had to. In the river they made easy targets.

Mike tried once again to reason with their unknown assailants. He climbed another rock and cried, "No más! No más!" This time no one shot him off of his perch. He realized that he was still carrying his camera—as if it had the least bit of importance to him now. "Maybe it's the camera," he said to no one in particular. "They don't want pictures."

He lifted the camera over his head to show it to them. And then he dashed it to pieces against the rocks.

Jamie looked upon her husband's futile gesture with pity. It was the first time she'd seen him so desperate, the first time he didn't know what to do. Her anger simmered again. Not only had the shooters frightened and injured her husband, they'd stolen a little of his pride.

Although there was no response from the gunmen, Mike knew the attack was far from over. He focused what remained of his energies on leading his party out of the canyon. They stomped through the tangles of cane and scrub trees and brush, one pounding step after another, until they collided with a second rock outcropping that jutted into the river, blocking their path.

Jamie Heffley, who by now had burned every bit of her energy reserves, stared at the rock barrier in defeat. She didn't see how she could swim the river again.

"I'm just too tired, Mike," she said, her lungs aching for breath. "Leave me here."

Before her husband could tell her that he'd never do any such thing, Jamie had another premonition. If they entered the river here they would all die. For the first time, she panicked.

"We have to turn around and go back!" she pleaded. "We can't get in the water again!"

Jamie saw defeat in Mike's face. "It doesn't matter which way we go," he said. "They're goin' to kill us. You know that, don't you?"

"Yes," Jamie admitted, "I know."

Mike reached out to her. "If we both have to die, I want us to die together."

"Yes," Jamie said. "That's what I want, too."

All along Jamie had uttered small pieces of old prayers under her breath as she'd run. She looked at her husband and told him that they should take whatever time they had left and do it right. Slumped against the rock face that had trapped them, soaked to the bone with foul, polluted water, bleeding and exhausted, they prayed to a God who loved them to forgive them for all their faults and transgressions. Once they had made their amends, they reminded Him that they had long ago yielded to His infinite wisdom and mercy and were now content to live or die as He saw fit.

After they uttered the last *amen* together, Mike sniffed and shook the water from his hair. He held Jamie's hand and drew fresh air into his lungs. Maybe they were destined to die that day, but Mike didn't see any reason to make it easy for their murderers. He surveyed the ridge across the river on the Mexican side. He looked at the rock outcropping and then in the opposite direction. Last, he looked for any sign of the shooters.

He thought *Lord if I had a weapon—any weapon—it'd be a different story.* Maybe he should swim the river now and go after those bastards with a rock, or a limb, or even his bare hands, and teach them a little about what he learned in Vietnam. All he had to do was single out one of the killers, knock him out or kill him—it didn't matter which—and then turn his gun on the others. Then it'd be their turn to run, and they'd better be good at it.

Mike could see it all unfolding just like that. They'd better hope he didn't make it across the river. He knew they had bigger rifles than the twin .22 rimfires that had been strafing them. They didn't have enough gun to stop Mike Heffley, though, if he got close enough to charge. But then he thought about what Jamie would do if she saw him killed. He realized further that he couldn't possibly risk leaving Jamie alone and defenseless while he went on the hunt. He couldn't live with himself if he were out stalking them while they crossed the river and shot her down like a dog. He then let go of all thoughts of retaliation unless they killed Jamie before they got him. All bets were off after that.

They'd run this far under fire and survived. Mike decided they'd run some more, at least until the night hid them, when they'd find a way out of the canyon on the American side. He didn't suppose the killers would dare follow them down CR 170. He stared downriver and then looked hard the other direction they had come. And then he chose.

"I go first," he said to Jim Burr with military authority. "Then Jamie, then you. You got it?"

Jim nodded and then Mike and Jamie slipped back into the river. They started swimming, with Mike's body between Jamie and the shooters. Mike held onto her elbow so she would know he was close by.

As soon as they cleared the outcropping's point, the canyon erupted with gunfire. Too exhausted to swim, Jamie pulled herself along the cliff, bouncing off the bottom instead of treading water. She was clawing the rock, fumbling for her next hand hold, when she heard a strange thud and felt something sear her abdomen. The force slammed her against the rock face. A strange warmth surrounded her, and a crimson stain ringed her body until it was absorbed by the current.

"I'm hit!" She started to flounder.

"No!" Mike yelled as he churned the water to reach her.

"I'm hit," she repeated before she lost her grip on the rocks and slipped beneath the surface. Mike plunged under the water to find her. He got a good hold and pulled her to the surface. He cradled her in a lifeguard's carry until they reached the bank, and then he hoisted her out of the water and laid her on the ground.

Jamie managed to stand. Mike yanked her shirt up to inspect the damage. What he saw unnerved him.

"Oh, God, no!" he screamed.

Mike was through running. He wrapped his powerful arms around his wife and walked her toward the cane. He could no longer hold back his tears. He no longer cared about his own life. He was telling himself he had lost everything when the big gun thundered from the bluff above.

Jamie was blown clear of her husband. She looked back to see him four feet in the air with his hands stretched above his head, as if he were trying out some new aerobic exercise and really didn't have the build or flexibility for it. Just as quickly, the impact slammed him back against the bank, where he landed on his back with his arms outstretched. Jamie heard the heavy bullet ripping through his bone and tissue, the thud of his body against the earth, the air rushing out of his lungs, and then a slow, agonizing groan.

Jim Burr, the last to jump into the river and the last to crawl out, was passing by Mike Heffley for the cane under a hail of rifle fire when the bullet struck down his client.

"Are you hit?" Jim said. He saw no wound, no blood.

"Yes," Mike stammered. "I've been shot."

"Are you dying, Mike?" Jamie asked him.

"I know one thing," he said. "I'm paralyzed." Silence drifted over the gravel bar, a portent as grim as the first black smoke had been. Mike blinked his eyes. He felt the blood draining out of him. He couldn't turn his head to look at his wife, so he just spoke the words. "Yeah, Baby," he said. "I'm dying."

"My husband is dying!" Jamie wailed the words over and over for herself as much as for anyone else. When she was spent, she stared at Mike. She knew he could not live much longer.

"I love you, Mike," she said.

"And I love you," he said, summoning the power to say the words he'd spoken to her almost every day. His voice trailed off at the end of this short sentence.

Jim Burr, who had the least serious wound, was terrified, too. But he also knew the only chance left was for him to run like hell for help. Panther Arroyo wasn't too much farther downriver. He yelled to Mike and Jamie both to advise them of his intent and then dove into the brush. By then his own bullet wound felt so numb. He looked back once or twice at the Heffleys lying bleeding in the midday sun.

Jamie heard the crackle of dense brush as Jim Burr plowed along the riverbank toward Panther Arroyo. She realized that she was exposed to more gunfire. Blood poured from her abdomen and also from a wound in her upper arm. She didn't know exactly when she'd been shot the second time, and she didn't care.

Jamie's survival instincts spurred her on. She crawled just a few feet from Mike into the deep weeds in a small grove of honey mesquite. The effort took everything she had. She felt as if she would soon lose consciousness and lay very still and listened.

Mike Heffley begged God to save him. When that was done, he lay very still.

Jamie sensed the men on the bluff were searching for her again. She couldn't really see them, but she felt their stares. Mike wasn't dead, but they didn't know that. Jamie started to cover herself with dirt, limbs, and dead grasses—anything to help her blend into her surroundings. She stopped when she heard her husband's voice.

"Lord, take me now!" Mike yelled. There was no longer any despair or agony in his voice. Jamie heard the same anticipation and excitement that he used to sell her on his exotic trips. Jamie prayed for God to deny Mike's request and leave him with her.

A lone gunshot downriver in Jim Burr's direction startled her. Jamie looked at her watch. It was noon. If Burr was gunned down, Jamie believed the killers would now return to make sure the job was done. She burrowed deeper into what she believed would be her grave.

She lay still. She held her breath to practice playing dead in the event she heard their feet on the rocks. The convulsions that racked her body betrayed her best efforts. When she could lie still again she reapplied the sticks and dirt.

The slow hours crept by, marked only by the constant rush of whitewater and the gusting wind. She continued to bleed.

Jamie thought she heard voices. She couldn't make out a single word or even what language it was. She thought she heard her husband cough, a sign that he was still alive. But logic told her that Mike was dead and what she heard could not have come from him. Slowly and quietly, she burrowed a little deeper, listening to every little noise.

Red ants clinched their pincers on the tender flesh around her cuts, scrapes, and bullet wounds. She endured their torment, moving only when involuntary convulsions racked her body. When the spells passed, she packed two more inches of soil on top of her clothes to replace what had been knocked off. She took turns applying direct pressure to both of her wounds. Fearing infection, she rolled to one side to let her abdominal wound bleed a little more and then rolled back to make it stop. She waited, she listened. She shook violently. And then she scraped a little more dirt from the ground and covered herself.

At sundown, the ants retreated and the cold attacked. She now shivered in addition to her spells of convulsions. Muscles that were not cramping ached. She pulled her shirt up over her nose and ears to warm the cold night air before she breathed it. She learned that there is no dark like the night in the canyon, lying close to your murdered husband, listening for footsteps, waiting to die.

The minutes passed slowly. She sang church hymns to comfort herself. Now numb with cold, she watched the moon reach its apex directly in front of her and then dive behind the black mountains.

She listened in the dark for a man wading across the river or a boot kicking a loose rock, the cock of a hammer, a cough or a groan from her dead husband. She listened for coyotes, the scream of a lone mountain lion, or the growl of a Mexican black bear, or any other predator that had caught the scent of blood in the wind. She could not stop herself from imagining the sounds of animals tearing into Mike's body or thinking of herself being dragged off to a shallow grave. She listened for the killers to emerge from out of the black canyon and put a bullet in her head. These thoughts faded as the light began to etch itself into the eastern horizon and push back her longest night. The sun climbed back into the sky, and still Jamie waited.

Sometime that cold morning she heard the unmistakable *whack, whack, whack* of a Black Hawk helicopter. The craft hovered for a moment when it came to a body lying in blood on a gravel bar, and then it landed on the canyon floor.

JAMES BURR RAN OUT of riverbank for the third time. He slipped back into the river until he reached Panther Rapids, where the killers shot at him one last time. He hid in the brush until dark. When the moon was up, he picked his way along the canyon wall until he reached Panther Arroyo. In wet shorts and river shoes, he climbed the sharp, abrasive rocks and crossed the low hills choked with horse crippler, Spanish dagger, agave, prickly pear, and ocotillo. A Lipan Apache warrior raised in the desert might have been hard pressed to match Burr's trek across some of the most hostile terrain in the American Southwest. I couldn't do it. I don't know how he did. I believe that Jim Burr felt a duty to his clients, and even with a bullet wound in his thigh, that obligation drove him on.

Jim Burr wandered County Road 170 until Ken Kempf picked him up around 8:30 the next morning, about the same time the chopper was rescuing Jamie Heffley. Their long nightmare finally ended.

Mine began.

I GOT THE CALL from Presidio County Chief Deputy Steve Bailey around three A.M. He reported that Far Flung Adventures was missing three people in Colorado Canyon. Searchers had found the boat tied up on the shore but not the occupants. They were most likely somewhere on the river, so the best thing to do was get some boats, put them in at Camp Nine, and hunt them up.

I dressed as quietly as I could, but the telephone had awakened Shirley and she asked me about the case. I told her what I knew and that I was on my way to catch a boat.

"Well, don't drown," she said.

My wife suffers from a phobia of large bodies of water. Two of her close relatives have died by drowning, so in her mind the danger of lakes and rivers is very real. For twenty-three years, however, I'd gone out on rivers, lakes, swamps, and wetlands, and she'd never before warned me about drowning. Her comment, delivered in a half-conscious, drowsy state, unnerved me.

I gathered my gear, careful to collect extra cigarettes and cigars. The trunk of my 1986 Chevrolet Caprice carried what it always did, along with full Border Patrol canteen and plenty of C rations. A case might take a day or it might take thirty. Rangers stay in the saddle until the job's done. I've always known that, and so did my wife.

By four A.M. I was dodging mule deer on the lonely eighty-seven-mile trek of Highway 118 south between Alpine and Study Butte, and from there on the twisting, turning asphalt road that leads to Lajitas, and then a dozen more miles on CR 170, which swings by the Rio Bravo and Camp Nine.

I arrived around 5:30 to meet up with Chief Bailey of Presidio County, several Border Patrol and U.S. Customs agents, Brewster County deputy sheriffs, and some personnel from Far Flung Adventures who had been out most of the night looking for their employee and clients. A regular flotilla, ranging from dented johnboats to fiberglass jet skiffs, all marked with various government insignias and corporate logos, was beached on the river. Daylight was our last requirement.

The Far Flung Adventures staff advised us that they had come upon the bullet-riddled raft. We knew then that we were dealing with an intentional act.

At dawn, the Border Patrol jet helicopter and U.S. Customs Black Hawk swung into the canyon for a first reconnaissance. Soon enough they located the abandoned raft, and then a few hundred yards from that the body of Mike Wayne Heffley, lying face up on the sandbar where he had fallen the morning before. While the pilots were radioing in their findings, a woman appeared out of the brush. The Black Hawk loaded her up and delivered her to the Alpine hospital for treatment of gunshot wounds and shock.

I'll never understand how that young woman survived that horrible ordeal in such rough country, in the cold of late November, knowing her dead husband lay just a few feet away. The pilots explained that she was nearly incoherent and suffering from blood loss, shock, and exposure. When she looked at the gray, bloated body of her husband, however, she was overcome with grief.

James Burr turned up at Camp Nine soon afterward. Wounded and suffering from shock and dehydration, Burr had climbed out of Colorado Canyon and walked over a mile of torturous country to reach CR 170. He'd walked quite a ways down the road until a truck came along. Burr told us the whole story before he was whisked off for medical care. After that, we knew a little more about what had happened. Among other crimes, we were dealing with a murder.

The suspects were most likely Mexican nationals, which opened the door on a whole host of complex issues. Relations with Mexican law enforcement were nothing like what I'd known in the 1960s. The victims had no earthly idea why anyone would want to kill them.

The plan was to position officers along the canyon bluff in case the shooters were still out there while we got a team to the crime scene to learn what we could about this tragic, senseless offense.

The river was up and running strong. I knew without considering it twice that I wanted to tag along with Texas Game Warden Robert Newman, a friend of mine who for years had run the Rio Grande under a variety of conditions. I made a step or two toward Newman's hard-used craft when the U.S. Customs agent implored me to ride along with him.

I assumed he wanted to discuss some of the international issues kicked up by this mess or something. I didn't mind jawing with this bird about whatever was on his mind, but my main concern was how well he knew how to operate Uncle Sam's fancy jet boat outfit.

To that exact inquiry, the customs agent responded with a confident affirmation. Still, there were plenty of rocks in the river, any number of which could splinter his boat. I suggested that the safest path would be in Officer Newman's wake. He agreed. Furthermore, with the strong current, I advised the agent that once we got caught in the grip of the current, he'd need to give the skiff full throttle to retain the craft's steering ability until we powered through to slower water, just as I'd seen Officer Newman successfully do in the past.

The agent responded that he knew all about that. I don't claim to have much boating experience, but I've developed a good sense for competent law enforcement officers. Despite this fellow's unbridled confidence and snappy new uniform, he looked like a screwup to me. I occupied the bow of the new boat and he the stern. Before we knew it, we were swept away by whitewater.

Fifty yards into our run we encountered slick, black rocks protruding above the water line. I braced myself for that thrust of jet power that would propel us safely around each of them. I was terribly disappointed when I heard the engine shut down completely. About then, the jet boat struck a glancing blow against the first of many rocks in our path and knocked me off balance.

I turned around to encourage the Fed to start up the engine and operate it in the manner we had discussed. I was alarmed to see that he had not only misrepresented his skill in operating the boat motor, he was now attempting to breast-feed it.

I don't know which collision had sheared the motor from its mount, but given our situation I was looking for something far more buoyant than an Evinrude outboard to clutch against my chest. The agent seemed confused by these unexpected events. I, on the other hand, was deeply vexed.

Hopelessly adrift, we careened off two more boulders in rapid succession, and then the river hurled us head-on against the wall of the great igneous bluff. Knowing that I would be separated from the contents of my trunk, I decided to tote much of my arsenal with me. I carried a .308 M-14 automatic rifle fully loaded with a twenty-round clip, which had to weigh close to twenty pounds. I had two more twenty-round clips tucked away in my military field jacket. Naturally, my Colt .45 pistol and two extra clips hung from my gun belt, as did my knife and other metal objects. I wore eighteen-inch-high cowboy boots and tight-fitting Wrangler jeans.

These items are not typically found on the greased bodies of your long-distance swimmers. I was burdened with fear and lots and lots of guns and ammo. Basically, I was a human anchor. It didn't take a lot of survival training to understand that if I went into the river, I'd soon be checking into Davy Jones' locker. I'd be the only Texas Ranger in the almost two-hundred-year history of the agency to be lost at sea. Undocumented workers crossing the Rio Grande would soon be using my *el rinche* butt for a stepping-stone. By the time I washed into the Gulf of Mexico, I'd be stinkbait for some Bubba's trotline. This was not the way I wanted to go out.

My next thought—impulse rather—was entirely inappropriate for a seasoned peace officer, but one never knows how the spirit will react in a crisis. I only knew that I was going down with somebody else's ship, and I planned to take that no-boat-driving, Barney Fife son of a bitch with me. I knew it was wrong.

The image of George Washington crossing the Delaware could not have been as glorious as watching Officer Newman adroitly navigate his tub close to ours to effect a rescue. Sheriff Bailey tossed me a rope, and as soon as I tied her off, Newman towed us safely to shore. That gritty riverbank silt and gravel never felt better beneath my feet. I thanked God for his mercy.

"Give me just a minute, Joaquin," the customs agent said. "I'll get this motor hooked back on and we'll be on our way."

"You can kiss my ass," I replied in a most unprofessional manner. "I'm going with somebody who knows what the hell they're doing."

He seemed at a loss as I stomped over to Far Flung Adventures' raft and asked if they'd mind if I flopped my butt in with them. They agreed and we resumed our journey to the murder scene. The wannabe mariner what's-his-name went it alone and smacked into nearly every black rock in Colorado Canyon. I liked watching him do it.

WE CAME UPON THE DEFLATED, bullet-riddled Far Flung Adventures raft tied to a limb on the bank. The scene reflected chaos: frantic footsteps leading into the brush, broken sunglasses, discarded rubber supply bags, and life jackets where the victims had thrown them.

All of us solemnly climbed back into our crafts (I did cast a menacing stare at the customs agent just to let him know I had not forgotten) and drifted downriver to the murder scene.

Three or four hundred yards beyond the raft we came upon the body of Mike Heffley lying on his back on the American bank of the Rio Grande. His head pointed southeast, his feet directly opposite, his right leg crossed over his left. His shirt was unbuttoned, and someone had unbuckled his belt and undone his pants and zipper, as if he were trying to relieve his agony—the searing pain and pressure of being gut-shot—before he died. Approximately four feet from his body was a large bloodstain where the hydrostatic force of the shot had slammed him facedown against the bank. He had rolled over on his back. Torn and dirty white socks covered his shoeless feet.

It didn't require a forensic scientist to observe the .44 caliber bullet exit wound eight inches below his left nipple. The round had entered from the back, expanded as it encountered tissue, the spinal cord, and maybe a rib bone, and exploded out of the victim's chest. Mr. Heffley's last moments were spent in a combination of fear and scalding pain. Looking at this young man who had his life snatched from him, I felt great guilt about harboring resentment over my own misadventure of a few moments before. This victim deserved justice. The responsibility to investigate his murder fell squarely upon me. For his sake, I wanted to be a damn good Texas Ranger. I wanted to do my job.

I patted the customs agent on the back as a token of my forgiveness and to restore a sense of professionalism and camaraderie. I spoke to all of my friends at the scene—Game Warden Bob Newman, Deputy Bailey, and Texas

Highway Patrol trooper David Duncan (Duncan would one day fill my boots very well as Alpine's Texas Ranger)—and I said, "Boys, I really want to find the son of a bitches who did this."

Maybe it was Bailey who pointed across the river, above the Colorado Canyon bluff, to the Chihuahuan desert that stretched to the blue Sierra Ricas towering to the south. "Mexican nationals, most likely," he said.

I didn't give a damn who they were. I'm pretty sure my expression made that clear. None of us felt like it was your typical drug deal gone bad. Dope killings are almost always at close range and intensely brutal—a .45 to the head or a twisting knife slash to the gut. Jim Burr had already told us that whoever did this opened up out of the blue. I'll be damned if it didn't appear that Burr was telling the truth. Without a motive, the suspects would be difficult to trace. We decided to prowl the area around the crime scene. We climbed through the cut on the Mexican side of the river to see what the shooters left behind.

We cut their tracks soon enough on top of the bluff, next to the piles of brass rifle casings in a spot overlooking the sandbar where Heffley had died. We followed their tracks south through an arroyo where they stopped and made a fire, ate sardines, drank sodas, and smoked a couple of joints.

Their tracks led to where they'd hobbled their horses and mules—the latter of the local variety bred with small hooves to better maneuver in the rocky country. I watched their prints trail off into the Chihuahuan desert.

We had to make some arrangements with Mexican officials to follow the suspects to wherever they went. But I knew we'd soon be back following their trail, and once we were, I swore we'd catch them. I didn't know any of the victims, but I'd seen what happened to them and it made me angry. Even if the woman lived, by our laws the two survivors were powerless to avenge themselves. I wasn't powerless by a long shot—at least not on the Texas side of the river—and from the moment I looked down at the body of Mike Heffley, I decided that I wanted to hunt down his murderers and introduce them to an American judge.

I wanted to do it for him.

CHAPTER NINE

Earth, Fire, Water, and Blood: II

(OCKHAM'S RAZOR AND THE DEVIL'S SWING)

The Colorado Canyon Shootings

1988

We choppered in Presidio Justice of the Peace Raul Ramos to pronounce Mike Heffley dead. The victim's body was airlifted to Marfa, where an ambulance transported it to El Paso for autopsy. Local Ranger Buster Collins was on hand to witness the procedure.

Those of us who spent the day on the river went to work on the crime scene, piecing the event together to see if it made any sense. There was a swarm of good officers working the scene, but I found myself leaning most on Border Patrol agent Wayne Weimers, who, among other talents, had developed an extensive intelligence network in Mexico, and ex-DPS narcotics officer turned U.S. Customs agent Bill Fort, who knew how to make use of the formidable federal resources, including snitch money to spread around if it came to that.

We photographed the body and the raft as we found them and started picking through all available evidence. We extracted bullet fragments from the oar and ice chest and sent them to the crime lab in Austin. We found .22, .30, and .44 shell casings all along the rim of Colorado Canyon on the Mexican side. We located Heffley's wallet, still containing some $537 in cash along with several bank and credit cards. These were later returned to Jamie Heffley, who at the time was fighting for her life at Brewster Memorial Hospital in Alpine.

Along with the complications posed by Jamie's blood loss, exposure, shock, and tissue and emotional trauma, a terrible infection had set in. The antibiotics were having little effect. She ran extreme fevers up to 104 degrees. Her legs turned black and swelled to twice their normal size. Her complexion turned yellow, while the flesh under her fingernails turned dark blue. She continued to sporadically convulse, and her heart rate raced off the charts. When her family felt like they might lose her, she was airlifted to Abilene for emergency treatment. She soon turned the corner, beating back the infection, anemia, and dehydration, and was released after only a few days to mourn the appalling death of her husband. Few have suffered more.

As they learned more about what this woman had been through, all manner of local, state, and federal law enforcement agencies put aside their petty bickering and combed every bush and cactus for evidence. We also had the full cooperation of the Mexican agencies. Fernando Lozano, comandante of the Chihuahua State Judicial Police, along with Officer Jesus Porras and others, was with us on the river. They were as keen to solve this case as we were.

It's possible that the Mexican authorities were worried about the effects the shootings would have on the tourist trade. Maybe they were embarrassed that Mexican citizens were the prime suspects in the murder of an innocent American or desperate to prove that the perpetrators had just cause. Cynics might tell you that these Mexican cops were inherently corrupt, knew exactly who had committed this crime, and were simply going through the motions of an investigation to appease American anger until it faded away. But I like to think that once Comandante Lozano and his men understood what had happened, they didn't like it any more than we did.

This was a fortuitous development, because no one on this side of the river had the authority to track these bastards down. That opportunity came by invitation from the Mexicans, who opened the door to the Chihuahuan desert for us to follow the killers wherever they fled.

The next day, Chihuahua Judicial Police Officers Jesus Porras and Loreto Quezada were again out in the field with me. They borrowed horses in the nearby village of El Mulato and put to work skills that they don't teach in schools and universities. They were desert trackers, some of the best I'd ever seen, and once Comandante Lozano cut them loose on the killers' trail they followed it like coyotes after a bleeding rabbit.

We worked our way from the crime scene through a cut in the canyon wall that rose to the desert plain paralleling the river. Walking the narrow cut, we came across a fire pit where the killers had enjoyed lunch. Most of the suspects wore boots, but one wore tennis shoes. We made a cast of the shoe print with dental plaster.

The suspects had left the area on three horses and one mule. The signs told us that the mule was missing a shoe. I needed to return to the crime scene. Porras and Quezada rode on for another mile or two, but eventually even these experts lost the trail on the hard, rocky ground.

We got the general idea that the killers were heading toward a series of villages strung along the Rio Grande east of Ojinaga in Chihuahua, Mexico. They had names like Barrio de los Montoya, El Marqueno, Monte Bustillos, Palomos (the Doves), El Ojito (the Little Spring), Valle Nueva, El Salitre (the Salt Peter Mine), Labor de Abajo (the Downstream Farm), La Bolsita (the Little Basin), and La Loma de Juarez (Juarez's Hill). Later, when we regrouped and the Mexican officers asked me where we should begin our efforts, I answered immediately. "El Mulato."

Without hesitation, they agreed.

EL MULATO ENDURES a notorious reputation older than the crumbling adobe buildings at its core. According to local legend, the village was settled by buffalo soldiers who had deserted Fort Davis. Proponents of this version assume that the African American outlaws harbored a natural contempt for American authority. They took Mexican wives, spawned Mexican mixed-blood children, and didn't give a shit about anybody except their own. They set to work smuggling candelilla wax across the river into Texas as a means to profit and thumb their noses at their former masters at the same time.

The Mexican government sought to regulate and tax the thriving candelilla wax market. The wax is derived from the native candelilla plant and used in lipstick, chewing gum, car wax, and countless other products. The buffalo soldiers bypassed the taxmen of two nations with considerable skill. They expanded their inventory with bottles of mescal and sotol packed along with the wax. Always keen to new markets, they coyoted in a few Chinese laborers, too, to work on the Texas railroads.

With Prohibition in full swing, the smugglers moved into the whiskey trade, which soon dwarfed the wax and desert spirits exports. By now, the sons and grandsons of the buffalo soldiers brought a new kind of profes-sionalism to the family trade. They were Mexicans by creed, soldiers by training, smugglers by nature, and they'd been bred to hate the gringos who bought their wares. Marijuana and cocaine were already trickling into the larger American cities, but nobody could anticipate what happened in American society in the 1960s, when the floodgates flew open for illegal drugs. Most in northern Mexico were new to the lucrative smuggling arts except the villagers of El Mulato.

The dope business was soon dominated by powerful gangsters from other Mexican states and other South American countries (except for Pablo Acosta, who was born in Santa Elena and worked as a roofer in Odessa, Texas, and Hobbs, New Mexico, before he dominated the trade around Ojinaga). Regardless of where the drug lords came from, they traditionally recruited their soldiers and "mules" from El Mulato—or at least this is their reputation among law enforcement folks.

It seemed pointless to nose around El Mulato in search of the person who wore sneakers and had ridden out two days before with plenty of guns on a mule with three horseshoes. No one knowing who fit that odd description would tell us. State and federal Mexican officials are not perceived as your friends in small Mexican towns, and few Mexicans place much faith in *los rinches,* the supposed henchmen of the arrogant gringo Tejanos. It never occurred to us that the killers had kept their secret to themselves and that the honest citizens of El Mulato had no idea who had committed the crime. We needed a plan to move the investigation forward, and I soon came up with one.

I don't know what pressure was brought to bear on El Mulato by the Mexican authorities. But I went to Hugh Rushton, chief of the Border Patrol stationed in Marfa, and got his permission to close down the border for several miles around Redford, Texas. I believed that if we stopped all illegal traffic across the border, the dope smugglers would turn over the shooters to get business back to normal.

Redford was a traditional crossing and farming area, inhabited for twelve millennia or more by Pueblo-type Indians, who first cut the irrigation canals still in use today. The Jumanos and Apaches, among others, once occupied this fertile plain. The Spanish castaway and chronicler Cabeza de Vaca crossed this way. The Spanish built a mission in 1683. In 1870, the village was formally organized as El Polvo, meaning "the dust." But for generations, the Indians and Mexicans called it Vado Rojo, or the "red crossing," based on the color of the stone bedrock that lay beneath the Rio Grande.

When locals requested a post office, the postal authorities insisted on an English name. The villagers happily complied with the literal translation of the Spanish name, Red Ford. But no one bothered to ask if the name was two separate words. Today, a very Anglo-sounding Redford boasts about one hundred full-time residents. Better than 90 percent can claim pure Native American ancestry. They, like most of the villagers on the Mexican side of the river, are hardworking, honest, truly special people perfectly attuned to their surroundings.

Redford and El Mulato are just a short distance apart, and although Redford in no way shared El Mulato's reputation, the two communities were socially and economically tied together. Each had family and friends living in the other. None of the locals thought twice about moving back and forth to buy groceries or visit a sick aunt. The children of El Mulato crossed the river to attend Redford's celebrated one-room school.

I asked Chief Rushton for the manpower to barricade all crossings for ten straight days. As far as the locals knew, however, the closing would last until the killers were brought to justice. Mexican citizens who attempted to cross the Rio Grande around Redford ran into heavily armed, humorless agents who turned them away.

Citizens found the blockade inconvenient, perhaps even insulting. The authorities struggled with the burden of manpower hours to keep it in force. It was hard on everyone. After six straight days of blockade failed to yield results, I began to sweat.

On the seventh day, several anonymous informants telephoned the Border Patrol with the names of four perpetrators. One was reported to have close family outside of Redford. Our informant claimed that at least one suspect was crossing the river each night to sleep with his relatives at one of two houses.

Such hearsay didn't leap the probable cause hurdle between me and swearing out a state arrest warrant, so we secured search warrants from the Immigration Service to scour the residences for illegal aliens. A multidepartment task force, complete with a helicopter, hit the houses at daylight on November 29, ten days after the shooting. We arrested Eduardo Rodriguez Piñeda, who confessed to being at the scene of the shooting. He claimed he wasn't the triggerman, but we already knew better.

Eduardo was wearing a pair of Reebok tennis shoes that were later matched to the print we found at the crime scene. He had stashed a Marlin .44 magnum carbine rifle that had been stolen from a residence in Odessa in 1984 and was later proven to have killed Michael Heffley. Although Piñeda lived with his family three miles downriver from Redford, he had close ties to Mulato. Among his scant possessions was $3,000 in cash. We knew from the evidence found by the river that he used drugs. None of this surprised me. The shocker was that Eduardo was only seventeen years old.

Two of his accomplices were only fifteen.

Subsequent interviews with the suspect concluded that none of the shooters had ever met Michael or Jamie Heffley or Jim Burr. They had never spoken. There had been no confrontation on the river before four Mexican boys gunned down three American tourists. The facts of this incident floored me.

REGARDLESS OF THE SUSPECTS' YOUTH, we went about our business like always. These boys were old enough to kill people. They were damn sure old enough to undergo a full-throttle murder investigation. Presidio Judge Raul Ramos arraigned Eduardo Rodriguez Piñeda on a murder charge. Meanwhile, Chihuahua State Police rounded up the other three, all of whom I believe lived in either El Mulato or Barrio de la Montoya.

The Mexican officers confiscated a Winchester Model 94 .30-30 rifle that fired the round retrieved from the ice chest and the two rounds that wounded Jamie Heffley, and two different models of Marlin .22 semiautomatic rifles, one of which had plugged Jim Burr. The three suspects and their weapons were transported to Chihuahua City, capital of Chihuahua.

Ballistics tests on the weapons in Mexican custody matched the markings on the shell casings found at the scene. Our Chihuahuan colleagues fired the .22's into a long wooden box full of cotton to extract the bullets, even though we told them that we were interested only in the fired casings, since we hadn't really recovered any intact .22 bullets at the scene. They gave us some anyway. We accepted them with thanks.

Test firing the .30-30 proved more challenging. A resourceful officer filled a rusted fifty-five-gallon drum with water and planned to pump a round into it from the bed of his truck. I told him he'd get pretty wet doing that. He smiled and pulled the trigger. The hydrostatic shock, explosion of gasses, and foot-pound energy of the 150-grain slug blasted fifty-five gallons of nasty water into a mushroom cloud that drenched our technician. We closed in after it was over, tipped the barrel to drain the last few ounces of water, picked our bullet out of the grit, and left after expressing our gratitude. The officer was still smiling.

We were handed copies of the suspects' written statements. They were, of course, in Spanish, but Border Patrol Agent David Castañeda was fluent in that language. It was my understanding that the suspects' parents had encouraged them to admit their crimes. If so, they shot the prevailing theory to hell that everyone in El Mulato is a criminal. We interviewed them in person with a translator until we felt like we had a coherent understanding of what had gone down in Colorado Canyon. I couldn't believe that such quiet, well-mannered boys were ruthless killers.

I didn't know what fate held in store for them, but incarceration in a youth facility in northern Mexico couldn't possibly have been a positive experience. Their detached demeanors told me that they were under the impression that the shooting was some video game. They were ready for it to end now. I didn't want to feel sorry for them, but I couldn't help myself. They had no idea what a horrific crime they had committed. And they couldn't imagine what it was about to cost them.

It's a two-hour drive north from Chihuahua to Ojinaga, through high mountain passes, dodging buses and burros—both packed to full capacity with people and products, wares borne by the weary. One impatient driver struck a glancing blow against a burro pulling a wooden cart. Knocked out of its harness, the indignant beast stared through the windshield at his assailant before he backed up and kicked in the side of the car with both hind hooves. I don't know if Mexican auto policies cover this sort of claim, but I bet they get a lot of them. There's no way those two vehicles—hundreds of years apart in technology—complement each other on the same one-lane road.

We passed by the state prison, its walls still peppered with bullet holes and cannon fire from the 1910 revolution. Chihuahua City holds better than a million residents. It's the largest city in Mexico's largest state. Everyone there seems so active, so busy, so engaged with each other, and far more alive than the people of Houston or Dallas. I don't know why that is.

We returned to Marfa to confront Eduardo Rodriguez Piñeda with everything we'd learned in Mexico. About this time, after he'd had ample opportunity to think things over and knew that his accomplices had told one tale, he sat down and told us what I think was the truth.

Later, Eduardo rolled the dice and took his case to trial. His brother-in-law, who was later convicted of drug-related felonies but at the time claimed to be a successful Dallas-area restaurant impresario, hired fancy Dallas lawyers to defend him. Eduardo's attorneys claimed, among other things, that Eduardo's confession was made under duress, that an INS agent had lied to a federal magistrate to obtain the search warrant, and that Jim Burr and/or Michael Heffley had shot at their client. They also maintained that Eduardo had not fired the fatal round. The jury heard both sides and convicted Eduardo Rodriguez Piñeda anyway. I testified in that case about what caliber bullet had killed Mike Heffley and who our investigation had revealed was handling that same gun at the scene. I was glad to do it.

Eduardo was sentenced to thirty years in the Texas Department of Corrections system. I heard that he was released a year or so ago. I don't know if it's true.

JIM BURR STILL LIVES in Terlingua. I don't think he guides on the river anymore, but he might. He was damn good at it. I've never believed he de-served any blame for what happened to his clients. It happened to him, too.

Jamie Sue Heffley spent two years recovering from her injuries. A friend once told her that the light in her eyes was gone. Her grief and loneliness were mitigated only by her strengthening devotion to God. She put her faith in the Lord as she had always done and lived each long day as it came. In 1990, she met a young minister named David Hill, who, like her, had lost his spouse. His wife left behind a two-year-old daughter and a nine-year-old son. One of Jamie's deepest regrets was never having children with Mike. She married David Hill and moved to Tennessee. She found purpose in life again. She went on.

The scars of the bullet wounds are still there, but the sting of memory has grown mercifully faint. If you ask her, Jamie will tell you only that she is the luckiest of all women to be so loved by two good men. I've always admired her.

But she didn't get real justice for the murder of her first husband, and everyone knew it. State Representative Pete Gallego, one of the prosecutors who worked on her case, asked her about her experience once the trial was over. Jamie expressed the deep void she felt, her sense that there had not been proper closure. What she truly wanted was to confront the young man who had killed her husband, tell him exactly what he had stolen from her, and say what she thought about him.

Gallego responded by sponsoring just such a bill to make indicted criminals face their victims. He fought like a dog for it, and today it is law in Texas that a victim of a crime can have a say if he or she wants it. That is the legacy left by Jamie Sue Heffley Hill to a state that she will never set foot in again.

LEGEND SPEAKS OF A CAVE near the peak of Sierra de la Santa Cruz, south of the Rio Bravo near present-day Ojinaga. Before the coming of the Span-iards, the Indians claimed that a great, evil spider inhabited the cave, where it had spun a magnificent web. The Indians made frequent offerings to ap-pease its hunger. They sang and danced in seasonal rituals to keep it enter-tained. For once the spider crawled out from its lair, it swung on its thread from one peak to the next, leaving sickness, famine, and feuds in its ter-rible wake.

Once the Spanish forced their culture and religion upon the Native Americans they had conquered, the spider became the devil himself, who on occasion swung from one peak to another on a silver chain hung over the crescent moon—to spread evil, bad luck, and ill will. The people maintained their rituals, but on rare occasions they became lax. The first time a great cholera epidemic decimated the population. On another, drought and famine struck. After a third, the Comanche burned the mission to the ground, slaughtering all who hid behind its crumbling walls.

In the wake of the destruction, the villagers climbed again with their offerings and their grief to the top of Sierra de la Santa Cruz to sing and dance to keep the devil locked in his cave. Whenever evil befell them, they believed that Lucifer had escaped long enough to ride the winds between the craggy peaks. The desert mountains he claimed as his home range became known as the Devil's Swing.

Colorado Canyon lies within its heart.

IN MY SEARCH over the years to understand the cause of the Colorado Canyon shootings—what it meant to my life and the people I served and protected—I finally came across the opinion of Redford's most educated man. He reminded me that the honest people who live and work along the Rio Grande are weary of the labels, of the racism, of the stereotypes brought on by the drug trade and the so-called War on Drugs.

He cites statistics that indicate the minuscule volume of drug traffic in the Big Bend when compared to the overall epidemic. Over 90 percent of drugs smuggled into this country arrive through legal points of entry. Contraband comes hidden in trucks, ships, and jets under the noses of trained officers and dogs and even X-ray machines.

He dares the United States to stop 100 percent of the Big Bend's burros and backpackers if that's what we want. He claims that if we do there will be no difference in the amount of illegal drugs available on American streets. If so many of the border people are involved in lucrative drug trafficking that generates billions of dollars, why do 48 percent of Presidio County residents live below the poverty line? It was never their idea to draw the line between Mexico and the United States down the middle of their river. The War on Drugs being fought in their backyard can only be won in American hearts and homes.

The sage asks us to understand that a river makes a lousy barrier between two desert nations. The Rio Grande has always attracted the desert people to both sides of her fertile banks. God never intended that she be used to keep them apart. A mountain range constitutes a better barrier, or maybe a brick wall, like the one the Soviets built in Berlin. People were shot dead trying to cross the Berlin Wall. The Soviets never understood that they had split German families apart. The same is true on the Rio Grande, where only a few inches of water—if even that much—separate cousins, lovers, and lifelong friends.

That's a lot to think about. And we'd better get after it.

But if I really wanted to distill the absolute truth about what happened in the Colorado Canyon back in 1988, my friend in Redford further suggested that I consider the principle of Ockham's Razor. I had to look that up.

William of Ockham was an English theologian and philosopher who probably laid much of the groundwork for modern scientific inquiry. In a nutshell, whenever Willie was presented with a complex problem, he first cut away all the unnecessary bullshit in an attempt to view the problem in its simplest terms. William of Ockham once said, "What can be done with fewer assumptions is done in vain with more."

Okay. Let's take Ockham at his word and cut this killing to the bone:

The formal account of the Colorado Canyon shootings has been left for posterity in the court record. Here's my own version, looking back these many years, flawed as it may be:

Four boys who knew each other only by their nicknames—the likes of "Cave," "Neck," "the Fourth," and "El Martillo," son of, would you believe it, "Bad Luck"—got together to go hunting. Attribute nothing ill to these boys from their nicknames. It is an Indian tradition to rename themselves after some significant event so subjective in nature that only their family may know what it means. They are not gangsters or pampered professional athletes. They are Native Americans hanging on to what culture has been left to them.

Anyway, Bad Luck Jr. and his buddies borrowed three horses and one mule from their neighbors one Friday afternoon. They took food, blankets, marijuana, guns, and handfuls of ammunition into the mountains to hunt rabbits or deer. They rode east out of El Mulato until they reached El Nueve, the Nine, where they hobbled the horses and camped for the night.

They rose before daylight, watered the horses and mule, and rode toward the mountains. They reached Cañon de la Engunena, called Colorado Canyon on American maps. For some reason, they set fire to an abandoned field most recently used by marijuana growers before they climbed up the cut that led to the top of the canyon walls. The sooty smoke hung in the canyon like a black blanket.

Like all boys out on their own, they were anxious to fire their weapons. They shot at a number of targets before they spotted a landlocked cow.

They fired on the cow. I don't know if they hit it. But with the fire burning below, and the thunderous shooting, and the bellowing, frightened animal, they had quite a show going on and there was no authority figure around to stop it. Out here in the wild they recognized no boundaries. They loved the thrill of firing something as dangerous as a gun. Maybe they smoked a joint; maybe they didn't. But they became excited. Their hearts beat faster. A little adrenaline rushed through their veins. They were like a group of sharks who catch the first hint of blood in the water, or dogs whose hair stands up on the back of their necks when they smell a female animal in heat. Caught up in the intensity of the moment, they suspended all reason and sound judgment. Impulse kicked in and it seldom thinks twice about anything. As they fired round after round at the cow, it no longer seemed that they were living in real life. It felt more like a movie, and it was far more fun. In the midst of all this, they saw the raft coming around the bend.

One of them—I don't know who—shouted, "Shoot the gringos!" They lay down on the rocks to get a good rest and did just that. The first rounds punched holes in the raft and shot Jim Burr's oars in half, but the veteran guide still managed to steer the raft to the American shore. As he tied the boat to the limb of a mesquite, the first round—a 40-grain .22 hollow point— pierced the meat of his thigh.

One of the two fifteen-year-old boys pulled the trigger. They were shooting semiautomatic .22 rifles with open sights. The distance from the rifle bore to Burr's leg was later confirmed to be almost nine hundred feet.

Confused and panicked, Burr and the Heffleys hid behind the big rocks and tried to decide what to do. Had they stayed behind the rocks, in my opinion, their chances of survival would have increased tenfold. But they did not know where the shots were coming from, so they felt like they had no choice but to run.

The shooters hesitated after they had drawn first blood. At first, shooting the gringos was the same as shooting at the cow. The rafters were targets of opportunity, a game, a spree. It didn't feel like that anymore. They were now in the grip of their own adrenaline. If there was a reason not to shoot at the gringos anymore, they couldn't think of it. One of the older boys didn't see any way back now. They had to shoot down all three of these people so that no one would ever know. He raised his rifle and fired again. The others joined in. It was easy to keep pace with the gringos walking along the level rim of bluff.

They laughed when Mike Heffley begged them for their lives. The shooters were in control of these foreigners and they liked it. Heffley offered them money and a camera. They took aim at him and again pulled the triggers. They saw the wall ahead that would trap their prey long before the rafters encountered it. The killers were young, but they'd hunted enough to know to let their game come to them, so they ran ahead a little to set up and wait.

When the three gringos jumped into the river, they were sitting ducks. All four boys fired at them, but only "The Cave" had any luck. He drilled a 150-grain .30-30 soft point slug right through Jamie Heffley's abdomen. Even from that height, they all saw the blood in the dirty water. I'm not sure if they ever knew that they'd also shot her in the arm. But either way, they figured her for dead. Only Mike Heffley was left unwounded. Eduardo Rodriguez Piñeda lined him up in his sights.

Eduardo had brought only twelve or thirteen rounds on this trip, and most of these he'd wasted on the cow. He had four rounds left when the raft turned up. Two of these had failed to draw blood. For him, the fun was about to end. The competitor in Eduardo wanted his two last shots to count.

About that time a strange thing happened. Mike Heffley inspected his wife's wound and screamed in despair. He walked with his arm around his wife slowly toward the brush. It was the easiest shot Eduardo had tried since the cow. He took his time. Lined up his sights. And squeezed the trigger.

He was delighted when his .44 magnum bullet ripped between Mike Heffley's shoulder blades, began to expand immediately upon contact with tissue, blasted through his spinal cord, sending lead and bone fragments to shred most of his internal organs before the mushroomed bullet exited through a hole the size of a fist near Mike's belly button. The impact of the bullet knocked Mike hard to the ground.

This shot was made with a lever-action rifle outfitted with open sights. The distance was later calculated to be just under three hundred yards. Because gravity has less impact on bullets fired perpendicularly to the earth (straight up or straight down as opposed to a trajectory parallel to the earth), even the shots of accomplished shooters fly high. A competitive marksman would be hard pressed to match Eduardo's skill. Nevertheless, during the last forty-five or so minutes, three school-age amateurs with barely enough resources to buy bullets had placed four rounds on the nose at that same distance without the aid of telescopic sights. What were the odds?

"I made a shot!" Eduardo yelled.

Mike Heffley rolled over on his back and tossed his arm over his head.

Later he loosened his belt and pants to relieve the pressure and agony of a gut wound, but the shooters didn't remember seeing that. Instead, they chased after the last man standing. They got one last crack at Jim Burr, who was clearly still bleeding from his leg wound. They didn't know if they'd hit him or not. But he didn't run again.

It was over now. They backtracked to their horses, all the time watching over their shoulders, staring down into the canyons, just to make sure that no one was coming after them.

A few minutes later, one or two of the killers climbed down from the top of the canyon and approached Mike's body, lying still on a gravel bar. I think it was both of the seventeen-year-olds, Eduardo and "Bad Luck Jr.," who risked the trip for a close-up inspection of their trophy.

I believe that one of them felt guilt for the first time. It would grow in power until it overwhelmed him. Later, he went to his mother and confessed what he'd done. But for now, standing near their victim, seeing Mike's blood seep into the little white and gray rocks, he felt only this numbness, the first comprehension that he'd done a terrible thing.

They saw Jamie Heffley lying half submerged beneath scrub mesquites in the grave she'd clawed out with her fingers. She lay still with her eyes closed, but they knew that she wasn't dead. Not yet. Jamie later said that she had heard their footsteps, but she never believed that they'd seen her. But they did.

At this point, I'm not sure what happened. Either they held Americans in such contempt that they didn't believe Jamie was worth another bullet, or maybe they were both out of ammo and none of them could stomach the idea of walking up to her and bashing in her head with a rock. It's possible that the image of Mike dead on the gravel bar snapped them out of their trance and all they wanted was to get away from that place as fast as they could. They knew that she'd never live long with a wound like that anyway.

But if the killing bothered them while they were at the scene, it didn't show in the evidence. They walked back to their horses, untethered the reins, and led all four animals to the river to drink, because even though they left three strangers to die they couldn't face their neighbors if they hadn't cared properly for the borrowed horses and mule.

Then they rode up the cut a little ways to where they felt safe enough to eat a late lunch. Mike Heffley's body was probably four hundred yards away. They peeled open cans of green chilis and sardines and ate them on crackers. They drank some Tecate beer. Then they smoked a joint together as they talked over the shooting. Killing people was not much different from shooting the cow. When they got good and ready, they mounted their borrowed animals and rode home.

Avoiding all assumptions, phrased in the simplest terms, I say some black-hearted boys set fire to the field to watch it burn. They fired at the cow to hear it bawl. They shot down three people to watch them die. They had lunch. They went home. All of this is fact. The question that remains sixteen years later is who or what is to blame?

Spree shootings happen all too often anywhere in America. A Luby's in Killeen, Columbine High School in Colorado, a McDonald's somewhere. Some kids fired at speeding cars from an overpass on a Florida interstate highway. In 2002, a father and his stepson systematically assassinated several people in Virginia and Maryland at random from the trunk of their car. This type of violence has become a fixture in modern America.

In 1988, it happened over the course of about an hour in Colorado Canyon. I will never understand why. Maybe that was the day the devil rode his swing. That explanation is as good as any. And that's a crying shame.

CHAPTER TEN

My Heroes Have Always Been Rangers: The Captain

1969

HURSDAY EVENING, APRIL 3, the year the Apollo mission reached the moon. My friend, Uvalde County Deputy Sheriff Morris Barrow, and I are barreling south down Highway 83 to Carrizo Springs. Wherever people settled in this part of the world, jails sprang up like mushrooms right behind them. Carrizo Springs built one like most every other small Texas town. The only difference was that today armed inmates were trying to break out of it.

The jailer and his wife had been feeding the prisoners when felons jumped them both. They broke weapons and ammunition out of the padlocked pantries. They shot their way out until they confronted some local law enforcement officers and Company D Captain Alfred Y. Allee Sr., who in turn shot the prisoners back inside again. The inmates decided to barricade themselves behind the walls and fight it out.

Captain Allee radioed dispatch to summon all available units. My 1969 Dodge sedan swallowed fifty miles of ranch country in twenty-eight minutes. When my captain calls me, I come.

I had been a Ranger for close to three years. My second son, Lance Sterling Jackson, was seven days old. I had a better understanding of my job and a reasonable amount of experience in doing it. My family ties and responsibilities were beginning to balance me. I was proud of who I was, and nobody had to tell me that I had a lot to live for.

When Deputy Barrow and I screeched to a halt in front of the Dimmitt

Ranger Captain Alfred
Allee Sr., Company D
Headquarters, Carrizo
Springs, Texas, 1968

County jail, however, I was dumbstruck by the chaotic violence raging in the streets. Several officers were firing at the Dimmitt County jail from behind abandoned police units. Sirens blared. Guns boomed from every angle. Citizens hunkered down behind trees and around corners, watching the show. I'd never been invited to a party quite like this one.

Morris and I took fire almost immediately. I saw the muzzle flashes from the second story of the jail. Bullets snapped by my head as soon as I got out of the car. I was wearing a brand-new Resistol silver belly felt cowboy hat. Although it was a factory second, it still set me back $65, which ain't chicken feed for a cop supporting a family of four on less than $1,000 a month. I was young and dumb enough to think of myself as bulletproof, so I worried mostly about them desperate sons of bitches drilling a round through my new cowboy hat. I just couldn't bear it. I grabbed my M-2 .30 caliber carbine out of the trunk. I flicked the selector switch to automatic fire, intending to inform the prisoners in the clearest terms possible that lead flies both ways.

I first ran into Alfred Allee Jr., son of Captain Allee and a Texas Ranger stationed in Ozona. He had picked a great day to visit his parents' ranch. "Little Alfred," as we all affectionately called him, was short of shells for his Remington riot gun, so I pitched him a couple of boxes of .000 buckshot. As soon as Alfred reloaded, he laid into the shooters inside the jail. People were running every which way with bullets ricocheting all around them.

"Where's Cap?" I asked Ranger Allee. It wasn't professional to ask "Where's your dad?" in the middle of a gun battle. He pointed toward the east face of the jail. Deputy Barrow and I laid down short bursts of covering fire as we scrambled that direction, only to find Captain Allee launching the last of his 40 mm tear gas canisters. None of his previous shots had passed through the bars. His last attempt failed also. Tear gas shrouded the entire scene in an eerie fog.

Captain Allee's furrowed brow warned anyone who knew him that he was irritated, probably because he had gassed everyone in Carrizo Springs except the inmates. Always mindful of his manners, he thanked us for coming so quickly and then said, "Boys, if we can't smoke them bastards out, we gotta go in."

"Yes, sir, Cap," I said. Captain Allee was surveying the shortest and safest approach to the jail when he paused to regard me with his bright brown eyes. Not sure what to expect, I leaned in to listen.

"Is that a new hat, Joaquin?" he said.

"Ah, yes sir, it is," I said, making damn sure I stayed squarely behind that elm tree we were all sharing.

"Looks mighty fine." He shoved three more cartridges into his nickel-plated Winchester .30-30 carbine (a birthday gift from his wife, Miss Pearl) and made his move toward the barricaded building. He didn't have to look back to know we would follow him.

CAPTAIN ALFRED ALLEE SR. was sixty-four years old in 1969 (if we can rely on his DPS file—which we can't), about a year away from forced retirement. His daddy was a Texas Ranger, as was his daddy before him. Both of them met violent deaths in the maelstrom endemic to the South Texas of their time. His grandfather, Alonzo Allee, was stabbed in a bar in Laredo. Captain's father was a rancher who was involved in a running dispute over maverick cattle with a neighbor named Butler. Tensions came to a head on the streets of Crystal City in 1920. With three shots in his Colt .45 revolver, the elder Allee shot down Butler and his foreman. Allee turned toward the Mercantile to get more ammo when Butler's sixteen-year-old son, still mounted, yanked his father's .30-30 out of the scabbard and shot Allee dead in the back. Captain Allee was fatherless at age fifteen.

Years later I worked a theft for a rancher named Butler, the very same one who as an adolescent had gunned down the elder Allee. I asked my captain if he still bore any anger toward his father's killer. "No," he said without hesitation. "He was defending his daddy. If it had been me in his boots, I'd have done the same thing. Fact is, we both lost our fathers to that feud."

Captain Allee's short, bristly hair was graying when I met him. He carried a little paunch. But all 5'10" of him was built like a cedar stump. He wore starched white shirts, a thin black tie, starched khakis, and a short-brimmed Rancher's Stetson. His size-eight-and-a-half feet seemed almost dainty as the foundation for his frame, although I never found the nerve to mention that observation to him. His little black boots were always perfectly polished. Once he fixed you with those stern brown eyes, he owned you. But he shot people straight, said what he meant, and meant what he said. When I screwed up, he chewed my ass down to the tailbone. But once he was finished, that was it. "Now, let's go get a cup of coffee, Joaquin," he'd say, shifting from a blistering assault to a fatherly tone. That was the last I'd hear of his anger unless I made the same mistake twice—when the volcanic cycle would simply repeat itself. All of us serving in Company D received the same treatment. Captain Allee played no favorites. He carried no grudges.

Captain Allee had a notorious reputation behind the wheel. He wasn't a wild driver. He was simply more focused on where he was going than how soon he got there—and I can assure you that he always arrived in record time. Legendary DPS Director Col. Homer Garrison once summoned Captain Allee to Austin to discuss the operation of Company D. In what must have seemed like only minutes since he'd hung up the phone Colonel Garrison was informed that Captain Allee had arrived.

"Alfred, exactly how long does it take for you to drive from Carrizo Springs to Austin?" Colonel Garrison asked him.

"Two cigars," Captain Allee said.

Headquarters in Austin mandated that Captain Allee upgrade the Company D shooting range in Carrizo Springs and modernize his handgun qualification process. Captain Allee preferred to watch his boys blister prickly pear cacti behind the Dimmitt County headquarters. He knew that his old-timers, like Walter Russell and Zeno Smith, were horrendous target shooters. But put those point-shooting buzzards on the back of a horse or in a speeding car and they could knock the gnats off a goat's ass at fifty paces.

Captain Allee had his own standards for handgun qualification and didn't appreciate Austin's efforts, especially when they sent down a "rangemaster" who blew a whistle before all of us Rangers could draw our weapons and fire at the fancy new silhouette targets. Captain Allee was especially amused when the rangemaster yelled, "Ready on the right! Ready on the left!" and then blew his whistle like a basketball coach.

After the first session, Captain Allee was shaking his head over his coffee in the local café, his patent cue for one of us to ask him why. Somebody finally did. "Well," he began, "it's going to be a sad day, a very sad day." Why? We all wondered. "I'm afraid one of you Rangers will be killed. Maybe two or three of you, and it's going to be sad, very sad indeed." Disturbed, we asked him what he meant. "After all this fancy new training Austin sent down here, I don't expect that you boys will fire back at anybody until you hear a goddamn whistle."

Captain Allee and Miss Pearl made a handsome couple. In their sixties, they still held hands while they rocked on the porch swing. She was every bit as feminine as he was all man, but there was a quiet substance behind her sweet smile. In the company of men, Captain Allee could be a salty, rancorous dog. He had a great sense of humor, frequently entertaining us with colorful and sometimes racy anecdotes. But around his wife—and all women for that matter—he was a perfect gentleman, respectful in words and demeanor.

In those days Rangers worked impossible hours. I never once heard Miss Pearl complain about her husband's relentless commitment to his job. Almost always, she left a hot meal covered in tinfoil on the stove or left a sandwich for him in the icebox. One night, Captain Allee, as usual, came home late. He fumbled around the shelves until he found a Tupperware of tuna fish salad next to a loaf of Wonderbread. He slapped a little mayonnaise on a slice and made himself a sandwich. It was so good that he made himself a second one before he crawled into a warm bed beside his wife.

Over coffee the next morning, Miss Pearl, dressed like an angel in the floral print dresses she favored, was digging through the icebox.

"What're you hunting, honey?" Captain Allee asked.

"I know that I had a container of cat food in here somewhere," she said.

Tasted close enough to tuna fish to suit him, he dryly told me later.

Captain Allee ranched 1,200 acres of chaparral country north of Carrizo Springs. His annual crop of spring calves supplemented his meager Ranger salary. To help make ends meet, Miss Pearl worked as an elementary school teacher. The Allees were a family of modest means, but I never saw Captain Allee file for his per diem reimbursement from the department when we were in the field, mainly because he was too proud to eat out of Austin's hand. He never let one of his Rangers buy his own lunch either because he wanted us to use our allowance when we were off by ourselves on a case. His worst fault was that he gave away too much.

In a way, he treated us all like sons. I, in return, thought of him as a father. He was quick to discipline us when we failed; quick to inspire us when we faltered; quick to support us when we weren't sure what to do. "To hell with a supervisor," he always said. "Men follow a leader." I had never known loyalty from an authority figure until I met him, a man who lived his life by example. I aspired to become the man I saw in Captain Alfred Y. Allee.

Did he have a quick temper? Yes, he did. But it was the product of the violent times that produced him, when men slow to anger in the chronic border skirmishes with professional bootleggers and rustlers were quick in the grave. Was he a racist? I suppose that he was. But this is a blanket indictment of his entire generation. He was perhaps the last of a long line of Texans bred to think of Mexico and her people as an enemy of the Lone Star State and, as such, at odds with the Anglos in authority, whom the Texas Rangers had sworn to uphold. He was incapable of seeing the world in the gray tones readily accepted today. He adhered to a code too simplistic to guide us in modern times, but he lived or died by it. This was honor as he understood it.

After Captain Allee retired, I served under better-educated and more politically astute captains. They were good men and damn good Rangers. But none of them stood above Allee's kneecap as a natural leader and a force to be reckoned with in the field. The heroics historians have long celebrated in nineteenth-century Rangers like Jack Hays, Samuel Walker, Big Foot Wallace, Leander McNelly, Rip Ford, and Ben McCulloch, I witnessed for myself in Captain Allee. On occasion I saw him angry. I *never* saw him afraid.

When Miriam "Ma" Ferguson was named governor in what many considered a sham election to allow her corrupt, impeached husband to continue to orchestrate that high office, Captain Allee resigned in protest along with many of the best Rangers. It was one hell of a sacrifice. When Ma passed from office, the state gladly hired him back.

Thirty-some-odd years later Captain Allee was still in the field commanding his Rangers, taking heavy fire on this particular day from armed convicts. While preparing to storm the barricaded building through clouds of gun smoke and tear gas, he took a moment to admire my new $65 Resistol hat. God, I loved that old man!

He ordered us to follow him to the north wall of the jail. The inmates opened up on us and I answered with a full clip from my M-2. As I was reloading, we heard shouting from inside the jailhouse. Now they wanted to talk.

"I'll give you sons of bitches till ten to lay down your arms and come out!" Captain Allee barked. He only reached three before he let them have it, not because he believed the inmates couldn't count but because he had run out of patience and was in no mood to negotiate. To him, there was only one way this situation could end honorably for the Texas Rangers.

He led us around to the west-facing entrance. We met up with my good friend, Ranger Tol Dawson, "Little Alfred" Allee, Highway Patrolman Art Rodriguez (who would one day become a damn good Ranger), and two or three solid local sheriff's deputies. We cleared the bottom floor first and then moved toward the stairway that led up to the jail cells.

Tol Dawson and I, guns cocked and loaded, assumed that as younger men we would be the most likely candidates to storm the second floor. We took one step toward the stairs, when our sixty-four-year-old captain grabbed our arms and jerked us back.

"None of my Rangers are gonna get killed in front of me!" he said. He paused long enough to snatch Deputy Barrow's World War II–era .45 caliber submachine gun, nicknamed a "grease gun" by the marines who carried it in combat. In an instant, he checked to make sure that the weapon had a full magazine, cocked the action, took a breath, shoved his cigar to the opposite side of his mouth, and charged screaming up the stairs, gun blazing. We were so awestruck that for a moment we didn't think to follow.

The jailhouse was primarily constructed of concrete and steel. The grease gun spit out 230-grain full-metal-jacketed bullets as fast as the action could slap them into the chamber. The jail was engulfed in a storm of fire, lightning ricochets, and booming thunder. The floor trembled. There was nothing for any sensible man to do but duck and cover as the bullets rocketed off the gray walls.

After a few anxious seconds, I heard Captain Allee's voice. "All clear!" he yelled. "Come on up."

Dawson and I were the first to climb the stairs. As we moved through the debris of the second floor, the effects of Captain's lone-man assault became obvious. Handguns lay abandoned, still cocked and loaded, on the floor. Two revolvers were stacked on the food trays like dirty dishes. We found a tossed rifle here, a shucked riot gun there. As the dust and gun smoke settled, an eerie quiet descended, like the stillness that follows a tornado. Everything had a bullet hole through it or in it. Inspecting the carnage, I was mighty glad the captain was on our side.

We moved from cell to cell until we came to two pairs of jailhouse slippers protruding from under a mattress. We excavated the owners, their expressions blank. The deputies identified them as two regular drunks that had nothing to do with the jailbreak. Shell-shocked, pasty with dust, they were led to safety. The search for the others went on.

We soon came across all fourteen inmates, huddled together in a corner cell. Some whimpered like children. Others appeared resigned to their fate, no doubt gripped by the early stages of post-traumatic stress disorder. Regardless, they all wanted to be excused from the business end of Captain Allee's borrowed grease gun—and quick.

"Your vacation's been canceled, boys," Captain Allee said. "But room and board is free here for five extra years."

We patted them down, cuffed them, and stretched them out on the jailhouse lawn while things were sorted out inside. Dimmitt County would later have to contract with a mason to undo some of the damage. Once the jail was close enough to operational, however, we led the prisoners back in and slammed the doors on them.

Standing out on the lawn just before sunset, Captain Allee put a match to a fresh cigar and gathered his Rangers around him. "Y'all hungry?" he said, as if we'd just walked out of an afternoon cowboy matinee.

Months later, Captain Allee told me in passing that since the jailbreak both of the drunks had yet to touch a single drop of spirits. "That's better results than AA, ain't it?" he said with a wink. "And quicker, too."

Rest easy, my captain. You are well remembered by those who knew you best.

CHAPTER ELEVEN

⊛ A Goat and a Guitar

THE STORY OF A TEXAS
COUNTRY MUSIC STAR
1969–2004

No lyric poems live long or please that are written by water drinkers.

HORACE, ROMAN POET, 14 B.C.

See by this image . . . how utterly thou hast murdered thyself.

FROM "WILLIAM WILSON" BY EDGAR ALLAN POE

I SAW THE BODY sprawled across the caliche shoulder that framed U.S. Highway 83 just north of Uvalde, not too far from the entrance of Garner State Park. A discarded human being by the side of the road typically catches my attention. The victim didn't so much as twitch when I pulled up to investigate.

Garner State Park drew vacationing families from urban areas like Houston and San Antonio. That summer of 1969, the RV slots and camping areas looked like a patchwork quilt of sheet metal and nylon under a shroud of camp smoke and river mist. Folks spent their days floating the Frio River in canoes and inner tubes. At night, they drifted to the park's pavilion to mix with locals and listen to a live band or dance to a jukebox. The revelry sometimes escalated to all-out rowdy. My initial suspicion was that the victim curled up in the fetal position by the side of Highway 83 was an early casualty of the pavilion's festivities.

Uvalde Deputy Sheriff Morris Barrow and I approached the victim. I could see right off that he was a good-looking, clean-cut Mexican kid way too young to be drinking, much less passed out drunk. I nudged his butt with my boot. No sign of life. I tried again. Nothing.

"Hey," I said in my business voice. "Wake up."

Joaquin Jackson and Johnny Rodriguez, 1973

His eyelids trembled and slowly cranked open to half-mast. It's got to be sobering to awaken from the comforting arms of Bacchus and behold a Texas Ranger who's heard it all and ain't got a lot of time to listen to much more. The kid's dark eyes focused on the toes of my boots, rose toward the shank and on from there until he'd surveyed my 6′5″ frame.

"Damn," he said, his voice hoarse, his sluggish eyes widening. "I never thought I'd get to the top of your head."

I liked him from that moment on.

"What the hell are you doing lying out here on the side of this road?" I said.

"Oh, I just got tired," he said. "And then I laid down."

"Got tired of doing what?"

"I was playing for the people tonight," he said.

"Playing? Playing what?"

"Music," he said. "I play guitar. I write and sing songs."

"The hell you say," I said. "Where's your guitar?"

He pointed toward the park. "Down at the camp."

I asked him for some identification. Of course he didn't have any. I said I'd settle for his name. He said that he was Juan Raul Davis Rodriguez from neighboring Sabinal, seventy miles west of the Rio Grande. His family called him Raul. His nickname was "el Charro," the rider. Folks knew him as Johnny on the Anglo side of town.

I told him to go and fetch that guitar and let me hear him. We followed him down to a row of tents and bedrolls under the stars. He pulled out an old, beat-up six-string and broke into a repertoire of five original songs. His voice was pure and powerful, but also smooth and almost sweet. Rodriguez was maybe seventeen years old, but already his songs told convincing stories of the road and the border and the hard life his people had known there. As soon as he started singing, he wasn't a drunk anymore. His music rallied him. There was no mistaking his talent.

I had other crimes to attend to, so I cautioned Johnny to find himself a safer bed than the shoulder of a U.S. Highway and by all means to keep that guitar close.

I started talking about that boy after our first encounter. A lot of people already were. Johnny Rodriguez was the next-to-youngest of nine children born to Andres and Isabel Rodriguez. Andres worked as a welder at Kelly Air Force Base in San Antonio, a position that provided for his family while it kept him apart from them.

On those rare occasions home, Andres loved to play the guitar and sing traditional border *corridos* along with Texas standards like "Cattle Call" and "Strawberry Roan." Andres could yodel, too, when the tune called for it. Isabel was also the product of a family steeped in country music in a line drawn all the way back to Jimmie Rodgers. Amid her never-ending housework and feeding and mothering nine handsome children, Isabel often broke into "Jealous Heart" and "Faded Love."

Johnny Rodriguez was a competent student at Sabinal High School, but he was far more interested in athletics. He ran the mile in track, played varsity baseball, and was selected to play end on the all-district football team.

He started elementary school in Spanish-speaking classes but soon moved into the mainstream curriculum. Exposed to Anglo culture, Johnny ran around with Anglo friends, especially Austin "Hot Shot" Schaefer. Johnny virtually lived with Hot Shot's family, a traditional rural Texas household where Ernest Tubb and Merle Haggard records perpetually blared out the screen door. By the time I ran across Johnny, he had established himself as a performer at Sabinal's Ranch House Café and more informally at Garner State Park. The Schaefers had also scratched up the money to help Johnny record his first single, "Golden Tears." Despite early signs of success, though, Johnny's career was high-centered around Sabinal.

Johnny rustled an Angora goat from a ranch that adjoined Garner State Park. Some people dismiss this story as some sort of publicity campaign, but it happened. Johnny and some friends pinched the goat and barbecued it. By some accounts, Johnny, a naturally fast runner, was the wheelman and later the cook. Johnny had the misfortune of making tacos out of a registered Angora goat worth maybe $200, far from the usual $10 value of this nappy breed of animal. He was arrested by a police officer and jailed. A number of Johnny's friends raised a stink because of the nine perpetrators involved, the only one arrested was a Mexican American. The judge suspended Johnny's sentence and gave him three years' probation. I had nothing to do with any of this.

The next time I saw Johnny, he was behind bars in Uvalde for failing to pay a fine for minor possession of alcohol. I was checking in a guest with Sheriff Kenneth Kelley, and as we strolled through his office I caught a glimpse of Johnny. After Sheriff Kelley told me the details of Johnny's return visit, I asked if he had ever heard Johnny sing. When Sheriff Kelley expressed his skepticism, I shucked it over to my house to fetch Shirley's momma's old Gibson F-hole six-string.

Soon enough, Johnny was strumming to a handful of sheriff's deputies and jailers. He played songs he would later record, like "Riding My Thumb to Mexico." After he sang for an hour or so, Sheriff Kelley said, "Well, I'm gonna cut you loose. You pay $25 a week on this fine and we'll call it even."

I felt like there was something great stirring around in this wayward kid, but I wanted my wife to hear him. Shirley played professionally before we married and had once toured with the Jimmy Dean Band, among others. She's a wonderful singer and musician. If the kid had any talent, she would know.

Shirley looked him over with a suspicious eye. Johnny was wearing faded jeans, scuffed cowboy boots, and a cotton shirt with his shiny, dark curls draped over the collar—a risky ensemble for 1960s South Texas.

I play the guitar a little, too, but neither Shirley nor I can tune it worth a damn. Don't know why Shirley can't manage it, but I've shot too many guns. Anyway, when I want to play, I call up Frank Harrison and pluck a string. Frank tells me "down" or "up," and I adjust the tuners accordingly. When Frank says she's right, I hang up the phone and get to picking. Shirley wanted Johnny to play her personal instrument, and Johnny didn't need to call Frank Harrison to tune it.

As soon as he broke into his first song, Shirley put her reservations aside. She really enjoyed listening to him, a sure sign of his professional potential. We sat on the sofa and listened to him play for an hour or two. Then we looked at each other and silently agreed that we ought to help this talented but troubled young kid.

There were plenty of beer-and-blood joints in the area where Johnny could play for redneck rowdies, but only one place where he could really *perform*. J. T. "Happy" Shahan was a rancher and entrepreneur, a tall, slender man who had once played basketball for Baylor University. His natural enthusiasm and charm ultimately lured actor and producer John Wayne to his ranch near Brackettville to film the 1961 epic *The Alamo*.

After Hollywood cleared out, Shahan decided to capitalize on the public's curiosity about the movie set and fashion the faux Alamo and early San Antonio village into a tourist attraction and theme park, including restaurants, gift shops, and live music and skit performances. Most of the staff were college students who dressed in vintage Western clothing and looked like they had a good time earning Happy's minimum wage. Alamo Village seemed like the best place to get Johnny started off right.

I took Johnny out to meet Happy, and straight away Shahan stuck him on stage in his cantina to get a sense of the young man's potential. After just a few notes, Happy's eyes lit up and they soon struck up a professional relationship. Johnny sang. Happy sold tickets and *turista* mementos.

Shahan knew Johnny had star material, but he also recognized that the young Chicano was not quite ready to tackle Nashville. During the summers of 1970 and 1971, Shahan groomed Johnny Rodriguez's style and showmanship while he performed for Shahan's crowds. Happy also hired him to handle horseback rides, drive a stagecoach, and ham it up as a comic character named "Ortho" in the melodramatic shoot-outs. During the rest of the year, Johnny worked at menial jobs and played the same old local venues and worked on his original material. He drank a little beer, too. Then summer rolled around, Happy threw open the gates to Alamo Village, and the whole cycle repeated itself. Shahan was like a father to Rodriguez, but he was also his boss. Johnny never seemed to chafe under Shahan's firm hand, though. They were a good fit.

Shahan booked touring acts to appear alongside his local fare. On Labor Day 1971, Tom T. Hall and Bobby Bare played a set each to a packed house. Johnny caught the eye of these country music veterans when he opened their show to enthusiastic applause. Both men encouraged Johnny to come to Nashville. They promised to see if they couldn't kick open a few music industry doors for him.

I don't know if Happy talked Johnny out of it or Johnny didn't believe he was ready for Nashville, but he let the opportunity slip away. When Happy closed for the season, Johnny went to work on a construction site. Nevertheless, Johnny Rodriguez told me for dead certain that one day he would be a country music star.

In fall 1971, Andres Rodriguez was diagnosed with cancer. Johnny became a fixture at San Antonio's Nix Hospital. For twenty-one days he stayed by his father's side. Andres lost his battle with cancer in January 1972. Johnny was devastated.

His oldest brother, Andres Jr., called Andy, struggled to fill the void left by his father's absence. Andy entered his adult years as a hard-drinking, hard-living, brawling rebel who had several run-ins with the law, mostly for alcohol-related offenses. He even served time in a Wisconsin penitentiary.

Johnny, who saw Andy at his best, idolized him for his courage, his wit, his arrogance toward authority, and his carefree, bohemian attitude. Andy gave Johnny his first guitar, the same one he played that night in Garner State Park in 1969. Andy probably didn't fill his father's boots when it came to setting a respectable example for young people, but Johnny saw him as a handsome, misunderstood romantic who knew how to stand up for himself. He admired him above all other men, second only to his deceased father.

Andy was singing in some honky-tonk when he confronted a drunken heckler. When the argument came to blows, the drunk smashed Andy's guitar against his face, an injury that rendered him partially blind. That probably came to bear a little later, in May 1972, when Andy was killed in an automobile accident. He was only a year or two into his thirties.

Before he was twenty years old, before he had any real direction, Johnny Rodriguez had lost the two most important men in his life—men he cared for deeply and who, in turn, truly loved and accepted him. Their tragic deaths broke his heart and pushed him off center.

Johnny used his last paycheck to buy an airplane ticket to Nashville. Johnny told Happy Shahan that he had other ambitions beyond Alamo Village. He borrowed $8 from his mother, and stuffed three pairs of pants, three shirts, and a shaving kit into a sorry suitcase that looked like an old baseball glove. He wrapped his brother's guitar in cellophane, and he and his friends convened at the Schaefers' home for his farewell hurrah. I believe, in Johnny's honor, they served goat.

The next decade reads something like a dream. Johnny flew to Nashville and checked into the seldom-celebrated Sam Davis Hotel and immediately placed a call to Tom T. Hall. Hall was short a guitarist and hired Johnny on the spot to back him up in his band, the Storytellers. Hall came to believe in Rodriguez's ability and put him in touch with Mercury Records executive Roy Dea, who signed him before he had finished his second song.

Shahan came running after him and they continued their relationship as manager and artist. As far as I'm concerned, Happy fulfilled his role beautifully. He mentored Johnny Rodriguez as well as Colonel Tom Parker managed Elvis Presley. There was a time when there was no mistaking the similarities between these two singing sensations.

Johnny's first single for Mercury, "Pass Me By," reached number nine on the Country and Western charts. The second, "You Always Come Back to Hurting Me" (cowritten by Johnny with Tom T. Hall), blew the first one out of the record racks, reaching the number one spot on June 9, 1973. The next single out of the chute equaled the second, as did three of his next six. Each of his fifteen singles cracked the Top Ten, despite the fact that Johnny defied the conventional wisdom of the day and sang some of the lyrics in Spanish. Americans had never heard anything like Johnny Rodriguez. Once they did, they hungered for more.

In 1973, Johnny, then twenty-one, went on tour with another rising young star, sixteen-year-old Tanya Tucker. Together the pair proved to be a Nashville smash, pumping fresh blood into a stale, aging art form and introducing country music to a new generation of fans. His meteoric rise sure was fun to watch for us folks back home.

Johnny married a flight attendant in 1973. The wedding took place at Hall's Nashville estate. Shirley was asked to be a bridesmaid. I proudly served as an usher. It seemed like all of country's A-list performers paid tribute to the new kid in town. Mooney Lynn, Loretta's husband, presented Johnny with a black goat. Johnny gave me a beautiful over-and-under Beretta shotgun. The buttplate read "To Joaquin from Johnny R." I'm telling you all this to remind you of the goodness of Johnny's heart. He was a good Texas kid who remembered to dance with who brung him. Seeing him in the middle of all that success was really my reward. It was a great time for Johnny. Shirley and I enjoyed it, too.

We made some of Johnny's Texas gigs. He was always good to us—gracious, warm, and kind. He remembered Shirley, too, and later talked Mercury into recording two of her songs on a single. Johnny produced the record himself. I was knocked out by it, and I think Johnny was, too, but it never got much attention. I think Mercury didn't want Johnny to get too comfortable as a producer. The label wanted him out on the road, supporting those wonderfully commercial singles and meeting his fans.

Mostly woman fans. I've seen them lined up around a city block just to have him sign his name on something, give him a brief hug, or maybe peck him on the lips. It was flattering at first, but soon Johnny had to hire body-guards to manage the deluge. Gorgeous women were throwing themselves at him. Seems like quite a temptation to me.

There were others far more dangerous than the women. Johnny's happy-go-lucky nature, the availability of drugs, and the relentless pressure to perform and loneliness of life on the road began to take their toll. In 1975, Johnny cut Happy Shahan loose, severing his last ties to the man who had the *juevos* to tell him no every now and then.

Johnny's first marriage cratered after three years. His last number one hit was in 1975. In 1981, he switched record labels. His single "Down on the Rio Grande" broke the Top Ten, and while the other singles fared re-spectably, they failed to match his early success. In 1987, Johnny switched labels again, with even less favorable results. By then, everybody knew what was happening to him.

It's an old and sad story. The artist lets the bottle or the dope get be-tween him and his art. He spends half his life achieving success and the second half throwing it all away. How many talents have self-destructed before him? How many more will follow in his wake?

Johnny was already a blackout drinker as a teen. He was raised in a four-room shack on the wrong side of the tracks in a small town in South Texas, near enough to the Rio Grande to still feel the pull of Mother Mexico, at a time when the Anglo and Mexican American communities were beginning to put aside their two-hundred-year-old feud.

Johnny, the unintentional product of a cultural compromise, sang his crossover songs in both English and Spanish. He was born with the voice of an angel, movie star looks, a personality that could charm the skirt off any Anglo sorority girl, and more raw talent than any 1960s Nashville cookie-cutter performer. These gifts fueled the meteoric rise of one of the most original country singer/songwriter phenomena of the 1970s. The same traits, however, also conspired to destroy him.

For those who love him, Johnny's career has brought both joy and deep disappointment. We all had plenty of advice for him, but what did it mat-ter? Johnny occupies an arena that he must enter and negotiate alone. Elvis Presley traveled a dirt road to riches before he took a wrong turn on the downhill slide. Hank Williams Sr. walked it for a while before he snuffed himself out. Johnny Rodriguez came to know the hard road well, too.

Few among us have faced the horde of personal and professional pres-sures that hound Johnny every day of his hectic life, all endured by a kid

Shirley Jackson, Johnny Rodriguez, and Joaquin Jackson, 1973

from a fatherless home on the poor side of a Texas town, who was born equally with an incredible talent for music and voracious propensity for alcohol and drug abuse. Both traits very real. Both very powerful. Both perhaps so deeply rooted in his nature and psyche that he has consistently failed to abandon one to embrace the other.

No one is more aware of the destructive cycle than Johnny. Six times he has entered substance abuse programs to rid himself of this crippling monster. His battle with drugs and alcohol still rages. Three times he has settled down with a good woman to start a home and a family and anchor himself. Three times his marriages have failed. And no one has paid a greater price in this tragic conflict than Johnny.

He can look back on his career and see one of two things: a wall full of gold records heralding the success of America's first great Chicano country music star; or a patch of scorched earth littered with empty beer bottles and cocaine vials, wrecked cars and professional relationships, divorces, lawsuits, criminal charges, alienated friends and family, and a string of dopers and leeches too wasted to hold on to him whether he was rising from the ashes or spiraling into the abyss—and he's always doing one or the other, usually with a winning smile. He is, after all, a professional performer.

We see each other now and then. I sat in a Uvalde courtroom as a measure of support when he faced a murder charge in 1999. I don't know the facts of the case. I just know that the entire tragedy was saturated in alcohol. There was an altercation in Johnny's mother's house, the very house he built after he bulldozed the shack he'd grown up in. Johnny pulled the trigger. A young local man and father died. The law called Johnny to account for it. A jury of his peers in a town where he had none ultimately acquitted him. It was a chance to turn his life around, and Johnny's had plenty.

He still calls me. Sometimes he even comes by the house. I still feel pride in knowing him, along with the pity that swells within me watching the hard course of his life now that he's passing through middle age. I usually plead with him, like all of us who love him do, to get his life straight and deliver that God-given talent to his fans, who are always willing to forgive him.

Sure, it's an old story. We all know how it ends. Elvis, who tried everything he could to ruin his career and failed, didn't live past his forty-second year. Hank Sr. didn't see thirty. Johnny's in his early fifties now. You can see the hard living and the endless parties in his face. But by the grace of God he's still with us. He still has that voice. He'd still rather play music than eat. Despite his failings, he's still one hell of a nice guy. He's a friend of mine. For as long as he flashes that grin and tells me that he's finally turned the corner on the alcohol and the drugs, I'll believe him.

CHAPTER TWELVE

Just Folks

ME AND THE MUJAHEDIN

(The Seven Tribes and a Crowd of One)

1987

I'LL TELL YOU RIGHT OFF—this is where the story gets a little weird. I was doing my job while I was helping a friend, so I'm okay with Texas and the law. But I was out of my league politically and in over my head professionally when it came to the big picture during the last gasp of Cold War politics. All I know is that I once helped train a bunch of Afghani warriors. That's where this is going, and getting there's quite a ride.

It starts with a man. For reasons that will become apparent, we should call him "Agent X." I'm not going to do that because Agent X is a damn good friend of mine. Instead, I'm going to call him "Jake." I think he'll like that better, and he still won't lose his job and retirement benefits.

Jake was the son of a Custer, South Dakota, blacksmith and farrier who abandoned his young wife, three sons, and two daughters when Jake was five years old. Jake's early life was filled with poverty and deprivations, including the four years his family survived in a tent around Missoula, Montana. But his struggles also engendered in him self-reliance, drive, and a physical and mental toughness that made him one of a kind.

Jake grew up hunting bull elk and mule deer bucks on the western face of the Montana Rockies and fly-fishing for rainbows in the crystal streams around Missoula. He worked on ranches where the grass grew knee-deep and the cattle were wild as hell. He served as a fire lookout in the St. Regis drainage, the tail end of the remote Bitterroot Range. He cut roads and trails and marked trees for select cuts by the lumber companies in rugged areas where there were no electricity and no contact with the outside world.

Many of Jake's traits were a family tradition. In the 1870s his grandfather had homesteaded in South Dakota, where he worked as a civilian packer, freighter, and scout for the U.S. Cavalry around the Sioux Standing Rock Reservation. He learned the Sioux language and also served as an interpreter. He was at Standing Rock in the winter of 1890 when Sitting Bull was shot dead by Indian police just two weeks before the massacre at Wounded Knee Creek. The old man even transported Sitting Bull's body to its first grave in Fort Yates, North Dakota. Jake's grandfather told him the chief's body was covered in quicklime to hasten the end to the Ghost Dancing. Anyway, Jake was tied by spirit to the American West and by blood to the pioneers who had settled it. In that respect, he was kin to me.

When the time came to commit to a profession, Jake's love and knowledge of the Big Timber convinced him to join the smoke jumpers—an elite force of firefighters who parachute into remote mountain regions to snuff out forest fires. It was nothing for smoke jumpers to parachute to a wilderness blaze, deal with the situation, and then hike thirty miles to the nearest trail or road with sixty to one hundred pounds of gear on their backs.

The smoke jumpers also dropped supplies of food and water—tons of materials that had to be parachuted from an airplane. Jake soon mastered airdrop techniques and started to experiment with a few of his own ideas. Before long none knew this specialized art better.

Jake served with the smoke jumpers for three years before Uncle Sam sent him a draft notice. After basic training he was assigned to the paratroopers, where his natural inclinations—parachuting, rigging, and survival and forage skills—meshed well with the standard military training. The only difference was that Jake was now jumping with hundreds of men in full gear, with weapons and live ammunition, at one time. He adjusted. In fact he was soon selected as the 101st Airborne's senior scout.

Upon completion of his paratrooper service, Jake returned to smoke jumping. Two years later, the Department of Defense came knocking. It seems that Jake fit the special operations profile at a time when that sort of man was in demand. The DOD sent him to train in the techniques of long-range patrols and guerrilla warfare. But with the Bay of Pigs operation looming, the department was mostly interested in his unique talent to rig and drop supplies from an airplane. Jake was keen to take his art to a new level and signed on for a second military stint. The strange thing was that he was no longer in the army.

After World War II and through the late 1980s, the world was generally divided into three political groups—the communist bloc, which included the Soviet Union and satellite communist countries, the United States and her allies, and the developing nations that were occasionally up for grabs by either one of the first two. Wherever conflict erupted, the United States tended to support whichever side claimed to favor democracy over the communist model, or at least the side more sympathetic to American interests than to those of the Soviet Union. This is, of course, a blatantly oversimplified representation of forty-five years of global politics, but this is a book about a very simple Texas Ranger.

Once the American powers chose their side in any given foreign conflict, they sent in Jake and men like him as frontline Department of Defense advisors to support grassroots initiative and stiffen rebel resolve. If the insurgents had the will, Jake had the way—"sheep-dipped" as it was, that is, with no discernible military connection to the U.S. armed forces. Jake was a subcontractor in the shadows.

Some of Jake's campaigns include the ill-fated Bay of Pigs invasion, operations in the Indian Himalayas in support of Tibet's struggle against the Chinese invasion, training rebel troops during the Congo civil war and South Vietnamese troops in the Mekong Delta, as well as initiatives in Thailand and Cambodia. Perhaps Jake's signature operation was his support of some 30,000 Huomg tribesmen in Laos at war with the Viet Cong and NVA. On any given day during this campaign, Jake dropped anywhere from 100,000 to 300,000 pounds of cargo.

Jake went on to train military units in aerial delivery—in Italy, Sardinia, England, France, Norway, and Holland. He soon developed a system to drop a 500-D Hughes helicopter. Later, Jake designed a parachute system to drop a 4,000-pound Boston Whaler or an up to 12,000-pound, 21-foot Sea Craft boat. The navy couldn't do it, but Jake could.

The early 1980s brought Jake closer to home, where he was involved in operations in Central America. He once flew twenty-two missions in forty-one nights. He also worked with a Libyan contingent in rebellion against Muammar Khadaffi.

Jake excelled when he developed cooperation between military and civilian units that seldom spoke the same language. Jake was a people person, a gifted teacher and instructor who understood how to get soldiers from any army to work together. He also began to train on a new generation of surveillance equipment, including unmanned aerial vehicles, the UAV's. Jake's employers gradually returned him stateside to develop his vision of wilderness area training sites to teach others what he'd learned in over two decades of guerrilla warfare.

Jake had grown increasingly frustrated with the regulations that hamstrung special operations training around military bases and other federal installations. Given the politically sensitive nature of everything he did, he also wanted to avoid public scrutiny of his training camps. A chance meeting with a Texas official encouraged him to lease vast acreage in the Lone Star State—where 97 percent of the land is privately owned. The rugged, sparsely populated ranchland of West Texas appeared particularly inviting, especially when Jake could lease a ranch the size of Eastern Seaboard states. As luck would have it, West Texas also looked a lot like Afghanistan.

Afghanistan is perhaps best known for its chronic anarchy, symptomatic of its crippling ethnic and religious diversity. For centuries, the Afghani people have failed to develop a coherent national identity. Governments come and go, but political power is generally spread among feuding tribal chieftains, local warlords, and religious leaders. Most of the cities and villages are located in rugged, mountainous terrain. Communication and transportation systems are outdated and poorly maintained. In short, Afghanistan is perfectly suited for guerrilla warfare.

In 1979, the Soviet Union invaded Afghanistan to support the leftist regime du jour. The idea was to expand Soviet influence over a bordering "client" state, bolster the communist bloc, and maybe exploit Afghanistan's wealth of natural resources. With their puppet government firmly in control of Kabul, the Soviets planned their sweep of the mountain rebels.

There are seven dominant tribes in Afghanistan, and even they fray into hundreds of clans and factions, many of which bloody each other's noses. But when the godless Soviets invaded, the tribes, sometimes called the Peshawar Seven, united around their common Islamic faith into one force of formidable guerrilla fighters known collectively as the *mujahedin,* or holy warriors. They knew their country, were intensely motivated to defend it, and have never been afraid of war.

The Soviets' invasion quickly disintegrated into a quagmire involving over 120,000 conventional Soviet troops. The mujahedin, by comparison, operated from some four thousand bases spread throughout the mountains of Afghanistan and Pakistan. Each time the Soviet technology swatted one mujahedin command, a hundred more swarmed out of the mountains to cut supply lines and ambush demoralized troops.

In 1986, the United States equipped Afghani rebels with Stinger antiaircraft missiles, which the mujahedin used to knock Soviet helicopters out of the sky. The invaders began to send thousands of their young sons home in body bags.

After these initial successes, Afghanistan's holy warriors soon developed a keen interest in Western technology, especially unmanned aerial surveillance vehicles (UAV's). The United States offered to train them, and soon thirteen of the best and brightest Afghani tribesmen arrived on a 130,000-acre ranch in West Texas. They met two men—a former Montana smoke jumper who knew how to train foreign guerrillas to fight like hell, and a Texas Ranger who didn't know Afghanistan from a gopher hole.

IN THE SPRING OF 1986 Jake waltzed into my Alpine office without his customary grin. He slid his DOD credentials in front of me. I'd heard rumors about Jake's mysterious profession and was well aware of his extended absences over the years, but this was the first time I'd seen documentation. Jake was for real.

When I looked up at him, he said, "I need your help." He presented me with some additional documents from the Texas DPS authorizing me to assist his operation. I was cross-designated as a U.S. Customs agent to give me the latitude to deal with illegal aliens and drug traffickers. I had worked on several investigations with the FBI, DEA, Customs, and the Border Patrol, so working with the Feds was nothing new. But Jake approached me with a strange proposition.

"What the hell do you need me for?" I said. Before he could tell me, I had to sign a confidentiality agreement that stated that I would never reveal information vital to the security of the United States. Okay, no big deal. I didn't think Jake was about to entrust me with the nuclear launch codes, and I don't even tell people what kind of underwear I buy.

After I signed away my civil rights and agreed to let some assassin whack me if I got too gabby, Jake briefed me on the small part I was to play in the operation. Basically, he and his sponsors needed me to help find the right ranch for their training exercises and then run interference when their activities caught the eye of local, state, and federal law enforcement agencies. Aerial drops in this part of the country tend to attract the suspicions of the DEA, and Jake hoped to route all inquiries along these lines to the local Texas Ranger to prevent an on-site incident investigation.

I'd be fielding a few calls from civilians, as well. I'd explain that there was nothing unusual about mujahedin warriors parachuting out of the sky or bouncing boats off mountains or learning to land unmanned UFO's in Billy Ray Bubba's cattle chute.

Folks were to ignore the C-130 transport planes, fighter jets, and Black Hawk helicopters swarming the area; disregard the fleet of black, unmarked semis hauling mobile living quarters and airplane hangars; and remain blind to satellite communications, computer terminals, and power generation modules crossing over the clanky cattle guard. They should forget about the radio antennas and laser targets on scraggy peaks and ignore the Islamic insurgents facing east as they bowed in prayer five times a day in between learning how to spy on Russian soldiers that they wanted to bomb into oblivion.

Regardless of all appearances to the contrary, it was just another day on the ranch, just a few vaqueros busting loose on payday. Don't worry, boys. Old Joaquin's got her under control. It's really no big deal, and some Rambo special ops spook will kill me if you don't believe that.

I don't expect Captain Allee saw this doozy coming, but I'd love to hear what he'd have to say about it. Oh, well. I had successfully guarded liberal Democrat Ann Richards during her campaign through West Texas. I figured I could protect the mujahedin, too. I didn't understand either one of them, and they both scared the hell out of me.

AT JAKE'S INVITATION, I finally rolled into the ranch to behold whatever was transpiring there. The camp looked like a military operation. Jake wore jeans and boots and had a bandana tied around his neck. I dressed for work like always—which except for the leather leggings looked a lot like the cover I later shot for *Texas Monthly* magazine. I wore my Colt .45 auto with the engraved silver-and-gold grips, a silver badge pinned to my shirt, cowboy boots, and a buckskin Resistol hat, and I smoked a big cigar. I was also carrying a favorite Winchester Model 94 .30-30 carbine that I wanted to show off to Jake.

Jake seemed in his element orchestrating the activities of the many military officers, technicians, bureaucrats, and instructors milling about the command hangar. But he's still a country boy and a hunter, and I knew he'd be interested in the way my Winchester handled. We had both been around guns enough to know that he couldn't fully appreciate the weapon without popping off a cap. It was loaded, and I motioned for him to have at it. He swung on an appropriate target and let her rip right inside the hangar.

The percussion was loud but tolerable. Nevertheless, Jake's staff came unglued. They jumped up from behind every gizmo with a horrified look on their faces.

"Who authorized that round?" one woman said, her tone demanding an official response.

"Nobody," Jake said, winking at me. "And that's why we're out here."

I first saw them before everyone had settled down. The first two walked up, and then more drifted in singles or pairs to stand in the sun. The wind caught their flowing white robes and *ghuthras*. Their black eyes sparkled in the brilliant light. They looked like extras in the epic film *Lawrence of Arabia*.

I stood holding the carbine by the action, my hat brim covering my face in a half shadow. I puffed on my cigar, regarding tribal warriors who, on occasion, still galloped with sabers drawn in cavalry charges that had stopped the Soviet army in its tracks. Texas had seen nothing like them since Comanche Chief Quanah Parker rode into Fort Sill to surrender in 1875. They, in turn, regarded their first and only Texas Ranger. We had all come face-to-face with a creature of myth. I stared. And they stared, too.

They were small and dark with bits of black curls poking out from underneath their *ghuthras*. They were alien to this place, and yet they walked gracefully as if they owned the Texas ground. There was a haughtiness about them, an assurance that belied their dainty frames and thin, smooth fingers.

At first I didn't care for their demeanor. I wondered why our country needed these cocky people. I reflected their own attitude back at them. I was a shitty host, I guess, but it wasn't my job to hitch up the welcome wagon. I intended to keep my distance and allow Jake plenty of room to do his job.

The mujahedin began to whisper. They pointed at my guns or my boots and covered their mouths. The translators leaned in to listen to the Afghanis, and then they smiled, too. At last, they approached Jake with an array of questions. I found out later what they said, and this is the basic exchange as I remember it:

"Who is he?" they asked.

"A Texas Ranger," Jake said. "A state policeman with many powers."

"Who gives him such magnificent guns and why is he shooting them?"

"He bought the guns himself and out here in the desert he shoots them when he wants. But don't worry. Only criminals need fear him."

"And small people, too, when he moves among them," they said. "By the Grace of God, he's a giant! Are there many his size in this country?"

"No, not too many," Jake said. "I'm of average size."

"Then truly he's a giant even among Americans. God help my wife and children if this man came inside my home. He's a crowd of one!"

Here even Jake smiled. I didn't need an interpreter to translate their final comment. They uttered sentences that all ended with the words *John Wayne*. I caught their drift and it tickled me. They were just people after that, just folks a long way from home to do a job. I tipped my hat to the holy warriors, walked with my best John Wayne swagger back to my state vehicle, and carried my ass back to Alpine.

I expect there were any number of cultural clashes and hiccups as the training moved along. I don't have many to share, however, because I wasn't that involved in their day-to-day affairs, and even Jake didn't get too personal with them. We were never told the names of their handlers. Jake broke out the UAV's and transmitters and they got down to business.

Feeding the mujahedin proved quite a challenge. They adhered to strict religious rules when it came to their food. In order to avoid suspicion, Jake sent his men to grocery stores miles away, but if he thinks buying a truckload of pita bread from the H-E-B in Uvalde or El Paso didn't raise a few eyebrows he needs to consider another line of work. Jake shipped in fruits and vegetables by the truckload, all of which passed the scrutiny of the mujahedin before they agreed to eat them. Once the grub passed muster, however, the men had voracious appetites and ate like teenagers.

Fresh meat was another matter. The mujjies wanted it on the hoof and in their possession before it was butchered. There was some sort of religious ritual involved, I guess. Jake started them out on Spanish goats and lamb, which they grilled over burning coals and ate with gusto. They left the skull, four hooves, and a hide, and that was about it.

Pretty soon they got to eyeing the Santa Gertrudis cattle roaming the pastures. Jake kept cash in his pocket for just such expenditures, and he quickly struck a deal with the rancher. The mujahedin watched in delight as the vaqueros drove a few head into the camp's makeshift corral. After that, the steers were their problem, to bless and eat them as they saw fit.

Now I don't know what sort of cattle the holy warriors were used to, but it became obvious that they'd never fooled with the Texas breeds. A group of mujjies, decked out in their flowing dress whites, carried a long, shiny dagger and a new galvanized bucket for the blood and reverently approached the steer. They commenced to kneel and pray, which we do as well, only a little later in the process. They stood and sang a few songs, which, judging from the steer's walleyed stare, started to spook him a little. Then a couple of the wiry little fellers put the Santa Gertrudis in a headlock, another grabbed him by the horns, a third positioned the blood bucket just right, and the meanest-looking out of the bunch came at the steer's throat with that big-ass knife. As far as the Afghanis were concerned, it couldn't have gone any more smoothly.

About the time they tightened their grip on the steer, however, the Santa

Gertrudis decided he'd had enough. He bawled and pawed the ground. He shook his head, tossing three skinny warriors like clean dishrags. The steer punched a hoof through the blood bucket, which he dragged until he finally kicked it loose. The mujjies started hollering as they ran for everything they held dear. Seemed like here would have been a better time for them to pray. For the steer, all this racket was the last straw. Something inside him just snapped.

When the Santa Gertrudis lit out, the boy with the knife was shit out of luck. The steer ran right over him and packed him facedown into a fresh cow pie, burst through the fence, jumped the cattle guard, crashed through brush dense enough to rip the fenders off a pickup truck, and didn't stop running until he reached the big house seven miles away. It was leftovers for the mujjies, who resigned themselves to a microwaved pizza for the evening meal.

But the mujahedin hadn't whipped the Soviets only to lose to a steer, and so a bruised, embittered, and newly emboldened crew hit the corral the next evening with a whole new game plan. The vaqueros had roped the steer and left him cinched off tight between a couple of mesquite trees. The mujahedin performed the same prayers and ceremonies, but this time they kept their distance and only closed one eye. When the time came to cut its throat, they didn't bother with the headlocks. They slashed the steer from behind like a Sicilian assassin and caught what blood they could in their little plastic replacement bucket. I have to hand it to them boys. They knew how to improvise and still keep it right.

That night they ate fresh red Texas beef, and they were proud of it. I still remember them sitting around the campfire, rubbing their bloated bellies, laughing about everything that had gone wrong the night before.

The mujahedin stayed out on that ranch for four months. Jake and I had grown quite fond of the gamey little hellions, at least as much as we could under the conditions. They worked hard at mastering a kid's remote control airplane before they moved up to full-size military-style UAV's—the kind that carried cameras, propaganda leaflets, and later charges of C-4 explosives. Before long the Afghanis could land one of them babies in your back pocket.

They were close-knit but very competitive. We watched them play their soccer matches, but Jake and his staff played in their volleyball and horseshoe tournaments. They scaled five-thousand-foot mountains like goats, learned the technology rapidly, played as a team, ate together, prayed alone, and sat around the campfire to visit when they weren't watching Western movies on the video machine. They loved John Wayne and went to great lengths to observe the ranch's cowboys during their daily routines.

Somebody—I don't know who—decided to take the boys into town near the end of their training. I didn't go. Neither did Jake. But Jake felt that with their handlers nearby it was safe to let them party a little bit. Staunch Moslems, the mujahedin would never touch alcohol, so Jake didn't worry about them getting into a barroom brawl. They also didn't look a whole lot different from your Sul Ross University graduate geology student or West Texas independent hotel owners. In a weird sort of way, as long as they kept their mouths shut, they sort of blended into this modern Texas of ours. Jake opened the ranch gate and cut them loose in their street clothes. They hit Van Horn first and then El Paso. They went to a steak house, of course, and then they did a little shopping.

"You comin' out this way, Joaquin?" Jake said the next day over the phone. "There's something you've got to see."

I pulled in and soon encountered Jake with that big, suspicious grin, your first warning that he's up to no good. "Come and look at my boys," he said proudly. Curious, I followed along.

We rounded the bend where the fire pit squeezed between the volleyball court and sleeping accommodations. There sat thirteen warriors under thirteen of the biggest, gaudiest, most outrageous cowboy hats I'd ever seen. I don't know where they found them. Looked like special orders. They stood and tipped their hats to me. New to their boots, a couple of them bobbled a little in the stiff breeze. The Afghanis flaunted their embroidered Western shirts, but they seemed especially proud of their shiny new manly footwear. You don't see a lot of patent leather roach killers around Alpine. They danced a little jig to make sure I noticed. I noticed all right.

"Evenin', boys," I said, proud to see our tax dollars at work on these delicate matters of national security.

"Howdy," one said, speaking for all of them. I believe his name was Muomaur or some such. I could tell by the way he was walking that his new boots were blistering his heels raw. But he'd rather die than admit it.

"I just couldn't say no," Jake said.

I believe, in the name of all Texans hold dear, that I could have. Lord, God. I knew I'd seen it all then.

Later, back home, I tried to slip between the sheets without waking my long-suffering wife. The nights she's sat up alone waiting for me probably number into the thousands. She could tell by the way I'd been acting that I was involved in something unusual and that it had nothing to do with investigation of serious crime.

"What have you been up to this time of night, Joaquin?" she said.

"If I told you, honey, I'd have to kill you," I said. It's an old joke, and she didn't think it was funny, but what the hell? Jake *never* talked about this stuff, and he made it clear that I wasn't supposed to, either. National security is serious business, even when it involves a bunch of Afghani dudes, who didn't know any better than to ask a Santa Gertrudis steer to dance, sitting around a fire in ridiculous cowboy hats.

I was beat. I pulled up the covers and scooted over to spoon next to my wife. I settled in. Everything got nice and quiet. Then I snickered. She socked the hell out of me and pulled away. She could fuss all she wanted. I wasn't going to talk, and there was no way she'd ever break me.

Well, there was probably one.

WHEN THE JOB WAS DONE the government flew the mujahedin back into the teeth of their war. Jake and I will never know what became of the thirteen warriors. We just know that the odds were stacked against them. The Soviets lost 15,000 soldiers before they pulled out, but the mujahedin dead numbered between 1 and 1.5 million in ten years of war. They triumphed regardless of how many were slaughtered, because the mujahedin never lost their will to fight. Jake and I saw a glimpse of their gumption every now and then.

True to their ancestral traditions, the seven Afghani clans squabbled among themselves after their victory against the Soviet Union. An Islamic fundamentalist movement originating in the southern Pashtun region, known as the Taliban, or "those who study the book," meaning the Koran, soon rose to prominence. After yet another civil war, the Taliban drove out the mujahedin leadership, ruling Afghanistan from 1996 until 2001. The Taliban were subsequently demolished by an American-led coalition in the wake of the September 11, 2001, terrorist attacks on New York and Washington, D.C.

I once asked Jake if he thought that some of the boys we trained were firing back at our American soldiers. I was at the time ignorant of the difference between the Taliban and the mujahedin. The United States was now at war with Afghanistan's Islamic warriors, and I couldn't help but see the irony that we were trying the kill the same men we had once trained.

"No," Jake said. "There's no way our boys could turn on us. If they survived the Russians and the Taliban, they're fighting with the Northern Alliance alongside our marines."

I don't know. I just don't know. But I hope it's true.

My time with the mujahedin was a brief, strange experience. I have no keepsakes from them. We weren't allowed to take any photographs of each other. Whenever I watch the news about Afghanistan, I find myself looking for someone wearing a big, ugly cowboy hat or maybe a pair of scuffed cowboy boots. And then it hits me that there are 2 or 3 million dead after twenty years of continual war. Most likely the violence swept away our boys with all the rest. It's still going on today.

I carry this one image with me of a late afternoon under a clear, cool West Texas sky. The sun sat blood red on the crest of the mountains. Everything was golden in the last light. I heard the first howl of coyotes sensing the fresh blood in the air from a butchered Spanish goat. I caught movement to the east and strained my eyes to see.

Soon I made out the white robes of a mujahedin warrior walking a rocky ridge alone, his robes fluttering slightly in the breeze, his back to the fading sun. The brilliant cloth was almost golden in that light. The Afghani laid out his prayer rug, a fringed rectangular tapestry highly prized among these men. I watched as he knelt to pray facing east, touching his nose to the Texas ground, his heart with his family so far away, his spirit soaring for these few seconds with his God.

It was one of the most beautiful things I've ever seen. When I think of the mujahedin, I remember this, and I always think well of them.

My Heroes Have Always Been Rangers: Just a Ranger

1987

J ANUARY 22. The dead of a Texas winter. A lone Lincoln Continental
pulled into the driveway of a residence in Horseshoe Bay, an exclusive resort community near the Hill Country hamlet of Marble Falls. The
white garage doors reflected the glare of the headlights, illuminating the
anguished middle-aged businessman sitting at the wheel. Beside him sat a
briefcase full of ransom money.

Inside the home, another man peered out through the blinds, making
sure that everything happened to the letter. Brent Beeler was a fugitive and
kidnapper bent on a violent, pointless crime spree. What no law enforcement official knew yet was that Beeler was also a rapist and cold-blooded
killer who had kidnapped, sexually assaulted, and tortured an innocent
woman for nearly a week before he smothered her to death and left her
body to rot in a boathouse storage closet.

Beeler worked in lawn maintenance and landscaping around Horseshoe
Bay. For months, he had cased the area until he possessed an encyclopedic
knowledge of what became his home range. He knew who lived in which
house, who were full-time residents and who used their property only as a
vacation home, what his clients did for a living and when they came and
went. He also knew that many homeowners designed their houses with
outdoor phone jacks to answer the phone from the patio or pool. Beeler
soon used all of this knowledge to perpetrate a shocking crime.

All the officers knew for sure that night was that, hours before, Beeler had abducted a beautiful, blonde two-year-old named Kara Lee Whitehead from her bed. He'd phoned her parents to inform them that he'd kill her if they didn't quietly come up with a large sum of money and a fancy car. Now, as both of those things waited for him on the driveway just outside, he watched to see if his third demand had been met. If he saw one single cop he swore he'd kill Kara on the spot.

When he was certain that Kara's father had come alone, Beeler began to bundle the child in a tablecloth for the long drive to wherever he thought he could get away with rape, murder, and kidnapping and live to gloat about it. He reached for his stolen .44 Smith & Wesson Model 29 revolver.

Inside the Lincoln, Kara's father, Bill Whitehead, went over the plan in his head. He checked to make sure that he left the dome light on as Beeler wished, but dimmed down enough to obscure the vehicle's interior. He left the motor running and the headlights on, and opened the door.

"Do not come back to this car!" a voice whispered from somewhere in the backseat.

Veteran Texas Rangers Johnnie Aycock and Stan Guffey lay beneath a dark cloth cover that had taken the place of the Lincoln's backseat. Bill Whitehead was beside himself with grief and rage. His impulse was to lash out at his daughter's kidnapper. Aycock had enough variables to deal with and didn't want Whitehead nearby when the exchange played out. When Whitehead hesitated, Aycock made damn sure the victim's father understood he needed to clear out. The Texas Rangers would attend to Beeler from this point on.

"Please bring my daughter home!" Bill Whitehead said. Then he tore himself from the car and hurried away. The two Rangers, seasoned colleagues and best friends, waited in silence, in the dark, under the covering, for whatever came next. All they had was their unwavering trust in each other and two loaded guns.

In a matter of moments, Aycock and Guffey confronted Beeler. None of the men knew Kara Lee Whitehead, but that didn't change the fact that all three were willing to die for her—Beeler for a chance at quick, dirty money; Guffey and Aycock because they were Texas Rangers.

LIKE A LOT OF RANGERS from my generation, John Earl "Johnnie" Aycock grew up hard in the ranch country of rural West Texas. His daddy was a drilling superintendent, a toolpusher who followed the oil and gas booms from one Texas town to the next. His parents divorced when Johnnie was just a kid. To make ends meet, Johnnie worked all kinds of odd jobs around

San Angelo, like running the projector and catching sneak-ins at the drive-in theater, pumping gas as the Site Oil Company filling station, and washing dishes at Cotton Kohler's café.

In 1965, Aycock enlisted in the army, entered basic training, earned his GED, and shipped out with the First Infantry Division. I'm pretty sure he was only seventeen years old, stood maybe 5' 8", and weighed 145 pounds, but soon he proved that he was every inch a warrior. He rapidly acclimated to a dangerous, tropical world that he could only have imagined a few weeks before.

For the next three years, Johnnie Aycock served in a frontline combat unit. He was eventually recruited into a five-man advisory detachment routinely operating on its own miles behind enemy lines. Between the chronic engagements, skirmishes, and firefights with North Vietnamese regulars and Viet Cong in the Mekong Delta and the hinterlands beyond, Johnnie and his men fought alongside SEAL teams and Special Forces in a different kind of warfare that few understood and none knew better. Johnnie doesn't like talking about any of these experiences.

Johnnie stumbled at first when it came to finding suitable employment upon his return to Texas. He held a short-lived job at a bomb plant in Fort Worth but soon applied for a position with the Highway Patrol. Fourteen years later, including nine spent as a DPS narcotics agent, Johnnie fulfilled his childhood dream in 1982 when he made Ranger.

Johnnie was assigned to Company F, then commanded by Captain Bob Mitchell, a leader of extraordinary ability, courage, and compassion who was revered by the men who served under him. Many promising young Rangers blossomed to their full potential under Captain Mitchell's command. Two such men were Stan Guffey and Johnnie E. Aycock, whose loyalty was so great that they'd both rather die than disappoint their captain.

FLASH FORWARD five stellar years of rangering to 1987, when Brent Beeler skipped a routine probation hearing in Houston, an event that didn't create a ripple in Johnnie Aycock's pond. Johnnie was married, balanced, had earned a university degree, and settled into his job. As soon as Beeler failed to show for his probation hearing, he became a wanted man who would probably turn up later at a typical traffic stop. Instead, something snapped. Beeler returned to Marble Falls hell-bent on destroying his life and the life of anyone who happened to cross his misguided path.

He abducted the Whiteheads' maid, perhaps thinking that she was Kara's mother, and spent a week jabbing her with an ice pick and burning her with a cigarette when he wasn't raping her. Ranger Johnny Waldrip handled the maid's disappearance as a simple missing person case. With no charge card, bank account, or telephone activity to tie to Beeler, Waldrip's thorough investigation had reached a dead end. No one knew anything about Beeler or what he was capable of.

Meanwhile, Beeler finished torturing his victim. He duct-taped her nose and mouth and left her to suffocate in a hot, dark shed. Aycock later discovered the body when he noticed a tarp covering a heap on the boathouse closet floor. Its stench told him that his search for the maid was over.

Beeler broke into the Whitehead home a second time and raided the kitchen for a bite to eat. He stole a watch, a little cash, and several fancy cigars before he went upstairs to Kara's room and kidnapped her, all while her parents slept. Kara's brother woke up in the next room. "Ssshhh," Beeler said. "It's okay. Go back to sleep."

Beeler broke into another home he knew would be vacant and locked little Kara alone in a bathroom. He carried a phone with him to plug in one of the outdoor jacks of yet a third residence—the first of many he would call from to confuse anyone who tried to pin down his location—and placed a call to Kara's parents. He demanded the money and the car and warned them not to call the police. "Or I'll do to her what I did to the maid," Beeler said.

The Whiteheads wisely disobeyed Beeler and contacted authorities. Word flew quickly up the chain of command to the Ranger stationed in Llano, who immediately placed a call to Captain Mitchell. All available Rangers in the company responded because of the distance typically covered in such cases and the number of men needed to field leads and stake out likely locations. FBI agent Sykes Houston, an experienced hand in kidnapping and hostage negotiations, was also brought in. Jurisdiction, however, belonged to the Texas Rangers.

A thorough examination of the known facts led Captain Mitchell to conclude that Beeler should not be allowed to leave the premises with the Whitehead child. It seemed unlikely that Beeler was aware that the Rangers were involved. Captain Mitchell felt like the best and possibly last opportunity to save Kara would be to foil the ransom transaction. He needed a man with solid instincts and nerve. Mitchell went straight to Johnnie Aycock. An instant later, Aycock's friend Stan Guffey volunteered to ride along.

The first vehicle for the job was Bill Whitehead's Porsche sports car, specifically requested by Beeler for his getaway. Aycock experimented with a number of bodily contortions, but found none workable. Captain Mitchell and the others watched on until Aycock approached him.

"I love you, Captain," Aycock said, "and I'll do this thing in this car if you ask me to. But if I go in that Porsche I ain't coming back."

The Porsche was replaced with a brand-new Lincoln Continental owned by District Attorney Sam Oatman. Bill Whitehead informed Beeler that the Porsche was not mechanically sound. By then, Aycock, who was close in size and general appearance to Bill Whitehead, was wearing Whitehead's clothing and driving the Porsche around in an erratic fashion, just in case Beeler was watching.

Bill Whitehead was understandably emotional during this ordeal. He clashed with some of the Rangers over the specifics of the plan, but he seemed to bond to Aycock, who in turn convinced him to comply with the Rangers' every request.

While Bill Whitehead and his father accumulated the cash, the Rangers went to work customizing the Lincoln. They ripped out the backseat to make room not only for Aycock and Guffey but also for food and supplies in case they had to wait hours or even days before they arrived at the kidnapper's drop zone. Aycock chose to dress in a drab-colored military jacket, while Guffey cinched his navy blue bulletproof vest over his light-colored Ranger shirt. Soon, everything was ready.

Beeler threw the Rangers a curve in his last telephone communication when he instructed Kara's father to park the Lincoln in the driveway of the house across the street from the Whiteheads' home. Whitehead was to leave the driver's door open, the headlights shining, the motor running, and the interior lights on so he could see the briefcase full of money on the seat.

Guffey and Aycock, stunned that Beeler had been holed up across the street, jettisoned most of their provisions. Two things became important: First, Aycock's impersonation of Bill Whitehead had yielded positive results. Even though Beeler was just across the street, he still had no idea that the Rangers were involved. And second, the critical exchange would take place in a matter of minutes rather than hours or days. Aycock and Guffey stripped down to the bare essentials and braced themselves for a short and violent ride.

Aycock lay down where the backseat had been, with his head closest to the passenger door. He could face Guffey and maintain eye contact with Bill Whitehead while he talked Kara's father through his part of the plan. Guffey settled on the floorboard with his head against the driver's side rear door, where he could cover the passenger's side of the car. The support team rearranged the dark cloth that concealed Guffey and Aycock and then dimmed the interior light. Things didn't look great to Captain Mitchell and the others, but they were as good as they were going to get, and Beeler was waiting.

Aycock and Guffey calmly discussed the silent signal they'd use when the time came to either arrest Beeler or kill him. In either case, rescuing the girl unharmed was their paramount objective. What became of Beeler was up to him, because the Rangers would never let him leave that driveway with Kara Whitehead in the car. Aycock and Guffey understood each other very well as the dark cloth was drawn over their heads.

Bill Whitehead pulled the Lincoln onto the driveway and parked it in front of the garage. Aycock ordered him away from the car. Bill Whitehead pleaded with Aycock to bring his daughter back safe and then grimly obeyed.

Within a minute, Beeler shot out of the door and ran up to the Lincoln. He carried Kara Lee Whitehead bundled in a tablecloth in one hand and a .44 pistol in the other. Beeler said, "Move over, baby!" as he shoved in behind the wheel. He left the car door open while he arranged everything around him.

Aycock, who could not see, was puzzled. Not knowing that Beeler had already killed the maid, he wasn't certain if the suspect was talking to the maid or the girl. He and Guffey could do nothing until they understood everyone's position in the Lincoln. He felt movement in the seat as the victim made room for Beeler; the body seemed too light to be an adult woman. In order to be certain, Aycock reached his hand around and felt the victim's buttocks. From the size he knew it was Kara Whitehead. She never made a sound.

Meanwhile, Beeler snatched the briefcase from the front seat and slapped it on what he thought was the rear bench seat. It was actually Aycock's chest and stomach. Then Beeler pounded on the briefcase with the .44 wrapped in his fist. The repeated blow forced the cloth covering down past Aycock's eye. He saw that Beeler's pistol barrel was cocked, with the hammer back and pointed directly at him.

The Rangers held their positions. Beeler continued to fumble with the case until he either noticed that there was no real backseat or caught a glimpse of one of the Rangers. Either way, in an instant, he knew.

"Oh, Goddamn!" Beeler cried and flew out the driver's door, aiming his pistol into the rear seat. Guffey yelled, "State police!" and rose to fire at Beeler. He found himself looking straight into the bore of Beeler's pistol. Guffey's first shot struck the car doorpost, the only thing of substance between him and Beeler, maybe three or four inches in width of hollow steel. He started to squeeze off another round.

Beeler fired his .44. The report blew out the window next to Guffey, spraying shards of thick glass into Aycock and Kara Whitehead's arms and faces. The rubber window seal peeled the brass jacket off the bullet, where investigators found it later. The bullet's lead core flew through the window seal and a few short inches before striking Guffey squarely in the forehead. Guffey's weapon fired once more when it fell out of the shattered window and hit the oil-stained pavement below.

Aycock rocketed out of the backseat and over the console and dove between Kara and Beeler. He reached for Kara with one hand and fired at Beeler with the other. At first, Beeler didn't understand where the shots were coming from. He probably knew that he'd eliminated Guffey's fire with his first shot. When Aycock's bullets ripped into his chest and body, Beeler assumed a sniper had targeted him. He made a confused effort to get back into the Lincoln, was driven out by Aycock's relentless fire, and then scrambled to the front of the car. Aycock continued to shoot through the windshield, pumping round after round into the kidnapper's body.

Each muzzle flash framed Beeler in varying expressions of shock, rage, and pain. Finally he spun on his heel and fell faceup beside the car.

Aycock moved slowly toward him until he was standing on Beeler's wrist. He wrenched the weapon out of Beeler's hand and studied him. Beeler would later be pronounced DOA at the hospital, but Aycock already knew that the kidnapper's criminal career was over. In Ranger parlance, Beeler was DRT—"Dead Right There."

Aycock turned to Kara. "I'm a police officer, honey," he told her. "A Ranger." He put her in the nearest safe place away from the people who were about to attend to a wounded Ranger. "Don't you move from here," he said.

As the Rangers and FBI agents rushed out to assist Guffey and Aycock, they saw Guffey's wounds. Aycock never missed a beat. He screamed for someone to bring him a car.

The first unit to roll up was Aycock's own car driven by Ranger Jim Miller. Aycock knew it was packed full of supplies and gear; there was no room for Guffey. "Get a car up here so we can take Stan to the hospital!" he shouted.

The next car belonged to the FBI. Aycock, FBI agent Nancy Fernari, Johnny Waldrip, and others carried Guffey to the backseat. Fernari held Stan's head in her lap as another officer sped to the local hospital.

Fernari was just out of the FBI Academy. Sprout green on her very first assignment, she had impressed the Rangers with her gumption. She coolly kept her head in the middle of the carnage and the chaos now that the storm had blown over. She also remembered her FBI first aid training that taught agents to speak to seriously wounded people in order to keep them from going into shock, a technique that has saved numerous lives.

"If you can hear me," Fernari told Guffey, "squeeze my hand." Fernari felt Guffey's pressure. Ecstatic, she told the others and then, turning back to Guffey, she said, "You're going to be all right, Stan. It's not as bad as you think."

Fernari continued to talk to Guffey as the car barreled toward the ER's runway. Just before they reached the hospital, Fernari again asked him to squeeze her hand. She felt the reassuring pressure, and then suddenly, there was a slow release. Texas Ranger Stan Guffey drifted away before the surgeons could attend to him. Beeler's .44 slug fragment fell out onto the stainless steel operating table.

Stan Guffey didn't live to see Kara Lee Whitehead being handed back to her parents.

STAN GUFFEY WAS THE FIRST Texas Ranger to be killed in the line of duty since Bobby Paul Doherty had been shot to death in a narcotics raid in 1978. There had been only two other Ranger fatalities, both resulting from motor vehicle accidents, after the Rangers had been incorporated into the Department of Public Safety in 1935.

Captain Mitchell, his company, and all of us who knew Stan Guffey were devastated to hear of his death. Simple words cannot describe how much Stan Guffey's colleagues loved and respected him. Even after Johnnie Aycock was awarded the Medal of Valor, the veteran Ranger was beside himself with grief.

After all these years, Johnnie's remorse has yet to leave him. He would later receive the Medal of Valor for his conduct in a second kidnapping situation in 1995 (the victim a girl who looked remarkably like Kara). He is the only Texas Ranger to be thus twice recognized.

But you won't hear about any of this from Johnnie Aycock. He refuses to speak publicly about his accomplishments as a Ranger. As his friend, I knew a little about what happened back in 1987, and in 1995, and about other remarkable things, too. Despite Johnnie's wishes, I think people ought to know what he did. If you believe Ranger heroes are only a thing of the past, you are dead wrong.

There is an unspoken code as old as the Rangers themselves that equates humility and modesty alongside courage, independence, and valor. The greater the Ranger's deed, the more stubborn he is about keeping quiet about it. And so it has been all these years with Johnnie, who suffers the misfortune of having a gabby friend with literary ambitions. After I begged him to allow me to include this story in my memoir, he reluctantly agreed.

"Don't make me out to sound like some kind of hero, Joaquin," he warned me. "I'm just a Ranger."

Joaquin Jackson and Johnnie Aycock on the set of *The Alamo*, Reimer Ranch, Dripping Springs, Texas, July 2003. *Photo by Shelton Smith.*

It's the first promise I couldn't keep to my old friend. Johnnie Aycock is "just a Ranger" the way that Elvis Presley was just a singer and Mike Jordan liked to shoot baskets every now and then. In my book we're going to call him what he is—the greatest Ranger of his generation.

Like me, Johnnie's retired now. He lives with his wife Estelle on a beautiful ranch in the heart of the rolling Texas hills that used to be his jurisdiction. Seems fitting that Johnnie has returned to the rural life he knew from his beginning, living peacefully among the people that he served and protected for so many years.

You might catch him peering out from a cedar brake, wearing a big grin and a goofy gimmee cap under a canopy of wild grapevines, or burning a welding rod as he builds intricate working pens that he designs himself, or stretching another strand of barbed wire across the five-mile perimeter of lush coastal and Klein grass and bluestem pasture. He believes he looks like just another stove-up old rancher who got thrown from one too many broncs. He doesn't think you'll notice him. Johnnie Aycock doesn't understand that his magnificence shines through all his futile efforts to obscure it—today, tomorrow, and for as long as the Rangers ride.

CHAPTER FOURTEEN

⊕ Desperadoes and Dumbasses
1966–1993

THE DEVIL'S IN THE DETAILS, SOLDIER

HE KILLER WORE black leather gloves. A passing motorist, the son of the local game warden, discovered the body in a bar ditch on Highway 57 between Batesville and La Pryor. The victim wasn't hard to notice. He was engulfed in flames four feet high.

The body was burned to the extent that we could not determine its race. Right away we noticed the bullet wounds to the head, upper right chest, and right forearm. Every effort had been made to destroy all means of identification. The soil around the body had been soaked with plenty of gasoline, set aflame, and allowed to burn for some time before it was discovered. Had the game warden not put out the fire with an extinguisher, very little of the body would have been left. We could not obtain fingerprints. There was no point in circulating a photograph of the unrecognizable corpse. We didn't have enough to go on to have any idea where to search for dental records. DNA technology was almost two decades away. I didn't know what to do, until the coroner handed me a numbered key to a military barracks that was found in the victim's pants pocket.

A quick call to the Criminal Investigation Division at Fort Sam Houston in San Antonio matched the key with Spec. 4 Mario Joaquin Mendoza of Thirty-fourth Supply Brigade, Sixth Air Combat Command, stationed at Fort Hood, Texas. A native of Panama, Spec. 4 Mendoza had lived in Brooklyn, New York, before enlisting in the United States Army. He was listed as AWOL, as were the two soldiers he had been traveling with. Known marijuana users, the three errant servicemen had boosted a Sansui stereo receiver from one of their comrades before they hooked them south toward the border on a wild road trip to make the big drug buy.

Mendoza, now a human charcoal briquette, was also carrying $2,000 in cash. His mistake was that his two buddies knew that he had it.

One of the two surviving killers was a Colombia native by the name of Prospero Orlando Pinzon Jr., who had prospered by $2,000, the Sansui receiver he later traded for Mexican black tar heroin, and whatever dope they had on hand for Mendoza's last great road trip. He and his partner carried their booty across the Rio Grande and whooped it up big in Piedras Negras. The big deal soon went sour. But Pinzon had formulated a backup plan. He bought a Rossi .38 caliber revolver and a gallon can of gasoline and kept his financier close to him on the long drive home.

Ranger Ed Gooding and I interviewed witnesses and suspects, including Pinzon, but it took us awhile to narrow down a list of likely suspects. We secured warrants for Pinzon after his cohort confessed and identified Pinzon as the shooter. By the time we showed up at Fort Hood, however, Pinzon had decided to go Greyhound and leave the fleeing to them.

We put out an APB when I was notified of yet another murder case, which involved a good friend of mine. I headed west out of San Antonio toward Hondo. Just west of Castroville there was a long hill, where I overtook a Greyhound bus. I couldn't help but notice that Pinzon, whom I had already interviewed, was casually visiting with the driver.

I pulled ahead of the Greyhound and off to the side of the road and motioned to the bus driver to pull over. He readily complied. When the doors opened, I identified myself as a Texas Ranger and told him that there was a murder suspect on his bus. Pinzon was reported to be armed and dangerous, so I had little choice but to pull out my Colt pistol and advance toward the rear of the bus.

Pinzon attempted to hide between two old and very nervous women. I walked straight to him and put a pistol against his forehead and said, "State police. You're under arrest. Put your hands behind your head." Pinzon looked cross-eyed at the pistol and surrendered.

I pulled him up by his hair to his feet and escorted him off the bus. To add insult to injury, I explained that there would be no refund on his bus ticket, but the State of Texas would pick up his hotel tab for a while.

In the end, it was a stupid crime by a mean, stupid crook.

The case that distracted me from the fugitive Pinzon involved Castroville City Marshall Frank Hayes. I had worked with Frank on a number of investigations, so I knew him well. I liked him.

Frank was interrogating a twenty-year-old Hispanic male theft and burglary suspect on a hill outside of Castroville. When the marshall didn't get the answers he was looking for, he decided to coerce the suspect with his hammerless double-barrel shotgun. He poked the kid in the gut with the bore. The suspect grabbed the barrel of the shotgun and jerked it forward. With the sudden tug, Frank's thumb flipped off the safety and he accidentally pulled the trigger. The weapon discharged into the suspect's chest, killing him.

Frank went to pieces when the inappropriate and illegal interrogation went so damn wrong. Instead of calling for an ambulance and reporting the incident as an accidental shooting, Frank loaded the body in his trunk, drove to his family's place in East Texas, and buried it. It didn't take long for investigators to put the pieces together.

By the time I was free from the Pinzon case, Rangers Bob Favor and Dan North (with North being the principal investigator) had already recovered the body, sent it to pathology to determine its identity and cause of death, and sworn out an arrest warrant for Frank Hayes. When I finally arrived in Hondo, the other officers were preparing to raid Frank's trailer.

Like many cops, Frank owned and used a number of firearms. He was holed up in his trailer. Word was out that he was deeply depressed by this incident and probably wouldn't allow himself to be taken alive. Accordingly, a number of officers had gathered to storm the trailer and either arrest Frank or kill him.

I worried about this plan, not only for Frank's sake, but for ours. I felt it was very likely that a bunch of people were going to get shot. So I asked them, "Has anybody just called and talked to Frank?"

Nobody had. So I talked them into letting me contact Frank before we did anything else. I picked up the phone and called his trailer.

"Frank," I said. "This is Joaquin."

"Hey, Joaquin," he said. His voice was flat. I knew that he was hurting.

"Frank, I'm sorry to hear about this shooting. I know that you didn't mean to hurt that kid. They've issued a warrant for your arrest. I'm wondering what you want us to do about it. I think it'd be best for you and your family if you just drove to Hondo and turned yourself in."

The phone went silent while he thought about it. Then he said, "I'll be right there, Joaquin," he said. "I'll come on in."

Whew. Frank was good for his word. He was later convicted in state court and sentenced to thirty years. Then the Feds came after him for civil rights violations and they tacked on another life sentence. Frank died behind bars. It makes me sad to think about it because I know he didn't mean for things to happen like that. But they did, and he handled them wrong, and he paid a heavy price.

THE SABINAL PSYCHO

The call came in from my friend Kenneth Kelley, Uvalde County sheriff, who advised me that he had a hostage situation in-progress with shots fired at responding officers. Kelley and I arrived simultaneously at the scene just before dark. We soon learned that an eighty-year-old Sabinal woman was being held at gunpoint in her trailer by her disturbed son.

When sheriff's deputies attempted to visit with Junior about this unpleasant situation, he fired a .22 round through the window of the front door, nearly wounding one officer and sending them all running for cover. Apparently, the subject continued to fire at officers and was observed slapping his mother around, too, whenever she made a move toward the door. Neither one of the subject's choices set well with me.

Upon our arrival, the neighbors advised that the man was unstable and had been threatening to kill his mother and also some of them for at least the past two weeks. He had also lost the use of his right eye some time ago. He shot with his right hand while attempting to sight the weapon with his left eye, which explains why no one had been shot yet despite a barrage of .22 fire.

Sheriff Kelley attempted to reason with this afflicted man with a bullhorn. The subject answered with a hail of bullets, many of which ricocheted off the concrete EMS building that lay in his line of fire. Of course, Sheriff Kelley and I were also in the line of fire. It became obvious that this tragic fellow faced a number of personal challenges, being a psycho only one among many. But I wasn't going to allow him to kill or injure me, his mom, or any other officer or innocent civilian if I had anything to do with it. As we were ducking bullets I advised Sheriff Kelley in no uncertain terms that I planned to take the crazy son of a bitch out and in a hurry.

Sheriff Kelley said it was early yet for that, and I guess his compassion swayed me to attempt less lethal measures. Our entire position was brightly illuminated by a streetlight. I wanted it shut off. The city couldn't do it soon enough, so one of the officers tried to shoot it out with a pellet rifle. The pellets only bounced off the lamp's thick glass. I cracked it with a .22 rifle, and then we had things like we needed them. We could now see into the subject's trailer, while he could no longer see us.

His mother sat at the head of their dinner table, calmly talking to her son. She wasn't restrained in any way that I could determine. Junior visited with her while he reloaded one of two .22 rifles, which he then emptied at us. Other than the sporadic gunfire, the scene inside the trailer looked downright tranquil. For all I knew, the old woman was watching *The Dukes of Hazard* while her boy leered at us through the shot-out window with his one good eye. It didn't really look like your standard hostage situation, but then again it didn't look like anything else I'd ever seen, either.

Sheriff Kelley and I agreed that tear gas was the best way to break up this happy home. I didn't want to gas the man's mother with a grenade or standard projectile because I was afraid that the stress on her system would give her a stroke. I chose one of the newfangled weapons issued by the department, a shotgun-shell-sized canister stuffed with granules that released smaller quantities of tear gas on impact. I asked Sheriff Kelley to position his men close to the trailer while I eased up to the picture window with my fancy new gas gun.

The idiot emptied yet another magazine out the window and then sat down on the floor to reload like he was working a jigsaw puzzle or something. I stepped up to the front door and aimed the gun inside. The subject trained his eye on me and swung the barrel of his rifle my way. I popped him square in the chest with the canister of granules and then got out of his way to let the gas smoke them out.

Next thing I knew, I heard his mother say, "I ain't staying here in this shit!" She rose from the dining table and stormed out the door like I believe she could have done at any moment during this ordeal. I could only assume that she, like any concerned mother, wanted to support her son's professional ambitions by volunteering to be his very first victim. After he got the hang of the extortion business, he'd probably soon move on to abduct perfect strangers and even make demands for money, a getaway car, and what have you. She knew that all her boy needed to make it big as a criminal was a little confidence.

Everything was going beautifully until the tear gas enveloped their little wigwam on wheels. The old woman was keen to play her role until asphyxiation became a real threat, and then she made it perfectly clear to her son that her time as a hostage was at an end. Disconcerted, Junior followed after her.

"Come back, Mama," he said, pleading with her not to ruin a perfectly good hostage standoff. "Mama, please come back!"

Frankly, I didn't know what to think at this point, except that the incident then reminded me of the heartbreaking scene in *Shane*—a little different situation, maybe, but one with the same emotional punch once I suspended my sense of the absurd. I was going to pity the subject just as soon as I disarmed him. I approached him for the final coup de grace, when he once again pointed that rifle in my direction.

I had no choice but to raise my Colt, flick off the thumb safety, and prepare to fire point-blank into his chest, when State Trooper Leonard Vaughn jumped out of the bushes and onto the man's back and rode him to the ground. Other officers quickly piled on. Their swift and heroic action saved this boy's life. I was really glad that I didn't have to drill him with the .45 Colt. He had enough problems already.

They soon handcuffed Mama's little mom-napper and hauled his confused ass off to jail. EMS took his mother to the hospital for observation. She was okay.

Her son, however, was struggling with an allergic reaction to the gas granules, along with a host of other more deeply rooted difficulties. His head had swollen to the size of a pumpkin. He couldn't see but he could still yap.

"Who was that exterminator who shot me with that shit?" he asked Sheriff Kelley the next day.

"The man from Orkin," Kelley said.

YEARS LATER, the subject was released from a mental institution. His ever-dutiful mother took him back in, with the understanding that there'd be no gunplay around the house. They lived quietly without incident until the old lady passed on. Sometime afterward, the subject walked naked into the only women's fashions store in Sabinal. The authorities sent him back to the mental hospital, and what became of him after that is anyone's guess.

PLEASE, GOD, NO MORE GENETIC MATERIAL

The heyday of the safecrackers was in the 1960s and '70s, when professional artists created a national epidemic. In my jurisdiction, talented, organized burglary rings operated around Lake Worth, San Angelo, and Odessa, Texas, and Hobbs, New Mexico. They tended to target small-town banks, lucrative local businesses, and wealthy ranchers, all holding large amounts of valuables and cash.

Most of the victims of these crimes relied on outdated safes and had not yet installed the routine electronic security and on-site surveillance systems available today. This turned out to be a bad combination for honest people who kept large amounts of cash around their homes or offices.

The crooks targeted small, sleepy towns away from their home area. They sought out likely victims, entered the business as a normal customer, and then cased the joint for lighting conditions, business hours, location of the safe, and whatever security measures were in place. They would also establish the routine of the local police—how many officers were on duty at nighttime and when and how they made their rounds. Once they had cased a promising joint and patterned the local cops, they struck.

The true professionals adopted a signature MO. First of all, to avoid a violent confrontation with law enforcement, they *never* carried guns. For them, no amount of money was worth getting shot, and they didn't see the need in aggravating the charges against them if they were caught.

They also owned the fanciest, most expensive drills and other state-of-the-art tools on the market. They typically used jeepers, a lookout usually in radio contact with the safe technician. Most were apprenticed to an old safecracker or some jailhouse talent encountered in the prison system. They developed a locksmith's education and skill when it came to locks and tumblers.

If the crooks didn't simply pick the lock to the front door of the subject business, most tended to gain access to the crime scene by cutting a hole in the roof, which was more difficult to detect by the casual observer. The idea was not to leave any blatant signs of entry, like a broken window or a jimmied door. Everything looked normal when a skilled safecracker went to work. Once inside, safe men worried about time, lights, and noise.

Since the professional already knew from his research the make and manufacture of the subject safe, he was able to bring only the appropriate tools for the job, usually hauled to the job in a tradesman's bag used by plumbers and electricians. Real pros always relied on their own equipment. Some chose run-of-the-mill crowbars, hammers, and punches, and others customized with great forethought and creative genius. They knew what it took to crack a particular brand of safe, and they went out and acquired it.

One of the cruder safecracking methods involved knocking off the combination knob with a sledgehammer and punching the securing pin back into the safe. Valve stems from typical car engines of the time were the perfect size, diameter, and temper to handle this basic operation. Once the pin was driven out, the safe swung open. If they couldn't knock out the pin, they had equipment on hand to drill the pin out into so many metal shavings.

Some crooks were "peelers," cons who knew how to separate the layers of steel that formed the safe's door. Starting from a corner, they'd chisel one layer from another and peel them back until they got to the fire clay. They'd chisel through fire clay to gain access to the locking lug, which they dismantled, cut, or pried out of the slot. They were grabbing the green after that.

Some enterprising safecrackers with blue-collar roots resorted to acetylene cutting torches. This operation was messy and created a brilliant light. To overcome these problems, professionals used a tarp as a tent to shield their activities. To protect the cash, they'd drill a hole and hook in a garden hose and fill her up with tap water. These guys looked guilty as sin, though. You'd find them with pinholes burned all over their clothes. A cutting torch was not the true artist's choice.

In the late 1960s, I first came into contact with the thermal bar technique. Developed in Europe, the thermal bar was a heavy metal cylinder with some sort of alloy or compound in the middle. It looked like a giant sparkler with three or four welding rods in the middle. Once ignited with an acetylene torch, a thermal bar could melt through a concrete slab. They really did a number on the company safe, but with their intense heat and brilliant glow, successful use of the thermal bar proved to be a real challenge.

Once during a bank job in D'Hanis, Texas, a group of felons used a thermal bar to burn a doorway through a brick wall. In the process, they'd set fire to the tarp, among other items. The ensuing smoke drove them out long before they could get to the safe. These suspects, obvious amateurs, were never apprehended, probably because they were hospitalized for smoke inhalation.

Professional safecrackers all relied on a fairly standard MO. But even the best and most traditional burglars left some idiosyncratic sign or symbol to differentiate them from others in the business. Crooks that specialized in grocery store jobs left behind particular items—an opened tin of sardines or discarded can of Big Red soda or ginger ale. If we found a bottle of Grapette next to some Fig Newtons at two or three jobs, we assumed that we were dealing with the same bird.

But by far, the crook with the most peculiar crime scene habits was a San Angelo–area career cracker by the name of Zack Goorigan. Goorigan mastered the techniques described above that were used by all professionals. Yet, it was obvious to criminal investigators when Zack had pulled a job. The reason was that Goorigan's MO included a BM.

It's absolutely true! To add to the insult of having their property violated and valuables purloined, Goorigan's victims also encountered a large pile of human feces near the scene of the crime—once on the owner's business desk.

For today's forensic investigators, this wealth of genetic materials would be considered a boon when it came to identifying a suspect. For us poor Stone Age saps, though, it was damn disgusting. Law enforcement wits soon nicknamed Goorigan the "Shit 'n' Git Safecracker." Obviously, local business leaders as well as the DPS brass in Austin wanted this appalling felon—I'm sorry, but there's no other way to phrase it—wiped off the books.

I forget the particulars concerning Goorigan's arrest (except the stench—that sticks with you), but he was eventually flushed out by criminal investigators, tried in a court of law, and convicted. Once we had him behind bars with a toilet safely there by his bunk, I interviewed "Shit 'n' Git" about two outstanding safe jobs. It was obvious that he had been the perpetrator in both cases. My question was why he made it so damn repugnantly obvious.

During our interview, Goorigan claimed that he got so excited once he'd cracked the safe that his bowels engaged. He couldn't help himself, he said. It was like trying to control a sneeze.

"Why didn't you just use a toilet?" I asked him.

"Too far away from my work," he said.

I hope they tacked a few extra years on his sentence for that. Or maybe put him to work in the prison sewage facility so that the punishment fit the crime.

THE BUNKER MENTALITY

Two rural Atascosa County neighbors stopped to visit near their mailboxes, when a bullet slammed through one of their hands. Turned out the shot originated from a third neighbor, an irascible character who seemed hell bound to take private property rights to a new extreme. His neighbors got a little too close to his property line for comfort, so he figured that he was within his rights to let them have it with a high-powered rifle. Merciful God!

Perhaps it was the nine-foot-tall perimeter fence he had constructed around his home that provided the first clue that he was a little particular about his privacy. Or maybe it was the watchtower he climbed every day to keep a close eye on his neighbors' activities with his binoculars. There was no escaping the several fifty-five-gallon drums, old washing machines, and refrigerators arranged around his house to protect the perimeter and discourage a frontal assault. I guess you could consider the montage of rusting appliances and junk metal contraptions as a sort of economical white-trash moat.

The house itself had been bolstered to withstand a siege—at least this moron seemed to think so. He'd cut slits and gun ports in all of his exterior walls. He had a basement refuge full of weapons and ammunition. He reared a like-minded son. He didn't like people, but he loved guns. The man was strange and he was violent, but at least he was prepared . . . for *something*.

So, when his neighbors strayed across the property line, he felt obliged to shoot them. And when the victims notified the sheriff's department about the incident, the first deputies to respond got their windshield shot out with an M-16. This type of behavior attracts more police officers. Eventually it summoned me, my sergeant Lefty Block, and Rangers Dan North, Glenn Krueger, and Gene Kea.

The first thing I did was replace my .45 Colt sidearm with standard issue .357 magnum, basic procedure to ensure that all of us Rangers shot the same ammunition. I didn't rely on my bulletproof vest as much as I should have—and it's ineffective against rifle fire anyway—but I strapped it on just in case it might help me. As I slid my AR-18 Armalite assault rifle out of its protective case, a wounded policeman on his way to an ambulance happened by. "You're gonna need that," he said, with the blood dripping from his fingers. "He's got one just like it."

Fair enough, I thought, angered that a good policeman had been shot over a chickenshit deal like this. Let's dance.

I moved toward the house and crouched behind a handy washing machine and studied the situation to get the lay of things. By now the man and his boy were really going at it with the police. He focused on me long enough to shoot the control panel off my washing machine. Boy, howdy!

Some sheriff's deputies located a can of gasoline. They quickly fabricated some Molotov cocktails and set the side of the house on fire. The subject attempted to extinguish the flames by daubing them with a wet mop through the window. I fired a steady burst at him with the Armalite and he gave up the mop.

After the fire caught on, the explosions started, and soon I heard someone holler, "He's comin' out!" He did, but with a pistol in his hand, and when we ordered him to drop it or else, he receded back into the burning house. He next shoved his son out of the door to see if we'd shoot him or not—which we didn't. We handcuffed the boy and led him away.

Meanwhile, his daddy stood at the door with the pistol in his hand and deliberated about what to do—burn up, get his ass shot, or surrender. In the end, he chose the third alternative and the jig was finally up.

We found out later that he had a .50 caliber machine gun and thousands of rounds ready to go. If he'd have rigged up that baby, we'd have all been in serious trouble. He also had land mines buried around the place. Luckily no one tripped one, but you've got to wonder where this lunatic came up with all this stuff and why he felt it was necessary to have it on hand. I mean, land mines? I'd hate to be his UPS man.

I'll never forget his parting words as they hauled him off to jail. "Well, you sons of bitches got me this time," he said. "Next time, I'll build a house that you can't burn down."

With three officers and one neighbor wounded, he had plenty of time to think through his design.

HOME IS WHERE THE RANGER IS

Before Gary Ball actually escaped from the Brewster County jail, he threatened to kill his girlfriend. Since he was crazy enough to break jail, we figured he was crazy enough to kill the only woman crazy enough to put up with him. We took her into protective custody. Short of manpower, I volunteered to sit inside her Alpine trailer and greet the man of the house if he showed.

Forty-five minutes after I climbed inside, I heard the dog barking. I heard the footsteps of someone walking up to the dog's pen and then the dog quit yapping. The dog obviously knew the guy.

Ball came around to the south end of the trailer and attempted to pry open the back window. I found out later that he had a pencil stuck in the window jamb to keep his girlfriend from latching it, but she'd smashed it down good and the window was locked. Ball fooled with it for a while before he gave up and went around to the front door.

Ball was a career criminal, but he wasn't a very good one. At least he didn't know how to pick a lock or jimmy open a door. After he monkeyed with the front door for a while, I finally reached over and unlocked it and let her swing open just a little. I stepped back to see what he would do.

He pounced right in. I could see that he was holding something in his hand, but it was too dark to see that it was only a screwdriver. I identified myself and ordered him to hit the floor and get down on his face. I repeated the order again. There was no response and still Ball stood there.

I fired a warning shot at the floor to let him know that I meant business. Unfortunately, the bullet passed through his big toe. He didn't scream in pain or show any sign that he had been wounded. I repeated my instructions with greater emphasis. The son of a bitch just stood there and looked at me!

I fired a second round, this time a little higher, and definitely at his frame. This bullet passed through his upper thigh. He didn't holler or give me any indication that I had injured him in any way. I didn't know if this jailbird didn't understand that I was serious or was just a little slow in the head when it came to what I wanted him to do. I screamed, "Get down on the floor!" Seemed clear enough to me.

Instead, Ball lunged at me. I couldn't believe it. I fired point-blank. The bullet entered his lower chest, passed completely through his abdominal cavity, and exited through his buttocks. Ironically enough, I was using ball ammunition, as opposed to soft-, or hollow-, point, which mushrooms upon impact for maximum tissue damage. I'd been target shooting that day and hadn't switched back. It turned out that my oversight was lucky for me and very lucky for Gary Ball.

Ball hit the floor after the third shot. I stepped over him and flipped on the light. The lunatic was trying to get back up and have at me, but I stepped on his chest and told him he best lie still. I called the sheriff and told him to get an EMS unit on the scene.

Ball was evacuated to a hospital in El Paso for treatment of his wounds. One of the emergency technicians asked Ball how he was doing as they loaded him into the ambulance.

"Not too bad for a guy who's just been shot three times with a .45," he said. Amen.

Gary Ball recovered just fine. He finished up his jail sentence and continued to hang around Alpine. He was perpetually active in petty crimes and shady deals. He did develop a healthy respect for me, though, and even offered to become one of my informants. That's as close as he ever got to a righteous life. I'm not sure what happened to his girlfriend, but I hope she searched elsewhere for a mate.

Ranger Joe Coleman interviewed Gary Ball about the shooting, and Ball confirmed my version of the incident, which I appreciated. Toward the end of the interview, Ball said, "Should have known better than to come to a gunfight with a screwdriver."

And they say criminals never learn.

No Accounts

Ben "Doc" Murray was the longtime sheriff of Dimmit County. Doc knew his people and territory well and was probably the best civil servant that part of the country ever knew. We worked on many cases together. I learned a lot from that old-school Texas sheriff. He had to be in his mid-to-late sixties in 1991.

Doc Murray never trusted banks. I don't know if this decision was due to some scar he carried from the Depression or what, but he carried a huge wad of cash with him at all times. He basically banked out of his pocket, not only for personal needs but for county business, too. If the jail needed toilet paper and Windex, Doc shelled out the cash, bought the items, turned in the receipt, and was later reimbursed. Such accounting would never fly today, of course, but Doc was impeccably honest.

He also had a heart of gold. Everyone knew this, and some folks thought of Doc when they needed a little cash to see them through. Two such people were troubled young men. They asked Doc for $10. He pulled out his roll and peeled off the small bills and handed them their money. Doc didn't notice the gleam in their eyes or the way they looked at each other.

Late that afternoon, they'd summoned enough courage to knock on Doc's door with a butcher knife behind their backs. As soon as Doc answered, they slashed his throat. But the wound wasn't severe enough to cripple Doc Murray, who put up a desperate fight for his life. The entire house looked like a couple of bulls had gotten loose in there.

In the end, one of the murderers jabbed the butcher knife to the hilt in Doc's chest. Even that wound didn't kill him. One of the bastards held him down while the other one shot Doc in the head with his own .45.

I gave the eulogy at Doc Murray's funeral. It was a gloomy day in Dimmit County. An era had passed in South Texas with Doc's murder.

Ranger Doyle Holdridge worked the case in whirlwind time. He was assisted mostly by Coy Smith, but I helped a little because I wanted to. We arrested both killers in a couple of days. One got a life sentence. The other was sentenced to death.

THE LAST ROUNDUP

I was about ten miles south of Uvalde when I heard the radio transmission. A thirty-year-old Hispanic man had taken over the Uvalde Memorial Hospital ER. What?

Turns out this tormented soul had a history of severe seizures. When they struck he became extremely violent and had the strength of five men. Judging from the desperate voices on the radio, the patient was a real handful. I hooked over to the hospital to see if I could help out.

As I blew into the entry lane south of Uvalde Memorial, I spotted Patrolman Montgomery's unit, lights flashing, tires spinning, trying to back the hell away from the ER. Standing in front of Montgomery's unit was the subject, with an oxygen cylinder over his head. Looked like he intended to throw it through Montgomery's windshield—if he could catch him. The police officer was burning some serious rubber trying to reverse out of harm's way.

As Montgomery sped away, the subject lost his balance and fell backwards with the cylinder. He jumped up and lit out after the police officer. I get that sinking feeling when I see a cop trying to run away from an unarmed man on foot. Really worries me.

I made a semicircle around them both and came up behind them. When the subject accepted that he'd never catch Montgomery, he turned on me. What a hellion! What sort of disease had a hold of this fellow?

The subject grabbed the door handle on my side of the car and tried to pound out the glass with his fist. Spooked me a little. I goosed the engine to knock this guy loose. When I did, my rear tire ran over his foot. I didn't mean for that to happen. He went down and grabbed his foot with both hands and spun around on his butt like a hurt dog.

I jumped out of my car and popped the trunk. I had a variety of weapons at my disposal, but I chose my lariat rope instead. I couldn't shoot him. Seemed like he'd had all the damage to his brain that he could stand, so I couldn't knock him out with my nightstick, and there was no way in hell I was going mano a mano with a maniac who had chased off a police car. I roped his ass, dragged him fifty feet to a mesquite tree, and lashed him against its trunk. As soon as I had him cinched good, he passed out. Whew!

About then the hospital staff appeared, armed with syringes and a straitjacket. They pumped him full of something, and then I unwrapped him enough to get the jacket on him. I don't know what sort of person he was normally, but when those seizures hit, watch out! I heard that this poor, tortured man died a year or two later from this tragic illness.

HOLLYWOOD MAKEOVER

Around 1966, I was patrolling the Uvalde County fairgrounds with Sheriff Kelley. A carnival was in town, and we hoped that our appearance might inspire the gamesmen and vendors to treat our citizens fairly. We came across a neatly dressed man in his seventies strutting around with a beautiful young Mexican girl on his arm. Sheriff Kelley backslapped with him before we went on our way.

"Who's that old codger?" I said.

"Willis Newton," Sheriff Kelley said. And then he went on to tell me the story of the Newton Boys, the down-home bank-robbing brothers. They were famous in Uvalde long before Willis's and Claude Stanusch's book and later Richard Linklater's feature film portrayed them as Texas Robin Hoods. They hit something like sixty banks, many of them in Texas. Their success was obviously the Rangers' failure.

Only one of the Newtons ever worked, to my knowledge. None of them owned a business. Joe, the youngest and most affable of the brothers, ran cattle on leased land to get by. The rest of them had no visible means of support that I knew about, and yet Willis always drove a new Cadillac and wore fancy suits and fine felt fedoras. Whenever it appeared that he was low on funds he'd disappear for a while, only to return flush with cash. I didn't believe that they were still active as burglars, so they must have stashed some loot somewhere during their criminal career.

"We wasn't thugs like Bonnie and Clyde," Willis liked to say, "we was just quiet businessmen." Horseshit. The Newtons were common criminals. I found Willis Newton's arrogance repugnant and Sheriff Kelley's admiration of him and his brothers disgusting.

After that first encounter, I eyed Willis Newton from a distance, and he had the spit and vinegar to glare back at me. I always kept an ear to the ground for information about their activities, mostly because I felt like their celebrity sent the worst possible message to the young people in our community. All I needed was a reason to put them behind bars and I'd have done it in a heartbeat.

A few years later, Sheriff Kelley asked me to tag along while he served the Newtons with some civil documents. Willis opened the door and invited us in. There were four windows in that old house, and every one of them had a Winchester rifle leaning next to it. If they'd gone straight, they obviously suffered from a guilty conscience. They kept their distance from me, but they fawned over Sheriff Kelley. In this, they were wise.

I think it was Doc or maybe Jess who tried his hand at least once more at bank robbery after their retirement. He was caught inside the bank at Rowena by the local sheriff. The old fool pointed a saddle ring Winchester rifle at the sheriff before the cop took it away from him. I believe the gun was one of those I'd seen at the house.

Sheriff Kelley told me that the next day he received a mysterious call from Willis. "Hey, Sheriff," he said. "I've been down in Laredo for a few days. I just wanted you to know in case anybody came looking for me." And then he hung up.

Willis was jeeping for his brother in Rowena. And if anybody had gotten hurt in the robbery attempt, both brothers would've been back in jail where they belonged. As it happened, folks felt sorry for them. I don't know if Jess or Doc was ever prosecuted, but nobody got after old Willis like we could have.

I got on well with all sorts of crooks. I still get letters and phone calls from men I arrested who, for some reason, liked to keep in touch. It wasn't the same with the Newtons. I'm sorry that I can't be more romantic about my dealings with them, but the truth is that I never found them all that likeable. Let others believe what they want.

A LITTLE BLACK SPOT

May 5, 1991. I drove forty-two miles south of Alpine on Highway 118, where we discovered an abandoned vehicle registered to a missing person. Directly to the east loomed Santiago Peak, boasting some six thousand feet in elevation. We were looking for a twenty-year-old male. A likely scenario formed in my mind.

The Big Bend is not an environment to fool with, and yet tourists of all kinds take extraordinary chances all the time. Young males especially. The young man became enamored with the mountain during his trek with his mother to Big Bend National Park. He decided that before this trip was over he'd conquer Santiago alone. For some reason, he left his mother's hotel around eleven P.M. without telling her, took what he believed would be enough water to walk two or three miles across the brush country by moonlight, scale Santiago, and watch the sun rise from its peak. Sounds romantic as hell, doesn't it?

The problem is that it's actually eleven miles from Highway 118 to the foot of the mountain (a distance we measured by helicopter while we were looking for this fool). And even then one has a great deal farther to go to climb to the top. Daytime temperatures in May can still exceed 100 degrees, and the arid atmosphere depletes moisture much more quickly than most people assume. He was thinking hike when he was really going on an expedition.

To the guy's credit, he climbed close to the top of Santiago. I don't know how. He was out of water before dawn on the first day. He claimed he'd been attacked in an arroyo by a two-thousand-pound bear (which was most likely a Santa Gertrudis bull). As sunburn and dehydration exacted their toll, he decided to strip down to the nude to carry on.

When he failed to return by the following morning, we put a helicopter in the air and hikers and horsemen in the pastures popping the brush. We searched for three days before we found him—butt naked and sunburned like a lobster. Every square inch of this dude was blistered beyond belief. If he had planned on a spiritual quest he got everything he bargained for and more. Another day without water and he'd have been dead. A week later, he'd have mummified. By the end of the summer he'd have been a little black spot on a reddish-gray rock.

Now that I think about it, sounds like a pretty clean getaway. Beats a nursing home for sure. I'll consider taking that trek as the years roll by. But I ain't walking no eleven miles in the heat of the day. I'll putter along in my golf cart and be damn sure to keep an eye out for that bear.

CHAPTER FIFTEEN

With Friends Like These

La Puerta AND THE DAMAGE DONE

1990

For if gold rusts, what shall iron do?
GEOFFREY CHAUCER, *The Canterbury Tales*

RUMBLED OVER the railroad tracks that lay east of Marfa just past seven A.M., when I crossed paths with Presidio County Sheriff Rick Thompson and his chief deputy, Steve Bailey. Sheriff Thompson was headed away from the fairgrounds, which was not an unusual event, since he stabled several horses that his youngest child rode in competition. We had business together that morning, and I followed the sheriff and his deputy to their office.

I was working with INS agents on a case involving theft and extortion by a notary public who officed on the border. Some Mexican nationals alleged that they had fronted the son of a bitch as much as $600 to obtain a United States visa and then he burned them. Nothing riles me worse than a crook who preys on poor people. This guy was only a notch above your common coyote, in my book, or the scum who steal elderly people's Social Security checks. Lowlifes every one. Anyway, Sheriff Rick Thompson was interested in this criminal investigation, as he often was in others, and he asked to go along.

I had to be in Presidio by nine to complete preparations for the sting— wiring the victim, supplying him with the $300 cash he still owed the notary, and briefing him on how this deal needed to go down to get a conviction. We also had to swear out a search warrant. All of this takes time, and it annoyed me that after Sheriff Thompson finished fiddling around alone in his office, he began orchestrating the presentation of coffee and doughnuts in the office lounge. For some reason, catering for the instructors and attendees in town for the New Mexico State Police course on drug profiling fell personally upon his shoulders. I was focused on a crook while he was arranging éclairs on a cutting board. It gnawed on me.

Thompson finally got himself together and loaded himself in my Jeep Cherokee—absolutely the sorriest vehicle I ever drove in the service of Texas. We drove south to Presidio. Sheriff Rick was normally a talkative sort, and when he failed to speak I asked him if something was wrong. He told me that he was worried about the upcoming election and that he needed to get the required papers filed with the district clerk before the deadline.

We arrived at the Port of Entry, and I sat down to begin filling out the documents for the warrant. Rick Thompson, Joey Gordon (who was a DPS narcotics agent), and a couple of federal customs officers were milling around when a third customs agent came in carrying a printout from the teletype. She informed us that Robert Chambers had just been arrested for stealing a Presidio County horse trailer.

I knew Chambers. He was a young man of questionable character from a fine local family who deserved a better son. Chambers walked a hard road and a fine line, and even served as a sometime snitch for Sheriff Thompson. I suspected that his and Thompson's association went beyond that of a cop and his informant. It's not unusual for a good police officer to be on speaking terms with some seedy folks, and Chambers knew most of the bad guys on the border. I wondered if Chambers, along with being the sheriff's eyes and ears in the shadowy regions, performed little favors for Rick Thompson that were too dirty for his deputies. In return, Thompson always seemed to shield Chambers from scrutiny. "He'll only talk to me," Rick always said. Chambers's arrest was an odd development in a peculiar relationship.

I guess I'm not much on this multitasking. I had learned to rope one steer at a time. Although Chambers's arrest was definitely of interest to me, additional details would have to wait until after we nailed this dirty notary. Rick Thompson mustered a stoic reaction to the news. Chambers was in custody. I saw no urgency. I pushed the theft of a horse trailer aside to concentrate on the sting operation I already had in motion.

Later that same evening, the horse trailer theft started to churn in my head during the quiet drive back home with Thompson. Nothing about this situation really added up.

"Why would Chambers steal the trailer instead of just asking you to use it?" I finally asked the sheriff.

"I don't know," Thompson said before he resumed his uncharacteristic reticence.

We soon rolled up to the Border Patrol checkpoint located four miles south of Marfa. An exuberant young agent stepped up to the window and said, "Ranger, did you hear about the 2,500 pounds of cocaine found in the county horse trailer at the fairgrounds?"

What! Before I could react to this shocking news, Rick Thompson said, "Well, I guess they'll blame that shit on me."

Those words—and especially Thompson's tone and delivery—had the impact of a blackjack rapped against my head. I thought, *Why would they ever blame this on you, Rick?* But I said nothing. I dropped Sheriff Thompson back at his office, and then I drove home alone to Alpine. There was no silence in my solitude. Over twenty-four miles twisting through some of West Texas's most beautiful country, a series of images and voices began to play in my head. I considered five years' worth of quirky little incidents, strange though seemingly benign conversations, imperceptible warnings from unproven informants who seemed worried about how I would react to the news, and a shift in behavior over the last few months by a man who was my friend. Taken piecemeal, none of these things meant much. But over every inch of those twenty-four miles I began to connect the dots. I had to step back from the blindness of familiarity and the routine to understand how the fragments and pieces all fit together into one ugly picture. When my car rolled to a stop in my driveway, I knew.

Man, I never saw this coming. I couldn't accept the fact that a man I had worked with and trusted for the last five years could possibly be involved in drugs. I felt this sickness in my gut. But I *knew.*

I'D TAKEN A LONG and twisting road before I arrived at the beginning of the Rick Thompson affair. In Texas, the responsibility to investigate the use and sale of illegal drugs rests with the Department of Public Safety Narcotics Division. Technically speaking, the Texas Rangers don't fool with drug cases, although some of the very best Rangers emerge from out of the DPS narcotics squad. As it turns out, a clear delineation between drug use and trafficking and theft and murder doesn't bear up in the field. It's like separating the wind from the rain in a thunderstorm.

My first exposure to criminal use of narcotics had to do with the heroin traffic spilling out of San Antonio into neighboring rural counties. I handled an enormous volume of daylight thefts and burglaries of items that could easily be fenced for some quick cash—stereos, televisions, guns, anything they could haul off to the pawnshop. The trail of these suspects almost always led straight back to the rough neighborhoods of San Antonio, and from there to some junkie who didn't give a shit about his life or yours. Most disconcerting of all was that most of these losers were on the government methadone program for heroin addicts. From a law enforcement perspective, methadone kept hardcore users straight enough to commit more crimes to buy the real stuff. They stole from honest, hardworking people. They killed some of them, too.

Once I connected the rural crime with a San Antonio "ring," I worked with that city's detective division felony squad. Chief Hutton, an able administrator, handpicked his skilled, seasoned detectives. I learned about the seedy world of illegal drugs from great veterans, men like Wilbacker, Lauderdale, and Beckett.

We tried to round up as many suspects as possible in one sweep, mainly because they operated in little rings. Once we had sufficient probable cause to swear out the multiple search and arrest warrants, we assembled a team of local, state, and federal agents and swooped down together upon the dopers in the wee hours of the morning.

One such agent was named Maurice Rose. He stood eyeball to eyeball with me and weighed 250 portly pounds of firm muscle. To supplement his law enforcement income, Maurice moonlighted as a wrestler. One early morning our team swarmed a suspect's shack in a part of San Antonio where even the dogs are nervous. Maurice charged up to the front door with me at his side and proceeded to kick it in. He stuck his leg right through it up to his knee.

Horrified that some doper might be waiting behind the door with a dull axe, Maurice violently yanked back his leg, and in the process he ripped the door off its hinges, and so while the rest of us were clearing a dark house with known felons, Maurice was dancing out in the yard with his leg through a door. I don't know how well Maurice fared with the wrestling fans, but he sure put on one hell of a show for us.

In the late 1970s and early 1980s the heroin market began to taper off. Marijuana use became almost pedestrian, and cocaine emerged as the drug of choice. All of the small towns in my jurisdiction were infected with narcotics, shattering the myth that small-town Texas remained a bastion of American family values. In truth, we were fighting a war to salvage our young people from the grip of illegal drugs. On a percentage of population basis, I'd estimate that the problem was just as deeply rooted in Uvalde as it was in San Antonio and Houston. As law enforcement officials became more sophisticated in the ways of the drug culture, so did our investigative methods.

A reliable informant once approached me about a group of dopers in the Uvalde area looking to make a big hit. He suggested that we do a "reversal," which basically meant that law enforcement people posed as dealers to sell the dope to the bad guys. We proceeded to do just that in conjunction with the DEA task force active in Eagle Pass. The Feds fronted us two hundred pounds of marijuana, which we sold to some boneheads for $50,000 in cash. They stuffed the stash in a truck toolbox and motored down the road.

Unfortunately, they had not properly closed the lid of the toolbox, which flopped up and down advertising their burlap sack full of dope before we arrested these incompetent wannabe Capones.

The courts gave the cash back to Uvalde County to purchase equipment and whatnot, while our daylong drug lords went to jail. The first-ever reversal conducted in Uvalde County had gone very well. Local cops got a little wild with this type of sting operation, which eventually spilled into other counties.

Since addicts aren't particular about what they inject into their veins, methamphetamine labs cropped up all over the Texas Hill Country. We usually located them by their horrendous stench, second only to a decomposing human body. But even though they were easy to find, they were risky to raid. Any police officer will tell you that there is nothing more dangerous to confront than a subject high on meth. Speed freaks believe that they're invincible, and I've had several occasions where we were forced to bleed them a little to change their minds. Speed kills, but surviving speed freaks stink. They don't eat or sleep. They're psychotic enough to inject chemicals in their veins that are strong enough to unclog kitchen sinks. And they'll kill you or anyone else who gets in their way when they use it. Horrible people. Horrible drug.

Hallucinogens, such as LSD and peyote, were sold to the youth culture as a spiritual quest. The books of Carlos Castañeda and the influence of Ken Kesey and Timothy Leary inspired thousands of young kids to drop acid and explore their inner mind. I can tell you that the experience was nowhere near as pretty a picture as the one painted by these irresponsible flakes.

Witness the call I once received from a frantic farmer in Uvalde County: His twenty-five-year-old son was standing out on the family tennis court with a .357 revolver in his hand, in the grip of a flashback, shooting out the lights. Sound like a pleasant trip?

No medical personnel dared to approach an armed man in the throes of drug-induced psychosis. The responsibility to disarm him fell to me, and I took Uvalde Sheriff Kenneth Kelley with me. The suspect stared at us like a wild animal as we approached him, moving with us as we neared the gate. I didn't see his weapon, but upon arrival his mother reminded us that he had a nickel-plated Ruger Blackhawk .357 magnum. I figured that if he fired at us, I was terribly outgunned because of the eight-foot chain-link fence between us. And so was Sheriff Kelley, who I noticed, after we were engaged with the suspect, hadn't bothered to bring any kind of weapon. I was sort of peeved at the time. I told the young man to put his hands up and keep them there. Thank God that he did. We handcuffed him and herded him off to the hospital for observation. (I stayed at the scene and dressed down Kelley in no uncertain terms. What was he planning to do if the kid had shot me? Challenge him to a quick tennis match or what?)

In the aftermath of this brief, unfortunate incident, I think mostly of the mother peering through the window at her lost son, of the hard lines etched into her face from worrying.

I've seen far worse when it came to the use of hallucinogens. Consider the fate of a young adult Native American, a member of some Northwestern tribe whose name now escapes me. It was my understanding that his nation had obtained a permit for the purchase and use of peyote during tribal religious ceremonies. This young man was entrusted with $4,000 in tribal funds and dispatched to Zapata, Texas, where I understand that certain people are licensed to sell peyote to registered buyers.

But the Indian got hung up, as so many young men do, well north of Laredo and on the wrong side of the river in Villa Acuña. Somebody pumped him full of alcohol and God knows what all else, and then liberated him from his money after debauching his morals. By the time Boy's Town was finished with him, he had access to a pair of faded jeans and his old truck, which he had to hotwire. Someone had made off with his keys. He plowed the vehicle through a barbed wire fence. Three hundred yards later, he came to a stop in the middle of somebody's pasture.

Those somebodies were South Texas ranchers. They owned plenty of guns, and they knew how to use them.

Whacked out of his mind on acid and alcohol, the Indian saw but one set of lights twinkling in that infinite ocean of brush, and he stumbled toward it. He reached the house. He heard people playing cards on the other side and also running water. He moved toward the sound of running water.

There was a young girl showering in the house. The Indian pulled back the curtain and gawked at her with his glassy eyes. For some reason, she wasn't completely alarmed. Her father hired lots of Mexican nationals to work on the place, and she assumed that this was yet another, sent in here by her brother or dad as some sort of sick practical joke.

When he dropped his jeans and stepped into the tub with her, however, she naturally came unglued. She ran screaming at the top of her lungs out of the bathroom and down the hall to the master bedroom. The naked Indian followed her. I have no idea what he thought he was doing, but I don't believe that he intended to rape or injure her. Or maybe he did.

He caught her in the bedroom and they scuffled. They fell on the bed together. And that's where they were when the rancher, responding to his daughter's screams, first saw them.

The rancher's gun case sat in the master bedroom. He snatched a .20-gauge shotgun, pumped a round into the chamber, and hollered at the Indian to knock it off then and there. The problem was that the rancher assumed that the Indian was a Mexican. He spoke to him in Spanish, and the Indian couldn't understand a word of it. They ran out of things to talk about in a hurry, and the rancher peppered him good with the shotgun. Full of birdshot, the Indian made every attempt to pull himself together.

About that time, the daughter's brother entered the room with a .222 rifle that he carried with him in his truck. It didn't seem to matter to him that his father already had the situation under control. By then, I'm sure they saw that the suspect was out of his mind on drugs. But it was too late. Their blood was up. The kid shot the Indian through the heart with a .222 round. The intruder was dead before he hit the ground, and I don't think he ever understood what he had done to offend these people.

I didn't see any call for the boy to kill the Indian and said as much to a grand jury. But this is Texas, the deceased was deep onto private property, and there was just no explaining that a naked man on a bed with a naked woman didn't have rape on his mind. The jury No Billed the case. The rancher replaced the carpet and painted the walls and went on about his business.

I tracked down the man's parents and told them what had happened to their son. Ultimately it wasn't the rednecks who killed this boy. Drugs led him to a place where there was no turning back.

We saw it every day during my time in the Rangers—the wasted youth of Texas, lured to their own destruction by a culture that convinced them that drugs were a hell of a lot of fun. I watched so many trip their way into a prison cell and many more dig their own graves with a coke spoon. I saw so many stunned parents suffer the pain of burying their children. Lord, I hope we've turned back the tide of this tragic epidemic.

THE GREATEST THRILL for any law enforcement officer is to bust the commercial doper. The most interesting criminal I ever disappointed was John Webster Flannigan, a native of Crystal City who earned a law degree, opened a practice in Austin, and soon set the standard for shady deals and debauchery in a town where it's really hard to stand out.

Flannigan's clients included a who's who of local scum, including the ringleader of a notorious gang involved in white slavery, narcotics, and upscale burglaries, as well as the madam of the local whorehouse, who I assume paid his legal fees in kind. It was only a matter of time before Flannigan crossed the line. After he was disbarred, Flannigan returned to Crystal City looking for a new line of work.

He stuck with what he knew best. His clients soon became his colleagues, and God only knows what manner of crimes this affable guy got into. But he excelled in only one: flying dope. Flannigan soon emerged as the greatest bush pilot in the business. He didn't fly above the brush, he flew in it, blowing through thickets as well as any mourning dove. Flannigan never required much of a landing strip, which made him really hard to pattern. The boy could hang a Cessna on a mesquite thorn long enough to unload and then drop into some dark hole before he soared back into the clouds.

A task force including three DPS narcotics agents and myself once staked out Flannigan's stolen plane for four days. Flannigan had stashed this bird under black plastic in the brush. A rancher alerted me to its presence, and we were waiting for Flannigan to show when we received a call that the pilot had dropped eight hundred pounds of marijuana west of Crystal City. Damn.

U.S. Customs confiscated the load of dope and seized three other airplanes at the Crystal City airport. We dusted the hidden plane and found a single fingerprint on the yoke, which we later identified as belonging to John Webster Flannigan.

We secured a search warrant on his Crystal City residence and were stunned by the amount and variety of stolen property he had stashed around the place—ski boats, guns, appliances. In all, we seized four airplanes. I found a Ranger badge in his house in Austin. We turned in the hundreds of pounds of drugs and all the stolen merchandise, but I threw the badge in the Nueces River and it's still there. Anyway, knowing that he was a wanted man, Flannigan slipped across the border into Mexico. The only difference was that he now wore leather gloves when he flew.

He continued to smuggle dope for years until we finally arrested him on seven or eight state criminal counts. He cut a deal with the Feds, who gave him a ridiculously short sentence down in Florida. It didn't matter, because he never served it. The authorities claimed that one day he was standing in a line when he simply disappeared, but that's horseshit.

Flannigan turned up again behind a cockpit in Mexico, flying loads into the United States. In 1986 or '87, some agency finally caught him flying cocaine into Kansas City and locked him up in the pen. He may be there now. Or he may be back slipping in under the radar, the ultimate stick and rudder man—too smart for his own good, and too good to stay straight. John Webster Flannigan flew dope for close to twenty years. That's a lifetime career for his kind.

On January 1, 1987, I moved out to my new jurisdiction in the Big Bend. I stayed on the 101 Ranch, managed by my good friend Jim Phillips, until I bought a home. To be effective, a Ranger needed to learn his territory and the people who lived there. I'd been on the border all my working life, but everything out here was different.

I started exploring the Rio Bravo and the small villages that hugged her northern bank. Information about criminal activity began to trickle in after I developed a ring of reliable informants. The stuff going on seemed as exotic to me as the desert terrain. And at the time, most of it revolved around the network of the local drug lord, Pablo Acosta.

There was a lucrative exchange of automatic assault weapons for narcotics. One lawless character who went by the name of "Rosenthal" accepted cheap Chinese semiautos for his stash of marijuana. He then converted the weapons to full automatic and sold them to Pablo Acosta's men for more drugs. Rosenthal was so brazen that he once exchanged gunfire with Presidio County Sheriff Rick Thompson over some sort of running feud that had erupted between them. Thompson later sent his crony, Robert Chambers, to hold Rosenthal at gunpoint until the Mexican police could drive up from Ojinaga and arrest him. Rosenthal somehow escaped into the desert, with Chambers popping a few caps at him as he ran. Rosenthal returned a couple of nights later to dig up his stash of weapons. He was wanted by two nations.

Two weeks later, officials found a body in the Rio Grande in Big Bend National Park. The FBI assumed that it was Rosenthal, who had finally succumbed to wounds inflicted by Chambers during Rosenthal's escape attempt. Turns out that we weren't even close.

One of Pablo Acosta's nephews had been tortured to death during interrogation by Mexican cops. Acosta retaliated by kidnapping a deputy federal officer and torturing him in an attempt to learn who was responsible for the death of Acosta's nephew. I was told that Robert Chambers, who I believe was on Acosta's payroll, was present when one of the two armed guards accidentally fired a round into his own foot. The second gunman was so startled that he accidentally fired his weapon, striking the Mexican officer in the heart, killing him.

Enraged by the incompetence of his henchmen, Acosta ordered them to bury the body high in the mountains in a place only the coyotes would know. Instead, they cut it open to resemble the work of competing Colombian cartels operating in the area, and threw it in the river.

And Rosenthal? He later shot it out with Mexican federal police in the mountains a few miles west of San Carlos. The *federales* confiscated his stash of automatic weapons and buried him in a shallow grave. Or so the rumors went. His body was never found. But not too many were really looking.

Pablo Acosta's turn to reap the whirlwind came in April of 1987—the same month that Captain Alfred Allee and Ranger Arthur Hill passed on. I served as a pallbearer for both Texas Rangers. I wasn't invited to lay the drug lord to rest.

Acosta was a colorful character. Raised in Santa Elena, he worked as a roofer in Midland and Hobbs before he found himself an easier and far more dangerous way to earn a living. Like his Colombian counterpart, Pablo Escobar, Acosta generated millions from the drug trade and spread it around the local communities. He was a hero to the poor in and around Ojinaga and the villages downstream. They wrote traditional *corridos* to celebrate his exploits, particularly his success in foiling the gringo's attempts to destroy him. It didn't seem to bother the locals that their downtown plaza was a war zone while he eliminated most of his competition. There were cold-blooded killings in broad daylight every week.

Pablo Acosta was a ruthless murderer, but he also had a genius for organization. He paid off the right cops and influential politicians. Probably bought himself a general or two. If the local people didn't love him, they at least accepted him. He only killed other dopers. He quickly accumulated immeasurable wealth and power. He thought he was above the law—and, for a while, he was.

Two weaknesses ultimately toppled his mountain fiefdom: he developed a fierce addiction to his wares (and even hired one man to reroll his cigarettes laced with cocaine), and he had a flair for self-promotion, especially when it came to humiliating the Mexican government during media interviews. The local authorities were in his pocket, so Mexico City sent in the *federales*, who cooperated with American agents. Together, they stalked Acosta, waiting for the right moment to strike.

My local informants later told me that an American woman who ran with Pablo's lieutenants set him up with the FBI. She crossed the river, entered Pablo's compound in Santa Elena, ascertained which house the drug lord occupied, and then returned to notify waiting agents. The FBI, in turn, alerted a force of Mexican officers, waiting nearby in a Huey helicopter. In twenty minutes, they were on Acosta and his men, who fought to the death like the desperadoes that they were.

For a short while after that, the plaza in Ojinaga was again up for grabs by anyone strong enough to take it—when the violent cycle repeated itself. I witnessed all of this during my first year in the Big Bend. But it went on year after year, same game, different players, always ending in an early grave.

The Mexican attorney general's office put an agent named Calderoni on Pablo Acosta's case. I was led to believe that he was paid $90,000 in blood money by the Americans when Acosta was finally shot dead. I knew Calderoni back when he was the *comandante* of the *federales* in Reynosa, Mexico. He was a short, thick, confrontational man who made no effort to hide his contempt for Anglos. He was rumored to have earned millions in drug money payoffs from the cartels, but in the end he still failed to play both frayed ends against the middle. During the writing of this book, Calderoni was gunned down in McAllen, Texas, as he left his attorney's office.

As they live, they die. In between those two events, they infect good, honest people with their corruption and greed. In 1991, they ruined a good friend of mine.

GODDAMNIT, I knew.

Even though it was ten at night, I stormed into my home and phoned Dale Stinson, the agent in charge of all DEA operations in the Big Bend.

"I need to know, Dale," I said. "Is Rick Thompson involved in this horse trailer cocaine bust?"

Stinson hesitated. I didn't know what that meant. To some, Dale Stinson was an unemotional bureaucrat. But I knew he had years of field experience under his belt, including serving as an undercover agent in Mexico, an assignment that is not for the squeamish. Dale was an intelligent, resourceful, disciplined man who played his hand close to the vest. His conservative manner caused some to dismiss him as a pencil pusher. His effectiveness earned him enemies. God knows I've had my run-ins with the Feds, but I respected Stinson.

"We can't put anything at the moment on Thompson," Stinson said. "But at best his involvement looks suspicious."

I spent the next two days reconsidering the facts. I had never questioned why Thompson had always seemed curious about where I would be on this night or that day. I always assumed that he was trying to hook up for a cup of coffee or lunch. And why had his conversations with Chambers been so damned private? What could Chambers have told him that I shouldn't hear?

There were too many times when Thompson was out of pocket. Even his men did not know where he was. He spent a lot of time either in El Paso on "sheriff's business" or running around in his political duties as president of the Sheriffs' Association of Texas.

A few of my informants on the river had occasionally gutted up and told me that Thompson was involved in drug smuggling. They referred to the Presidio County sheriff as *la puerta*, the door. All attempts by me to corroborate this information failed. These tips smelled more like personal or political attacks by Thompson's enemies. I never got enough to go forward with anything close to a formal investigation.

Plus, these accusations just never rang true for me. I never saw Sheriff Thompson flash an unusual amount of money. He lived in a modest home in Marfa. He owned and traded horses, operated a trailer park with a friend in Fort Davis, and owned a dry cleaning business in Marfa, all of which were going concerns before I moved to Alpine. If any of these were lucrative enterprises, however, it didn't show in Thompson's lifestyle. I couldn't imagine what Stinson and his agents had on Rick Thompson to connect him to the 2,500 pounds of cocaine confiscated at the fairgrounds, but by then I knew they had something.

Two days after my first telephone conversation with Dale Stinson, the DEA agent phoned and we had a second conversation. He asked me if I had any business with the Presidio County sheriff's office. I told him that sooner or later I certainly would. Stinson then advised me that he had sent a couple of agents to interview Sheriff Thompson about this cocaine bust. Thompson had run them out of his office and told them not to come back. Pretty ballsy, I thought. And also predictable. Thompson never cared much for Stinson. His contempt reached outright animosity once Stinson's wolves began to circle him. I told Dale that I'd be glad to have a word with him.

The Presidio County sheriff's office exuded an atmosphere of doom when I entered to visit with Rick Thompson. The sheriff busied himself with files and documents, avoiding my stare. I could tell by his expression and body language that the pressure was really gnawing on him.

"Rick," I finally said. "Stinson would like for you to come down to his office and talk to him."

"You can tell that son of a bitch that I won't say one word to him," Thompson said. "But I might talk to the U.S. attorney."

I reminded him that even if he went to the attorney's office, there was no getting around Dale Stinson. As the case agent, he would be sitting in the same room. We made our first strong eye contact before I added, "Rick, if you, your friends, your family, or anyone else you know is involved in this cocaine bust, you need to go and talk with Stinson and the U.S. attorney. As long as you've been in law enforcement, you should know that the first to talk is the first to walk."

"Yeah, I know," he said. "But I ain't gonna talk to Dale Stinson."

Several uneasy weeks passed. Rick Thompson was still a free man, but I knew the DEA was taking its time and tightening the noose. Thompson was a high-profile sheriff, active in national associations and recognized throughout Texas. He was also admired and respected in a community that is contemptuous of the Feds. A number of honest, rational people, including many in law enforcement, truly believed that Thompson was being framed.

My last conversation with Rick Thompson took place the night before he testified before a grand jury. I called him at a hotel room in Pecos, where he was staying with his wife. I begged him to play it straight with the grand jury. "I'm going to tell it like it is," Rick said.

He didn't. The DA indicted him the next day. After he was arrested, Thompson was talking to Dale Stinson whether he wanted to or not.

But I know that Thompson told them nothing. He was 6' 3" and 220 pounds of pure hombre. His polite manners and looks concealed one tough, iron-willed son of a bitch that had been tested in combat in Vietnam and in countless scrapes since. Stinson could've ripped Thompson's fingernails out with a pair of pliers and Thompson wouldn't tell him anything. He figured that his friend Robert Chambers, the only man who could tie Thompson to the horse trailer full of cocaine, was cut from the same cloth. Thompson was pretty sure that he'd skate on his record and reputation. And that probably wasn't a bad bet.

What Sheriff Thompson didn't know as he prepared to defend himself was that Robert Chambers had already rolled on him. Thompson was the only man who didn't know that Chambers was scum—which is a pity given that Thompson was the man who relied on him most.

Chambers implicated Thompson in a long list of smuggling activities going back to before I was ever assigned to Alpine. If Chambers was involved in the Pablo Acosta organization, Thompson must've been, too. We always assumed that Chambers was little more than Thompson's snitch. If we were to believe Robert Chambers, Thompson worked directly under him, monitoring local, state, and federal law enforcement movement and radio bands during numerous shipments.

Dale Stinson knew all of this and more before he made any effort to speak with Thompson. After Rick stonewalled the DEA's investigation, Stinson yanked the noose tight around Thompson's neck. He had the man he needed to make his case. What he wanted then from Thompson was to make a very public example of what happens to a dirty cop.

Thompson chose an attorney that the Rangers were already investigating for misappropriation of seized drug money. From a publicity standpoint alone, Rick had made another poor choice in his associates. It didn't bode well.

I was in agony when I watched his press conference on Midland/Odessa television. He seemed out of his element trying to persuade the cameras of his innocence. Thompson claimed that he had obtained the 2,500 pounds of cocaine in order to conduct a reversal drug buy.

I shook my head. No one who has worked in narcotics would ever consider risking his life to sell one kilo to a doper without substantial backup. Rick Thompson would have us believe that he aimed to sell over a ton of cocaine alone without any discussion of the case with other law enforcement officials. That's not a sting operation, that's suicide.

In the end, it didn't matter much when it came to Thompson's explanation of the horse trailer cocaine seizure. He was arrested and arraigned, and eventually pleaded guilty to all counts in a Pecos courtroom. The judge sentenced ex-Sheriff Rick Thompson to two back-to-back life terms with no possibility of parole. Rick Thompson will die in prison.

THIS CASE DID NOT sit well with me. I felt used. I felt humiliated. I felt dumb. One of the primary functions of a Texas Ranger is to support the local law enforcement community. I had developed a great working relationship with Rick Thompson, the very same I enjoyed with Harvey Adams of Jeff Davis County, Terrell County's Chel Duarte, and Sheriff George Jones of Brewster County. I considered all of these men to be friends of mine. Only one of them betrayed my trust.

I've tried to stand by other friends in trouble, even when they faced criminal charges. I supported Johnny Rodriguez when he was tried on murder charges. I testified to the character of Kinney County Sheriff Norman Hooten when he was arrested on misdemeanor charges of attending a dog fight. Hooten's attorney, Charlie Butts, was a close personal friend and had consulted with me at no charge on Don Joaquin's case. At Charlie's request, I testified to the integrity of a man I had known both personally and professionally. Everybody knew Hooten bred and raised pit bulls, but he once told me point-blank that he never fought them and I believed him. All hell broke loose when Hooten was arrested, and the battle lines were drawn. I had no knowledge about the facts at issue in Hooten's criminal case. I simply told the jury that I knew Hooten was a good man and a fine sheriff, which he was. My testimony, however, couldn't overcome Hooten's mistakes and poor judgment. He was convicted and fined, and then the Feds amped up the case by filing additional related charges. The incident ruined Hooten's career and, as it turned out, splashed a little mud on mine.

Most retired DPS officers receive a special Ranger's commission—basically an honorary status that still allows us to carry handguns. Mine came up for renewal shortly after my involvement in the Hooten case. Ranger leadership at the time—or at least one senior official, so I was told—was of the opinion that I had perjured myself in Hooten's criminal case. No one can perjure himself when it comes to testifying about another's character, but enough of the politically appointed civilian DPS commissioners bought in to this absurd accusation that they denied the renewal of my special Ranger badge. It was a real slap in the face for the DPS to punish me for telling the truth. Assistant Director Col. Thomas urged me to appeal their decision and clear the air, but I couldn't see why I should have to jump through hoops to get something I had earned long ago. But the point I'm trying to make here is that standing by my friends has cost me plenty. I have no regrets. I wasn't raised to be a fair-weather friend. Jim Bowie once berated a friend who had abandoned him in a barroom brawl.

"Where were *you*?" Bowie demanded.

"You were in the wrong, Jim," his friend said.

"That's when a man *needs* a friend," Bowie said.

And so it was with my friends when they strayed.

Rick Thompson had been a good friend to me. If there were trouble under your roof, Rick would be the first to knock on your door and ask about what he could do to help you. The bad things he so suddenly dropped at our feet in 1990 had come along after he'd done so much good. I liked him, and I trusted him. As his case unfolded, I was at first conflicted about how I should treat him.

But by the time of Thompson's arrest, I knew that he was dirty, and that was the end of any personal conflict for me. A lawman gone bad is the worst kind of criminal. There is no gray area between an officer of the law and a criminal. The badge signifies the public's faith in one person. Whom do the people look to if our cops are corrupt? My friendship with Rick Thompson couldn't survive that. I distanced myself from him. I have not seen

Sheriff Rick Thompson and Joaquin Jackson,
Presidio County Sheriff's Office, Marfa, Texas, late 1980s

him since he's been in prison. My only regret is that I didn't put him there myself. Rick Thompson went to great pains to avoid my scrutiny, and he was wise to do so.

During the writing of this book it came to my attention that some people still believe that I was somehow involved with Thompson and his criminal acts. Such slander is guilt by association and I understand that. But nobody who knows anything about me or the facts of Thompson's case has ever accused me of any such thing. I've got no time or patience for gossips. Nearly fifteen years after the fact, I think more about Thompson's wife and children, and the many people who believed in this faithless man. Thompson left behind a community in shock when he was led away in chains. My sympathy lies with the innocent people who have suffered in the wake of Thompson's corruption.

Ahora, la puerta está cerrado . . .

CHAPTER SIXTEEN

Moving Pictures
1986–2004

I GOT A CALL FROM A WOMAN claiming to be Nick Nolte's secretary. She explained that the actor had just signed a contract to play a Texas Ranger in *Extreme Prejudice*. Apparently, Nolte had spoken with *North Dallas Forty* writer Pete Gent. I'd run into Gent at some function somewhere, and he'd suggested to Nolte that he should hunt me up. His secretary asked if the actor could ride around with me for a week or so. Well, as requests go, that was a new one on me.

I phoned Company D Captain Jack Dean to ask for his approval. Captain Dean seemed all for it as long as the arrangement didn't interfere with my normal duties and I didn't get Nolte shot. I called Nolte's secretary back and told her to send the boy on down to Uvalde.

About a week later he showed up with his handler, a man named Bill Cross. As we rode around together in the course of an average day, I started to teach him about how we worked and what sort of weapons we carried with us. He watched more than he talked, which I learned later was essential to the way he absorbed himself into any given role. My main goal was to keep Nolte out of trouble while I did my job, keep him far enough away at times to maintain contact with my network of informants, and enjoy the hell out of the novelty of a Hollywood actor wanting to base a character, more or less, on me.

Nick turned out to be a keen student of detail and equipment, constantly inquiring about the brand names of the clothing I wore and the materials I

Tommy Lee Jones and
Joaquin Jackson in a scene
from *The Good Old Boys*

used. Then, I took him around to acquire the items that were locally available. He bought seven Resistol hats in all—and I creased them just like I did mine—but he favored the first one I personalized for him, complete with its horsehair hatband, which he wore throughout the filming process.

Nolte commissioned local saddlemaker José Peña to make him three holsters, pistol belts, and double magazine holders just like the ones I wore. One rig was for him, a second for his double, and a third in case something happened to one of the other two. He even acquired Colt Commander .45 pistols, complete with silver-and-gold grips, that were similar to my own weapons. (During the filming, they switched to 9 mm pistols because the .45's failed to eject the blanks.)

I got to know Nick pretty well during our time together. I'd learn later that he got to know me better. Even so, he was a real nice guy. He hung around my house and was good to my family and friends. He seemed like a regular guy. We'd kick back after a long day of criminal investigations, sip a little Jack Daniel's, and contemplate all that we'd learned about Ranger life. Nolte was fast becoming like my little partner.

Nick was with me for Company D firearm qualification. Captain Dean suggested that Nolte punch targets just like the rest of us. I worked with him briefly on stance, technique, and basic firearm function and safety, and then let the actor fire away. Much to our surprise, he performed really well. In fact, he qualified by Ranger standards. It was just amazing to me how quickly he picked up different skills and mannerisms.

He had asked to spend one week with me. In the end, he spent three. And then he asked me to come to El Paso and be on location with him. Nolte's assistant had told me that Nick had recently kicked a bad cocaine habit. Of course, he still drank—as I did—but if he ever got drunk, I couldn't tell it.

Johnny Rodriguez accompanied me to El Paso in hopes of appending his new compositions to the film's soundtrack. Johnny and I were both knocked out when Nolte stepped out of his trailer and walked onto the set. He was a dead ringer for me—speech patterns, mannerisms, clothing, and with the three-inch lifts in his shoes, he stood just as tall. I was really impressed with his performance, and not because he was impersonating me but because not any actor could study a flesh and blood man and then portray him so vividly on film. There's no getting around the fact that Nolte is one fine character actor.

Watching them shoot the movie was a real treat. Veteran actors Rip Torn and Powers Boothe rounded out a superb cast. Boothe grew up in Snyder and Rip Torn somewhere in East Texas. Accordingly, they didn't need to hang out with locals to learn how to act like Texans. Torn also had no need of prop weapons. He showed up with his own shotgun and backed off all requests to surrender it. I liked both of these men. I golfed a little with Boothe and Nolte.

At Nolte's request, I read the script and suggested a few minor changes for the sake of accuracy, especially when it came to what a Ranger would say or do when confronted with certain situations. Some of that stuff actually made it on the screen. Together with the notion that Nolte was basically impersonating me for the lead role, the entire experience was a real thrill.

After a while, I realized that making movies is actually a slow, tedious process, boring as hell to watch. The most fun was slipping off to the local watering hole to knock a few back with the cast. I was sitting in a bar in El Paso with Nick and Bill Cross, when Cross spied a 6' 3", 210-pound, ponytailed dude strolling across the room. He punched me in the arm and said, "That son of a bitch who sold all that cocaine to Nick has followed us over here from Malibu! I'll be damned if he's gonna get that started up again."

Turns out that Cross had a pretty quick temper. He sat at the table and stewed until the alleged coke dealer got up to go to the restroom. Cross stormed after him. After a moment's hesitation, I decided that I needed to follow along.

By the time I arrived, they were already squared off, yelling at each other. Cross took the first swing. Then the dealer cocked back his arm to let Cross have it. I stepped up, grabbed a hold of his ponytail, and took him straight to the floor. (We always say, "Where the ponytail goes, so goes the heart.") I stepped on his neck with enough pressure to pin him down and told him to keep his ass still. Then I ordered Cross out of the restroom.

Cross stared at the man as he walked past him. "You know, Joaquin," he says, "now that I'm up close I don't think that's the right guy."

Oops. I took my foot off of his neck, helped him up, politely brushed him off, retied his ponytail, and apologized for mistaking him for a California dope dealer. He seemed as happy as I was that it was over and done with and lit out of there.

We got back down to business on the set. Most of the movie was shot in and around El Paso, but there were some scenes shot in California that were supposed to represent some big drug dealer's Mexican hacienda. The production wrapped fairly quickly and I went back to my Ranger work.

Later, Nolte flew Shirley and me out not only to attend the premiere but to tape TV and radio interviews for the publicity campaign. By that time, I had invested several weeks of effort in the film, some of which ate up my vacation time. I never asked for any compensation, but I guess Nolte felt like he wanted to reward me for helping him get the job done. He decided to help my son Lance with his college education. My wife and I were flabbergasted by this generous offer.

I didn't feel like *Extreme Prejudice* really fulfilled its potential. It was, in my opinion, an average film that could have been great. But I was told that it made money, especially with its stellar cast as a draw.

Months passed. I never heard from Nolte about anything, let alone his unsolicited contribution to Lance's education. I then told an attorney friend of mine in passing that Nolte had never made good. He wrote the actor a letter on my behalf. In response, we received a blistering letter from Nolte's attorneys, who alleged, among other things, that I owed Nolte several thousand dollars for flying me out to LA for the premiere and whatnot. I'm sad to say that I let Nolte's attorneys get between me and him.

We settled the case. I got paid. I went on. To this day, I regret that our relationship disintegrated like it did. I think it was Nolte's handlers who stirred up all the animosity. I don't think Nick had anything to do with it, and I know for a fact that it was not in his nature to be so ugly. He got busy with other films and let these other people work it out for him, which turned out to be a mistake.

I haven't seen Nick Nolte since the premiere. I've heard that alcohol has

Joaquin Jackson, Tommy Lee Jones, and Cliff Tienart on the set of *Blue Sky*

continued to haunt him, but I don't know of many actors who can match him when it comes to raw talent. He is amazing to watch as he performs his craft. I have enjoyed his work in so many films. I still think of him as a friend.

MY FIRST ACTUAL SCREEN appearance was in *Blue Sky*, starring Tommy Lee Jones and Jessica Lange. Cliff and Mary Jo Tienart, who own the Long X Ranch near Kent, were friends and neighbors of Tommy Lee. They asked me to go with them to visit the set in the salt flats near Guadalupe Peak. I got the opportunity to meet Tommy Lee, who later stuffed Cliff and me into air force officer's uniforms. We filled up the frame as extras in some obscure scene. I felt uneasy in the outfit, as it was completely out of character for me. Since I was a major and Cliff was a captain, I informed him that I expected him to salute me while we were in uniform. Cliff told me to kiss his ass.

In the fall of 1994, about a year after I had retired from the Ranger service, I was hired to do the security on the TNT production of *The Good Old Boys*, based on the Elmer Kelton novel. Tommy Lee Jones adapted the book into a screenplay, and produced, directed, and played the lead role in this wonderful film. Tommy Lee assembled an impressive cast—Sissy Spacek, Matt Damon, Sam Shepard, Frances McDormand, and Wilford Brimley, along with several gifted bit players. In the decade since it was first filmed, the movie hasn't aged a day. For me, everything worked in this movie.

As I made my security rounds, I noticed that Tommy Lee kept eyeing me. Finally, he walked up, slapped a dog-eared script against my chest, and said, "Ranger, I need you to play a sheriff. You've got three speaking parts."

Stunned, I managed to say, "I'm sorry, Tommy Lee, but I'm not an actor."

"I'd rather use a real lawman than teach some Hollywood actor how to act like a lawman," he said.

Okay. What the hell? Double pay. The costume people outfitted me in period clothing and dusted my face with some sort of crap while I studied my lines. I've been in all sorts of shoot-outs and serious scrapes, but this situation scared the hell out of me. I felt like a whore sitting on the front pew in a Baptist church. My mouth felt like it was stuffed with cotton. Shirley followed me around with two full cups of water, but it didn't seem to help.

My first scene required me to ride up on horseback to a windmill where Tommy Lee and Matt Damon were working. I was ordered to stop the black gelding quarterhorse on the mark. Okay. What's a mark? I asked them. Turns out that this is where they were already pointing the cameras. I just assumed that the cameras followed the actor. Not true in this case.

I soon learned where the mark was, but I couldn't get the fool horse to stand still on top of it. The gelding was also not an actor. We finally got the nag ironed out, and I delivered my lines over the withers of the horse like I was supposed to. Then I walked over just a few short steps to shake hands with Tommy Lee, when I discovered that I had another goddamn mark. Real confusing. Cut.

I walked through the whole scene. This time I counted the steps from one mark to the other. I got it right on the second take—which they tell me ain't too bad.

For the tavern scene, I strolled up and flipped a silver dollar on the bar and said, "Whiskey!" just like cowboys do in every Western I've ever seen. Colonels Garrison and Speir frowned on that sort of behavior for working Rangers, but it looked great in the film. The soundman looked like he'd been electrocuted when the coin hit the bar. I guess the noise was greatly amplified in his headset.

"Would you mind quietly setting the coin on the bar?" he asked.

Sure. I glanced at my marks to reorient myself and we shot the scene over. "Cut," they said and we moved on. Nothing to this acting business.

I shot one other talking scene, and one funeral scene where I didn't have any lines. I was greatly relieved when Tommy Lee shouted, "That's a wrap!"

Jones seemed pleased with my appearance. I only hoped that my scenes didn't bog down what appeared to be a great movie. The greatest compliment I received came from Elmer Kelton himself. I felt comfortable chatting up Elmer for some small talk. He watched us film my scenes with a blank look on his face. When they were over, Elmer walked up and said, "Ranger, when I heard Tommy Lee was casting you as Sheriff Wheeler, I had my doubts. But you done all right." Good enough for me.

I really enjoyed getting to know some of the actors. Sissy Spacek, a Texas girl, really impressed me with her manners and style. A gifted actress, she is foremost a mother. She had her daughter with her on location and brought along a tutor to look after her education. I just thought that Sissy was great. She does Texas proud.

I liked New Mexico–bred Sam Shepard, an intelligent man and splendid actor. He's sort of a man's man, but the women ogle him, too. A good guy. I spent most of my time with Wilford Brimley, a native of Utah who used to catch wild horses for a living. He'd once been a heavy drinker, too, and had learned to grow beyond it with wisdom. Really loved listening to his countless stories. Plus, that man could still sit a horse.

Tommy Lee Jones fascinated me. The son of an oilfield roustabout, Tommy Lee finagled a private prep school education in Dallas, went on to Harvard on a football scholarship (I believe he played guard), and emerged as a big Hollywood player. *The Good Old Boys* was Tommy Lee's directorial debut, and he was very focused on getting it made. He can be a bit temperamental, but if I were in his pressure cooker, I'd boil over into one hell of an asshole.

Tommy snapped at underlings every now and then, but he managed to swing by my house in Alpine to enjoy steaks and some cold beer. All business on the set, he was relaxed and wide open and funny as hell once rocking on our porch. The better I got to know him, the more I liked him. We've remained friends since he gave me the role in *The Good Old Boys.*

Every now and then I looked over at the novelist, Elmer Kelton. I could see by the sparkle in his eye that Tommy Lee had nailed the part of Hewey Calloway. Hewey was born with a wild streak that even a dying West couldn't tame. The love of a good woman almost rooted him to a farm and family, but when Hewey's running mates offered him one last chance at adventure, he knew that he had to saddle up and ride. Tommy Lee's performance was particularly moving for me, too. I saw a little of my daddy before the drought broke him in Tommy Lee's spry portrayal of Hewey Calloway.

I went on to act in several movies, but to date my role as Sheriff Wes

Wilford Brimley and
Joaquin Jackson on the
set of *The Good Old
Boys*, 1994

Wheeler has been the pinnacle of my acting career—if we can call those four scenes a career. People spend a lifetime trying to get the opportunity to act in a movie. It was handed to me by a friend because I had once been a Texas Ranger. Tell me that my life hasn't been blessed.

I HAD ONE SCENE in *Streets of Laredo*, which starred Jim Garner, an actor I've admired since his *Maverick* days. Garner and I golfed together in Lajitas and Del Rio. He's a real gentleman, let me tell you. He also plays to a three handicap. Because of some serious injury to the groin area, Jim couldn't run or ride a horse. The production company kept EMS personnel and helicopter on site in case of complications, filming all of his horseback scenes while he rode a dummy mounted in the bed of a dual-axle pickup. I walked up in the middle of one of his shoots and he said, "Ranger, I apologize for having to ride this hobby horse." I let him off easy.

I also worked security for this production with my friend, retired Ranger Bob Favor. Garner was the only actor who ever made a special effort to sit and visit with us when the production wrapped.

I handled security for *Dead Man's Walk*, adapted from the Larry McMurtry novel, starring Keith Carradine, David Arquette, Harry Dean Stanton, Edward James Olmos, and Eric Schweig. This project didn't fare well, I'm told. We locked Keith Carradine on the set one day, which pissed him off. He also had an inclination to wander around the ranch with guns and live ammo--strictly forbidden in the movie world. Had to straighten him out about that.

The most interesting thing about this movie occurred when armed Mexican nationals rode horses right through the middle of the set. Sort of startled the Hollywood people. The leader of the raid claimed that he was looking for a horse that had been confiscated by the USDA.

I knew these men. They were smugglers who operated out of an adobe hooch on the Mexican side of the river, where they kept their horses and pack burros in a corral of ocotillo cactus. They ran marijuana from the San Carlos area across the river to buyers on the U.S. side, and the movie production was really putting the pinch on their business. One of them, Roche Rodriguez, was the father of Eduardo Rodriguez, the boy who killed Michael Heffley in Colorado Canyon back in 1988. His son-in-law was Ruben Chapa, who smuggled dope out of the Redford area until he went to prison.

Roche was also a federal fugitive. He had been sentenced to ten years in the pen for his activities. The judge, a kindhearted sort, sent Roche home to put his affairs in order. Roche cleaned out his gear on the American side and walked across the river and kept on selling dope as if he had never been convicted. I wanted to set that right.

I called Texas Ranger Dave Duncan, who had replaced me after my retirement, and advised him of our situation down here on the river. Soon, Deputy U.S. Marshall Paul Evans and USDA agent Jerry Alarcon were also involved.

Evans and Alarcon drove up across from Rodriguez's hooch and told him that he could have his horse back if he signed the requisite documents. I covered them from two hundred yards away with an M-14 rifle just in case the exchange got a little hairy. Roche stood across the river, asking several questions about the particulars of who these men were and how exactly he was going to retrieve his horse. Convinced that he was dealing with USDA people, Roche jumped in his dented johnboat and paddled across the Rio Bravo. His border collie swam alongside the boat.

Joaquin Jackson, Nick Nolte, and Don Joaquin Jackson, 1988

Evans slapped the cuffs on Roche before he could say "reefer." I walked down from my perch to pay my last respects.

"Hello, Roche," I said. "It's been a while."

"Hello, Ranger," he said.

It was a better scene than anything they shot in that damn movie, let me tell you.

I PLAYED THE FATHER of a teenage girl in *Dancer, Texas: Pop. 81*, a successful independent production written, produced, and directed by native Texans. I was really proud to be given the chance to be a very small part of the production. I believe that the film was well received.

I had a bit role in *Rough Riders*, directed by my friend and fellow NRA director, John Milius. I was a passenger in a stagecoach held up by Brad Johnson and Buck Taylor. We spent the day with a woman—who I'm told once worked in a topless bar in Dallas—in a relationship with Gary Busey. She was a handful, that's for sure. Got to mix with Sam Elliot while this movie was being shot. Women swoon over him, but he's a family man.

I loved playing a hanging judge in a low-budget independent film entitled *Dirt*. I've never seen the movie, but I heard it played at some of the festivals around the country.

The State of Texas recently commissioned an IMAX production entitled *Texas: The Big Picture,* which is currently being shown in the Bob Bullock Museum of State History in Austin. I had a couple of small scenes in this entertaining tribute to my home state. I also helped the location managers with some security issues. They're good and reliable people, and I enjoyed working with them.

That about wraps up my scant movie credits. I want to conclude this chapter by saying that I never went looking for these movie roles. In every case, they came looking for me. I know that I'm typecast as a cowboy, but I never dreamed I'd have that chance back when I was a kid scraping up two bits to catch the powder burner matinee at the Wallace Theater in Levelland. Serious actors spend their entire lives hoping for a role in a movie like I had in *The Good Old Boys.* I always knew that I could not have been luckier. Some people advised me to move out to LA and pursue my film career in earnest. I'd sooner stick my ass on a fire ant mound than go to LA or any other big city.

The movies are about what you look like, not what you are. They stuck me in a few scenes because I look like a cowboy. I was once, in fact, a working cowboy—at least for a little while. But what I really was, and still am at heart, is a Texas Ranger.

CHAPTER SEVENTEEN

A Slow, Cold Rain

1990–THIS VERY DAY

It is beyond the province of this court, as it is beyond the capacity of humankind in its present state of development, to predicate ultimate responsibility for human acts.

FROM JUDGE JOHN R. CAVERLY'S DECISION
IN THE LEOPOLD AND LOEB TRIAL

THE FACTS, as New Mexico criminal investigators then understood them, are laid out chronologically in the Warrant for Arrest. "In regards to County of Bernalillo District Attorney File number CR1402-91 and CR1653-91, the subject is to be apprehended for Receiving and Transferring a Stolen Vehicle (Possession), Conspiracy to Receive Stolen Property ($100 or less), Tampering with Evidence, Firearm Enhancement, Armed Robbery, Conspiracy to Commit Murder, and Two Counts of Murder."

The warrant asserts that on November 24, 1990, hunters came across the bodies of two young men near Sandia Peak, close to Albuquerque, New Mexico. They had each been shot twice in the head with a .22 caliber pistol and then dragged approximately one hundred feet down a hill from a rural road. The victims had no wallets or other means of identification.

The warrant explains that investigators soon identified both victims. They were last seen together the night before leaving an Albuquerque nightclub typically frequented by homosexuals with two other males. Over the course of the investigation, which included interviews with a number of fact and circumstantial witnesses, both the subject and his accomplice were identified and placed at the scene with the victims.

The warrant clearly states that the subject is a twenty-seven-year-old unemployed male. He had served in the U.S. Marines and had recently been employed as a sheriff's deputy in Texas. He briefly worked at a Pizza Hut in Alpine, Texas. At the time of the murders, he had been unemployed for a few months.

In September of 1990, the subject had stolen a BMW automobile and driven it to Albuquerque, New Mexico, to visit a friend from the marines. He soon met and moved in with a young female college student and single mother. Over the course of their brief relationship, the subject claimed that he was on leave from a real estate company in Texas and also that he worked for an unnamed secret federal agency.

The young woman later threw him out of her house because he made no effort to either return to work in Texas or find suitable employment in Albuquerque. He also drank too much, had stolen cash from her purse, and had once absconded with her ATM card. In addition, he could not explain to her satisfaction his whereabouts on the night the two gay men were found murdered in the mountains.

The warrant further explains that the investigation soon focused on the subject and his accomplice. Under police pressure both men fled first to El Paso. The subject later phoned his ex-girlfriend from San Diego, California.

The accomplice returned to Albuquerque on January 22, 1991, and turned himself in to police. He gave a statement to investigators. The accomplice's version of the events claimed that he and the subject patronized the gay club with the express intent of picking up and then robbing homosexuals. The murder weapon belonged to the accomplice, but he claimed that the subject had borrowed the .22 pistol a few days before the murder. He claimed that he did not know that the subject had the gun in his possession on the night in question.

The subject and accomplice picked up two young men from the nightclub and bought Budweiser and Coors Light beer at a convenience store. The subject then drove them to Sandia Peak, also known as "the Crest." The men stopped in a remote area to relieve themselves. The accomplice got out of the car. According to him, he soon heard a gunshot. For reasons unknown the subject shot one of the victims in the head.

The second victim attacked the subject, punched him hard enough to knock the subject to the ground. The accomplice claimed that he grabbed the gun. The second victim then attacked him to gain control of it. In the ensuing scuffle, the weapon discharged, killing the victim.

The warrant does not explain why each victim was shot twice. The document does state, however, that both victims were dragged to a wooded area and left there. Their wallets were removed. The investigation later concluded that the suspect and his accomplice took a total of approximately $11 in cash from their victims.

The document makes it clear that on the date the warrant was issued, the accomplice had turned himself in, while the suspect remained at large. The State of New Mexico commanded any authorized officer to arrest the subject.

After reading the facts sworn to in the arrest warrant, any police officer would naturally assume the suspect to be armed and dangerous, would understand that he had been a soldier trained to use a variety of lethal weapons. He demonstrated some resourcefulness and appeared to rely on a network of noncriminal friends and associates to harbor him. He was known to be a heavy drinker. He was known to lie. He was a known car thief and suspected killer who allegedly murdered two young men for $11. He initially misled investigators about his involvement in this crime and then fled the state to avoid arrest.

Any police officer would have to assume the subject to be desperate and impulsive, with a tendency to react violently with the least provocation. It seemed highly probable that under the right circumstances the subject would kill again. Officers knew to use extreme caution if and when they attempted to apprehend him. The Warrant of Arrest told every officer what he needed to know about the suspect.

What the warrant doesn't tell anyone is that the suspect is my oldest son. His name is Don Joaquin Jackson.

I HAVE TWO SONS. My wife and I raised them both the same. One is the most honest man I know and followed me into law enforcement. The second is serving a forty-eight-year prison term for auto theft and double homicide.

My son's accomplice, a fellow ex-marine, gave two similar statements to police upon his arrest. He admitted killing one victim himself. He claimed that Don Joaquin killed the other for reasons that he did not know. After his confession he was sentenced to a prison term.

Nearly a year later, on September 19, 1991, the accomplice provided a second version to Don Joaquin's attorney and an assistant DA shortly before Don Joaquin's case came to trial. In this recorded and transcribed account, the accomplice admitted killing both victims. He alleges that he and Don Joaquin had considered picking up some homosexuals and then rolling them for spending money. After making inquiries, they selected a suitable location, met the victims, asked them to go drink beer, and took them up to the Crest in the automobile that Don Joaquin had stolen from a neighbor of ours in Alpine. The accomplice said that he never really intended to shoot the victims, but that he was "drunk and the gun was available."

By all accounts, the young men were all doing some serious drinking. (A toxicology report indicated that one victim had a blood alcohol level of .130 percent—close to twice the limit for a DWI arrest.) All hell broke loose after some inappropriate touching, at which time the accomplice shot one victim and then the other with a .22 High Standard pistol. He shot them once while they were sitting or standing. He shot them again once they were down. He originally blamed Don Joaquin for killing one of the victims because my son had some vague plan to avoid arrest and the accomplice did not want to be blamed for both murders. Or at least, this is the version he gave a year after the fact.

In the meantime, a jailhouse snitch approached the DA's office with information. In a letter dated October 21, 1991, the informant claimed that Don Joaquin admitted shooting one of the victims. In return for his testimony, the informant asked the State of New Mexico to "drop two felony residential burglaries [sic] and to reinstate [his] 18 month probation," along with another consideration. The DA believed the snitch above the accomplice and renewed vigorous prosecution of Don Joaquin Jackson for murder. The fact that the defendant targeted homosexuals aggravated the charges under "hate crime" legislation.

Facing either execution or a life sentence with no possibility of parole at trial, Don Joaquin pleaded guilty to some of the charges and threw himself on the mercy of the court. The State of New Mexico sentenced him to forty-eight years in a maximum security facility.

These are the facts as I have come by them. I don't know which version of the crime, if any, is true. These boys were so intoxicated at the time of the offense that I doubt either of them remembers what exactly took place. I only know that there was a killing in the desert. Two young men were murdered. Two other young men went to prison. Shirley and I learned all of this from the court documents.

But what about understanding? Where do my wife and I go for that?

IF DON JOAQUIN was troubled as a child I didn't see it. He was the spitting image of his mother, a busy little brown-haired, brown-eyed handsome boy who could not sit still. He could climb anything and did. He was cute and curious and performed well in school. He was an easy child to love. My wife and I could not help but spoil him.

Things changed during his adolescent years. His grades dipped drastically. His teachers claimed that he was capable of doing his schoolwork, but showed little interest in it. He became passive and withdrawn, both at school and with his friends. Where he'd once been active, we now saw him as impulsive. He exhibited a low threshold for frustration and little common sense. He threw tantrums. He ran away from home for no other reason than to worry his mother and me. We chalked up his behavioral troubles to his age and changing body. We hoped that he'd grow out of this difficult phase.

The film was called *The Deerhunter.* I've never been one to blame movies or rock stars for someone else's crimes, but it's a rare occasion when either one is fit to serve as a role model. Any influence pop culture has on our children is too much. One of the tragedies of our time is that films and rock music sometimes influence misguided kids with low self-esteem who are susceptible to poor choices. Don Joaquin and his closest boyhood friend are perhaps the best example of how things can go so terribly wrong.

Don Joaquin and his friend watched *The Deerhunter,* a story about personal relationships permanently damaged by the Vietnam War. One of the film's subplots revolved around the improbable premise that Christopher Walken's character could make a living for a year or two or more in Asia as a professional Russian roulette player. For some reason, this film made an impression on my son when nothing taught at his school could. He and his friend decided to duplicate the roulette scene with one of my pistols in my Uvalde home. They played the game only once. A seventeen-year-old boy was killed instantly.

The incident left behind a grieving family, a stunned community, and a lot of questions about how such a horrible thing can happen. I saw something die in my son. He seemed reluctant to accept his responsibility for his friend's death. He never considered that the odds would conspire against him—that there was nothing to be gained by playing Russian roulette, only everything to lose. Don Joaquin never seemed to understand that there was no sense in allowing himself and his friend to take such a huge risk with their lives! He saw the incident only as proof positive that he was doomed in this world. "There's no God," he said. And for him to conclude only that from this tragic experience probably made it true in his case.

This tragedy proved to be a pivotal incident in my son's struggle with behavioral anomalies. A confused boy spiraled downward in a journey that ultimately ended in his self-destruction. He kept everyone at a distance. He treated all authority with contempt. He recognized no boundaries. He abused alcohol. He broke little laws. He lied when the truth would have served him better. And none of us who loved him, and least of all Don Joaquin himself, could understand why. As parents, we grappled with the reality that Don Joaquin was wired differently than what is considered normal in our society. For his mother and me, the worry never ended.

Don Joaquin suffered through several failed attempts at college and a succession of hopeless jobs. The marines turned him around for a little while. Don Joaquin made the honor guard. He appeared to find his purpose, his niche in life, and we were all so grateful for it. Shirley and I hoped that our son had finally outgrown his troubles.

His marine enlistment ended two years later with a knee injury that left Don Joaquin physically unfit to perform his military duties. We found out later that Don Joaquin drank hard in the military and had been in alcohol treatment programs at least once. All appearances to the contrary, the deep cracks in his personality were always there, always crippling his best efforts to find his way in life.

Discharged from the service, he returned home to a strange community. His family lived in Alpine now, where he had no friends. He enrolled in Sul Ross University and soon lost interest. He got on as a sheriff's deputy and embarrassed me with his complete disregard for his duty to his employer and the community he served. He drank. He caroused. He drifted further away from us all. He grew more frustrated and anxious and shiftless as the hot summer days passed him by.

He got involved in some altercation with a local man. Humiliated, Don Joaquin responded with an angry outburst. I think I saw something snap in him that night. We quarreled. He later snuck out of the house like some kid and ripped off a neighbor's car. He drove to New Mexico to visit a friend who had no more sense than he did. They ended up together in a stolen car on a lonely mountain road that led away from the bodies of two dead boys. My son shot one of them. Or he didn't. But just the same he slammed a prison door on his life. And for what?

He can't tell you. And neither can I.

As I sat in the courtroom to support him, facing the parents of the young men he had killed, I realized that I didn't really know my son. An endless stream of what-if's crossed my mind. What if I had disciplined him more as a young boy? Or less? What if I had sent him away to military school? Or coached him another year in Little League? Or got him more involved in the church? Or Boy Scouts? Or taught him to play the guitar? Should I have read to him more at bedtime? Should he have been on medication of some kind? Should we have fed him less sugar? What did I do—or fail to do—that set this horrific event in motion? Should I have been less of a Ranger and more of a father? *Where did I go wrong?*

A wave of guilt welled up before me as my son's case ran its course. There was nothing I could do but let it swamp me. I wallowed in it through the rest of my son's case up to the moment I watched them haul him off to prison. If you want to kill a Texas Ranger, let him witness such a thing. I was never the same man after that.

After that first awful deluge, my guilt was like a slow, cold rain. I feel it always when I'm alone at night, here in the desert, little cold drops falling on the cold metal roof. If I lie quietly enough I hear it. Over ten years have passed, and I hear it still.

DEER SEASON HAD BEEN OPEN for only a week in 1973 when I yanked back the covers on a ten-year-old's bed. I told him once to get up and that's all it took. He was dressed, bright brown eyes gleaming, anxious for his first chance at a whitetail buck. I scrambled eggs and sausage in a single skillet and spooned them into warm flour tortillas. Don Joaquin helped me load the gear and guns into my state unit, and we were out the door without a sound. We left for our adventure, his mother and little brother sleeping in a warm house.

We drove ten miles south of Uvalde through patches of gray fog to the Kyle Ranch. A thick cloud bank seemed to be propped up by the live oaks lest it crash to the earth. We scooted along, under the gloom, through the black brush to a deer blind that climbed twenty feet in the air. I've never liked hunting deer from a blind, but with an eager, young kid what are you going to do? The only suitable rifle I owned at the time was a state-issued .30-06 with a cheap scope, and the boy needed a rest to handle it. In this instance, the blind was all right.

My son and I sat in silence as the day broke. I don't know why it always feels colder just after dawn, but the boy felt it, too. I wrapped him with my coat against my chest, and together we weathered the near-freezing temperatures. Don Joaquin kept his eyes trained on the long, dark *sendero*—the channel cut into the brush. Thinking of the kid's commitment to our task, I smiled. I had never seen him sit so still or be so vigilant.

Just a few minutes into the hunt, the big buck stepped out. He was a stout, mature eight-pointer. He took short, powerful, spring-loaded steps, his breath vaporizing in the cold, thick air. The animal's size and stately demeanor took away Don Joaquin's breath. The boy's eyes were the size of quarters. I slowly slid the rifle barrel out the window until the stock rested on the sill. Then I eased Don Joaquin out on my knee until he caressed the butt against his shoulder and pressed his eye near the scope.

"Put the crosshairs on the buck's neck," I whispered. "And then *squeeze* the trigger."

A few anxious seconds passed. It seemed a good sign to me that an impulsive kid could take his time on something so important to him.

Finally the trigger reached the point where it released the sear and the firing pin snapped against the cartridge's primer. The mechanism usually engages faster than the shooter thinks. There's a deafening explosion, a jolt to the shoulder that knocks your eye off the scope, and then there's no taking back that bullet or knowing for sure where it went. It flies true or it doesn't.

But I wasn't the shooter, I was the father, and I watched it all. The buck dropped in his tracks.

"You did it, son!" I said. "That was one hell of a shot!" I could feel his quick breath and the rapid beat of his heart as we waited. You don't want a wounded deer to run off anywhere, but it's particularly bad news in the dense South Texas brush. I wanted Don Joaquin to learn a little bit about patience, and a good deer hunter waits after the shot. He had to understand that certain rules govern all hunters, and if he were truly to become a hunter, he must comply. So we waited to learn a little about the law and to reduce all odds of failure. Then we climbed down out of the blind.

As we approached the deer, I finally realized how big he was. The outside spread approached twenty-two inches—a real trophy for a ten-year-old boy.

Joaquin, Don Joaquin, Shirley, and Lance Jackson, Uvalde, Texas, 1977

But to me as a father, nothing on this hunt was about the deer or the gun or the killing. It was about a father teaching his son to trust himself—to reassure him that he could set a goal and accomplish it. This hunt was about watching this kid enjoy his success and seeing the pride swell in his chest.

I pulled my knife and taught Don Joaquin how to dress out a deer. He watched every stroke carefully. When he thought we were finished, I told him to come near me. I dabbed my finger in the warm blood that had pooled inside the buck's rib cage and smudged it across Don Joaquin's cheek.

"That's the mark of a hunter," I said. "You earned the right to wear that today. You're in the blood."

He burst through the door to show it off to his mother and brother. I don't believe that he washed it off for another day.

We busied ourselves butchering the deer. When I was a young Ranger, Shirley and I could rarely afford to buy steaks. We lived off of fish, quail, and venison we harvested off the land, which is why it was that much more important that Don Joaquin had killed the deer that day. He had contributed to his family's welfare. He wrapped every cut in the waxy white butcher paper and delivered it to the freezer like it was gold.

That's the boy I remember. Sweet and good and warm and true, so proud of the blood mark on his cheek that his heart liked to beat out of his chest. That was a happy day for us, and for our family. I felt the natural bond between father and son. Everything was right. I would never place more hope and faith in him than I did on the day of his first hunt. I loved him then.

I love him still.

I HAVE TWO SONS. My wife and I raised them both the same. One is the most honest man I know and followed me into law enforcement. The second is serving a forty-eight-year prison term for auto theft and double homicide. I don't understand how this horrible thing happened. I only know that my guilt eats away at me. If you want to kill a Texas Ranger, send his son to prison. I die a little every day. At night, I hear the slow, cold rain on my roof. It torments me always that I failed to find a solution to my son's problems. Now it's too late.

And that's my last public word on the matter. Don't ask me about it again.

CHAPTER EIGHTEEN

 Saddle My Pony, Boys . . .

A FAREWELL TO ARMS

1993

Ranger management shoved mandatory retirement down Captain Allee's throat in 1971. All of us in Company D knew the Captain, a third-generation Texas Ranger, was at the end of the trail. None of us had the heart to tell him. And the bastards in Austin at the time didn't have the balls. But Captain Allee looked around real good and didn't see much of the Texas that he'd known as a young man. He never admitted any such thing to me, but he had to have realized that Texas had gone on and left him behind. He stepped down from the Rangers—not without controversy, of course—but he did let her go.

The department presented Captain Allee with a fine, customized Winchester rifle at his retirement party. My captain held the gun out for others to admire as he carefully regarded it himself. "Seems like a strange gift," he finally said, "now that they've taken away my hunting license."

He lived for sixteen more years. We visited often. He loved to tell the old stories and I loved to listen to them. Cap told great jokes. But I could see how the bitterness was eating into him. He was angry about how the Rangers had changed toward the end of his service. He felt abandoned by the people he'd served. He never understood that Texas had changed, while he didn't.

It was a hard thing for me to watch my old captain sink slowly into despair as he fought a losing battle against his tarnished reputation. He has been judged by history for how he handled the civil rights and labor struggles, movements that were beyond his scope and understanding. The more he tried to explain himself to reporters, the worse things got. He became a

Joaquin in Jacksboro, Texas, 1965

Ranger in 1931. He served four decades. There was so much more to the man than his failure to perceive civil rights as something other than a communist plot to undermine America.

In an interdepartmental memo to Wilson Speir dated February 9, 1967, I quoted Homer Garrison's letter to Captain Allee's file: "Alfred Allee is a traditional figure in the border country in the south part of our state. I am sure that he will go down in history as one of the real top Ranger Captains of all time."

And he would have if he had retired in 1965. I was a pallbearer at his funeral in 1987.

ALMOST TWENTY YEARS after Captain Allee retired, I was umpiring a baseball game. I coached both of my sons in the Uvalde Little League (Lance went on to play college ball). I later became the director of the league and was even elected president for two terms. I've umpired a few games, too.

I was behind the plate one night when little Bozo Alderson came up to bat. (When people hear "Bozo" they think of the clown, but among the Hispanics in my jurisdiction it meant "shorty.") Bozo was an all-star-caliber player who lived and breathed baseball. He was a real good kid and a joy to watch on the diamond. He played on a team coached by my good friend Frank Harrison. Anyway, before Bozo came up to bat, Frank told him, "Did you know that umpire there is a real Texas Ranger?"

Bozo usually trotted out to the batter's box. He was that anxious to take a swing. But this time, he dragged the bat behind him as he walked slowly toward me, his eyes wide with amazement.

When he finally got out to the batter's box, he said, "Say, are you really a Texas Ranger?"

"Yes, son," I said, straightening a little and probably puffing out my chest, too. "I sure am."

Bozo stared at me as he breathed this big sigh. I could tell he was a little awestruck. I was like that once.

"What position do you play?" he said.

No Texas-raised kid of my generation could have ever made the same mistake. We were inundated with the frontier adventures of the Texas Rangers in books, on the radio, and in film. Historians devoted a lifetime to documenting their true life exploits. As boys, we all wanted to ride alongside our heroes, the Texas Rangers. As a man, I did it. I had fulfilled every Texas kid's childhood dream, and Bozo thought I played for a goddamned baseball team. I realized then that as a state, as a people, we had undergone a dramatic social and cultural shift. Professional athletes, rock musicians, and movie stars now outshined a Texas legend.

"Wrong outfit, Bozo," I said. "Batter up."

I don't remember who was pitching that night, but it was entirely inappropriate for me, the umpire, to signal to him to come with the heater. I needed to see the heat. I wanted Bozo's misinformed ass back on the bench.

The pitcher threw a low curve that was just outside the plate. Anything near the backstop is a strike when you insult the umpire's profession. Three quick pitches and Bozo was cooked. Instead, he tagged the ball with the meat of the bat and roped it out of the park for a homer. I watched his victory lap around the bags looking like I just received news of a death in the family.

What position do you play? Set me back a step or two.

IN MY YOUTH, I dreamed of riding beside Jack Hays. He was only twenty-seven years old when he led a scouting party up near Walker Creek, a tributary of the Guadalupe River, a full day's ride north of San Antonio de Bexar. They came across ten Comanche warriors, who tried to bait them into an ambush where seventy more lay in wait. When Hays refused to comply, the Comanches rode to the crest of a hill, dismounted, and taunted the young Ranger captain in Spanish.

Hays wheeled his men toward the Indians, riding in the bottom of a ravine where they could not be seen until they were right on the Comanches' flank. The warriors' first close image of the Texans was when they were on top of them.

The Comanche who survived the initial charge regrouped and bore down on the Rangers, who they assumed needed to reload. Instead, Hays's men formed a circle with their mounts, absorbed the Comanche attack, drew .36 caliber Colt Patterson revolvers, and hammered those warriors. When, at last, the Comanche broke off the engagement, Hays and his men mounted up and chased after them. "Powder burn 'em!" Hays ordered his men. And by that he meant ride up damn close to those Indians before you pull the trigger.

Seventeen Rangers routed over seventy Comanche warriors on horseback in an open, running fight. Warfare on the plains would never be the same.

I wanted to ride with Captain Samuel Walker during his cavalry charge, with sabers and pistols drawn, against the Mexican garrison at Huamantla. Witnesses were in awe of the young Ranger's bravado. Santa Anna himself plunged into the battle until the main body of the American force also engaged. In the end it was a stunning American victory, but Captain Walker lay dead. He was thirty-five years old.

Wouldn't it have been something to ride alongside Captain Matthew Caldwell in what is known to history as "the Great Comanche Raid," when he confronted the Comanche warriors who had raided Victoria and burned Linnville to the ground? Caldwell pushed his men hard, frantic to get between the Comanches and the *llano estacado* at the crossing at Plum Creek. "Boys," he said, "there are eight hundred or one thousand Indians. They have our women and children prisoners. They have repulsed our men below. We are eighty-seven strong, and I believe we can whip the hell out of 'em! Boys, shall we fight?"

To the man, they shouted, "Aye!"

Caldwell and his riders were soon joined by Colonel Edward Burleson, Ben McCulloch, and a few friendly Tonkawa, and then they stepped out of the brush to confront their stunned enemies. They exchanged fire with the Comanche, finally killing a great war chief who wore a conquistador's breastplate. Then the Texans charged in force, dispersing the Comanche into a hundred small parties, all of them on the run. The Texans chased the Indians in a running scrape for better than fifteen miles. For years, pioneer farmers reported finding the bones of slain Comanche warriors in their fields.

Wouldn't it have been something to have ridden with Leander McNelly in the Las Cuevas war, the taming of the Nueces Strip? At the end of several running skirmishes and near international incidents between Mexico and the United States, McNelly's sheer audacity had brought about the return of the stolen cattle. McNelly had nine Rangers with him for the exchange. Twenty-five Mexican *charros* held the cattle back on the south bank of the Rio Grande.

"Well, bring 'em over!" McNelly said.

The formal answer from the Mexicans was, not until the animals had been properly inspected.

"Well, boys, we are in it again," McNelly told his Rangers. "We will go over again, if we never get back. What do you say?"

"We are with you, Captain," they all said, and they were.

McNelly loaded his men onto a Mexican ferry, crossed the river, and rode to within ten feet of the overwhelming Mexican force. McNelly ordered his translator to inform the Mexican leader that their *presidente* had promised to deliver the cattle to the Texas bank.

"Not until they are inspected," the Mexican officer replied.

"By God," McNelly said, "they were stolen from Texas without being inspected. You can damn sure drive them back without one."

The Mexican officer shook his head and said, "No."

McNelly ordered his men to form ranks. They cocked their rifles and aimed their barrels at the Mexicans. McNelly turned to his translator and said, "You tell that son of a bitch that if he don't deliver them cattle across the river in less than five minutes, we'll kill every man here!"

Well short of McNelly's ultimatum, the cattle were grazing on the Texas side of the Rio Grande. McNelly was dying of tuberculosis at the time. He was thirty-three years old when they laid him down.

We didn't have cavalry charges in my time, but I once stormed the jail in Carrizo Springs, Texas, behind my sixty-four-year-old captain. Under heavy fire, we shot our way up to the front door, shot our way inside, and then Captain Allee shot his way up the stairway to the second floor. I was part of that. I was there. I was thirty-one years old.

THERE ARE TOO MANY great stories about the Rangers to tell in any one book, but here I'd like to recount what I think is one of the saddest:

Twelve warriors, four women, and four children split off from the last Mescalero war chief, Victorio, shortly before he and his band were annihilated at Tres Castillos in Chihuahua, Mexico. The splinter group crossed the Rio Grande and entered Texas in the dead of winter, January 1881. Desperate and starving, they preyed on anyone they could kill for food and clothing or maybe just to watch their enemies die. We'll never know.

Ranger Captain George W. Baylor put two dozen men in the field and picked up the Apaches' trail west of the Quitman Mountains. Pueblo scouts followed the Apache stragglers across the plain that lay between Eagle Springs and the Diablo Range. The Mescaleros killed their horses for fresh meat and melted snow for water, climbing higher into the Diablos until they felt secure. They had no idea that the Rangers were stalking them.

Baylor's scouts came across a horse carcass so fresh that blood still dripped from its pink bones. A flock of late afternoon doves told the Pueblos that good water lay just an hour or two ahead. With sign so fresh, the Mescaleros were most likely camped around the fresh pool for the night.

Baylor's men hunkered down in their blankets in a fireless camp and waited for daylight. On the morning of January 29, 1881, the guards awakened the Rangers. They were up and mounted and over the mountain ridge before daybreak. The Pueblos walked stooped over to follow the moccasin prints on the rocky ground. Baylor and his men at last saw the campfires glowing in the distance. *"Hoy!"* whispered the Pueblos. *"Están los indios!"*

Baylor split his command to trap the Mescaleros in a crossfire. He himself stayed with the main body, creeping through the thickets of prickly pear, Spanish dagger, and greasewood until they were just under a hundred yards from the Apaches. When the sun rose, the Rangers opened up with Winchester repeaters on the hapless Indians.

Startled, the Indians broke and ran with their blankets wrapped around them. The Rangers claimed that it was impossible to tell the women and children from the warriors. They killed eight and probably wounded them all. They captured one squaw and two children. The historians don't mention what happened to the rest. If the Rangers wrote it down in their reports, the historians saw no reason to repeat it.

There was indeed good water up on that mountain—two small pools of snowmelt. But the Apaches left so much blood in the larger depression that the Rangers couldn't drink it. They threw fresh brush on the coals of the Indians' cooking fires to roast the Apaches' horsemeat and venison. They collected just enough fresh water to percolate a little coffee. None of them wanted the Apaches' supplies of stolen tack and calico cloth. So they made a huge, roaring bonfire and torched everything that burned. Then they sat down to the breakfast the dead Mescaleros had intended for themselves with the sun just rising over the Diablo Mountains, to the sobs of a wounded, widowed Apache squaw and a child with a bullet hole in its foot, with the bodies of dead warriors scattered around.

Sierra Diablo was the last Indian engagement fought in Texas. Sounded more like a massacre to me. At any rate, the Rangers who served under Baylor had come of age on the frontier. Their parents and grandparents had fought the Comanche, the Kiowa, and the Apache in the great and tragic contest for Texas—a battle that on both sides had consumed so many brave souls. For the Indians and settlers alike, it was an honor to kill their enemies.

Baylor's Rangers had lived long enough to see fortunes fade for the once great warriors of the plains. By Sierra Diablo, all but a few handfuls of the Texas Indians were either on Oklahoma reservations or dead. The Rangers may have hunted down the Mescalero band in anticipation of an epic battle on the same scale as those of the previous fifty years. Instead, they tracked down exhausted men, women, and children—the last free-roaming Indians in Texas—and without offering them a chance to surrender, shot them to pieces. What glory was there in that?

They were born Indian fighters who had come of age when there were no more Indians left to fight. One can look beyond the tragic violence of Sierra Diablo and see the sadness in the eyes of those young Rangers on the long ride home. The bell tolled for them that winter's day. There was no longer a place in Texas for what they were.

I OFTEN IMAGINED what it would have been like to fight for Texas at Walker Creek, against Santa Anna, villain of the Alamo and Goliad, in the Mexican War; to retaliate for the Great Comanche Raid at Plum Creek; or to ride with McNelly on the Rio Grande. I did serve with their sons and grandsons, men I respected but couldn't touch when it came to sheer toughness and force of will. I did my duty at the Carrizo Springs jailbreak of 1969, the wildest gun battle of my thirty-seven years behind a badge. As the last decade of the twentieth century loomed, all of these epic events were behind the Texas Rangers. They were all behind me.

Ahead, I saw only my personal Diablo Mountain. And I wanted no part of it.

SOMEWHERE ALONG in the early 1990s, the DPS issued a desktop computer to every active officer. Even in the comfort of my field office, I stared at my fancy new monitor like an old bull hung up in front of a new gate. I watched young, trained officers take to the machines like ducks to water. They were probably doing nothing more complex than running a set of license plates, but to me they looked like they were navigating the space shuttle. Technology had just fired a fatal round into my Ranger career.

It's a bad feeling when the times pass you by. I had watched the 1960s confound damn good men, Captain Allee only one of many who had come of age during the Great Depression. My youth had allowed me to adapt when my elders couldn't make the same transition. Toward the 1990s, young Rangers were beginning to look at me as I had once looked at the old cowboy Rangers of the generation before me, stamped as they were by a bygone era before television, air-conditioning, and two-way radios. I realized then that I had come full circle. The bell now tolled for me.

The younger officers were bemused by the clothes I'd worn in preparation to spend the day either in the saddle or in a helicopter cockpit, that I still carried a .30-30 lever-action rifle in a saddle scabbard next to the driver's seat of my car, that well-used spurs hung on the brake release lever. They didn't see how any of this gear fit into the modern Ranger service. I couldn't imagine being a Ranger without it.

The young Rangers are good men and a couple of good women, people of manners everyone. Nobody laughed out loud at me that I ever heard. But every now and then I'd catch one of the new men looking at me like I was some kind of cartoon character. And I couldn't bear it.

I was in the last bunch of Rangers appointed by Homer Garrison himself. I was the last Garrison Ranger to retire. In 1993 I was the senior Ranger in the field. I was hired specifically because I knew how to rope and ride, live off the land, read the signs a fugitive left on the Texas earth, and judge a man by his mannerisms and body language, and I had proven that I knew when to talk and when to shoot. When the State of Texas didn't need men like that anymore, they didn't need me, and I didn't need some stringy-haired, potbellied computer geek half my age gawking down his nose at me to tell me so.

IF YOU'RE EXPECTING ME to tear into the new generation of Rangers, you're in for a surprise. Not too long ago, I was asked to address a security problem encountered by the production company on the set of *The Alamo*. Almost immediately, I recognized that we were dealing with felony theft. In response to my report to the Austin headquarters, the DPS sent out this handsome young Ranger by the name of Chris Love. Chris was bright as a brass button, polite as hell, respectful to an old, worn-out blowhard like myself, and when it came time to bear down on the suspects, he did one hell of a job of that, too.

I was proud of that young man. He was every inch a Texas Ranger. I gladly stepped out of his way and let him have at it, and he was damn good. I can further guarantee you that there are a hundred more just like him.

The contemporary Rangers are every bit as magnificent in their time as my generation was in ours. They aren't better or worse, they're just *different*, mainly because they have to be. The Texas Rangers have adapted beautifully to their time and place, just as they always have.

HERE WE ARE FIFTEEN YEARS after Captain Allee's funeral, and I still miss that old man, and his wife, Miss Pearl, and Zeno Smith, Levi Duncan, Walter Russell, Tol Dawson, Jim Riddle, Bill Wilson, and many of those old Rangers who shaped my early career—and my life. I carried a little piece of them with me after they were gone. I hope maybe some of the younger men and women who ride on ahead carry a little piece of me. In that way, the legend of the Texas Rangers lives on, as strong as it was in the days of Jack Hays, Samuel Walker, Ben McCulloch, Leander McNelly, McDonald, Hamer, Gonzaules, and Company D Captain Alfred Y. Allee Sr. It lived on for a little while in me and in the Rangers of my generation. And then it was time for me to pass it on to the next man. I felt it in my bones.

I felt this sadness watching Captain Allee struggle against mandatory retirement. He couldn't imagine his life without being a Texas Ranger. But we all reach a point where, physically and emotionally, we can't live up to it anymore. Sometime around 1990 I started to feel that way. I didn't tell a soul. But there it was, just as certain as wrinkles, aching joints, and gray hair.

I could cite any number of excuses for retirement: my son's crimes and prison term, and the personal toll they took on my family, the Rick Thompson scandal, the increasing reliance by officers in the field on technology in place of old-fashioned police work, the general erosion of respect for law enforcement officials by the citizens we serve, the Rangers being run by men who weren't fit to hold a piss bucket in comparison to Homer Garrison and Wilson Speir, and Governor Richards's political meddling with the heart of the Ranger corps. At one time or another I publicly or privately blamed these events for my decision to retire from the Rangers. They seemed like damn good reasons. The only problem was that not one of them was true.

There was a time when I couldn't wait for the phone to ring. It could mean almost anything—a murder, a jailbreak, a fugitive on the run, a stolen horse, a lost child—but it always represented a *challenge,* and I hungered to meet it. The ring of my telephone conditioned me like Pavlov's dog. I was instantly ready, immediately engaged, and as soon as I understood what was demanded of me, I was in pursuit of my objective until the end. For me, it was always all or nothing, and each new adventure began with the ring of a phone.

As I passed my twenty-fifth year in the Rangers, I realized that I had developed an entirely different response to a ringing telephone. I started to dread it. I began to wonder if I still had what it takes to respond. I had to accept the fact that I was no longer physically and emotionally the Ranger I had once been. The long hours, the high stress, and the countless miles had exacted a heavy personal toll. In a word, I had grown weary.

Accepting one's limitations is not an easy thing for a prideful man. And so as 1993 rolled around, I became very vocal about what I didn't like about the changing Ranger service. I told anybody who asked that the Rangers were moving in the wrong direction. In particular, I said that I didn't like the fact that woman Ranger recruits were not held to the same standards as their male counterparts. I claimed that this was the main reason that I handed in my badge.

I know better now. The truth is that I didn't want to hear that phone ring anymore in the dead of night. Boil it down anyway you want, but it was time for Joaquin Jackson to move on.

STATE OF TEXAS
OFFICE OF THE GOVERNOR
AUSTIN, TEXAS 78711

ANN W. RICHARDS
GOVERNOR

September 30, 1993

Greetings to:

H. Joaquin Jackson

As Governor of Texas, it is a pleasure for me to congratulate you upon your retirement and to commend your dedicated career.

I hope you will find retirement as rewarding as your work for the Texas Rangers. You have provided years of valued service, and I know your contributions will be missed.

I join your friends and colleagues in wishing you all the best for a well-deserved retirement.

Sincerely,

ANN W. RICHARDS
Governor

POST OFFICE BOX 12428 AUSTIN, TEXAS 78711 (512) 463-2000 (VOICE) / (512) 475-3165 (TDD)
Printed on Recycled Paper

CHAPTER NINETEEN

⊛ El Último Grito

FOR A HUNDRED MORE

(With a Nod to Hemingway's Death in the Afternoon*)*

2005

MRS. JORGENSEN: *Now Lars! . . . It so happens we be Texicans. . . .
We took a reachin' hold, way far out, past where any man has
right or reason to hold on. . . . Or if we didn't, our folks did. . . . So
we can't leave off without makin' them out to be fools, wastin'
their lives 'n' wasted in the way they died. . . . A Texican's nothin'
but a human man out on a limb. . . . This year an' next and maybe
for a hundred more. But I don't think it'll be forever. Someday this
country will be a fine good place to be. . . . Maybe it needs our
bones in the ground before that time can come.*

FROM *The Searchers* (1956)

WHERE TO NOW after this long journey, my friends? To the end,
I guess. Where else but to the end?

I am only one Ranger. There was only one story that belonged to me. But
I couldn't tell you all of it. This wasn't a big enough book. If I could have
made this enough of a book it would have had everything in it. Maybe then
you would have known what it was like to have been a Ranger. And then you
would have understood without me having to say the words why I loved it.

Somewhere in this book I should have mentioned that day back on April 1,
1966, when Col. Homer P. Garrison Jr. himself pinned the five-point star
on my chest. The director might as well have run an electric charge through
my body I felt such a jolt. Maybe Bill Gunn and Charlie Neal felt it, too. We
three were the last of the Garrison Rangers. Charlie's dead now. Bill's still
kicking up there around Waxahachie, where he spent the bulk of his career
in Company F. But I bet if you asked him, he'd say that he felt the exhilara-
tion, too. I just bet that he did.

Col. Garrison loved to swear in new Rangers. He knew that badge stood
for something—something hard won by blood, grit, courage, and a gun.
Charlie, Bill, and I became a small part of the 160-year-old legend, a con-

Texas Rangers Company D, 1969. From left to right: Dudley White; Joaquin Jackson; Glenn Krueger; Sgt. John Wood; DPS Col. Wilson Speir; Capt. Alfred Allee Sr.; Homer P. "Trey" Garrison III; Tol Dawson; Jack Van Cleave; Bob Favor; and Jerome Priess.

nection so powerful, and for me abrupt, that it felt like being electrocuted. I swear that I felt different from that day forward. I think it was pride burning right out of my chest, and I'd never truly known it before. Not like that. Never like that. Somewhere in this book I should have mentioned that sensation. April 1, 1966.

I should have talked more about the old Rangers I once knew. I attended a poker game back when I was still wet behind the ears. Companies D and F gathered for a joint meeting. It was my first opportunity to meet Charlie Miller, who had once been Pancho Villa's bodyguard and who quit just a short time before the revolutionary was assassinated. It was great to see the bond between Charlie and Walter Russell, the former Arizona Ranger. If you wanted to see Texas and the West embodied in two flesh and blood men, you should have seen Charlie Miller and Walter Russell sitting down to play cards. It was a scene out of some movie—a damn good movie.

"Walter," Charlie said, "I've got this no good son of a bitch son-in-law. Everybody knows he needs killin'. But if I do it, my wife will know I did it, and I'd be in for it then. But I could be at home reading a book or watching TV and you could kill him and she would never know that I had anything to do with it."

Walter thought it over for a minute or two before he said, "Charlie, I don't believe I can kill your son-in-law for you."

"I don't know why the hell not," Charlie said. "I'd kill yours for you." They were fooling around, of course, but I'm not sure I knew that then, and anyway Charlie and Walter, long dead and gone, deserved to be somewhere in this book. I don't know what happened to Charlie's son-in-law, but I hope he straightened up. If he knew what was good for him, he did.

I never said a word about the time Captain Allee sent Walter Russell and Levi Duncan to the Rio Bravo to investigate shootings. Mexicans were firing on tick riders, and Captain Allee wanted to put an end to it. If so, he'd sent the right men. Levi and Walter rode to the river together and then started to ride up the bank. They had not gone three hundred yards before somebody shot at them from across the river. Levi turned his mount behind a salt cedar, but Walter put the spurs to his and plunged into the river. Two Mexicans jumped up and climbed on their horses, while a third ran with his burro cart. Walter rode all three of them down and shot them off their mounts and then rode back to Levi and said, "Let's go home."

Levi claimed that he went straight to Captain Allee and said, "Never send me anywhere with that crazy son of a bitch Walter Russell!" That story isn't in the history books anywhere, and neither is the fact that the King Ranch gave Walter a registered quarterhorse each year. He'd sell it to make ends meet. Next year, they'd give him another. There was no scare in Walter Russell. I knew him when I was a young Ranger. He's been dead nearly forty years, but why couldn't he speak one more time in this book?

I've got to tell this one last story about Charlie Miller. He retired to Mason, where he always kept some good mares and a stud horse. The stud had kicked him, breaking his leg and chipping off some lower teeth. Bob Favor looked in on Charlie, who was laid up but refused to go to a doctor. He called the vet instead, who brought out his portable X-ray machine. The vet said that no doctor could have set Charlie's leg as well as he'd done it himself. Then Charlie asked Bob to go fetch him a pair of pliers, and this he did, and Charlie took the pliers and a hand mirror and pulled three lower teeth. Bob Favor watched him do it.

"You know," Charlie said to Bob after he'd pulled the first one, "pain never bothered me much." I know that's hard to believe, but it's true.

And what about Zeno Smith, who always wore a black hat and died with his boots on in his backyard just two years after retirement? Who spoke for him?

I should have mentioned somewhere that soon after I was sworn in, two old-time Rangers appeared out of nowhere to sit down with me. They were about Charlie and Walter's age, but maybe a little older. Too old to ranger anymore, but too damn stubborn to admit it. I was handpicked by Captain Allee, and that was endorsement enough for most working Rangers, but these two veterans wanted to know me a little better before they got around to the purpose of their visit.

Finally they leaned in real close and spoke in a voice worn by years of long hours, rough assignments, a little whiskey maybe, and filterless cigarettes and said, "Joaquin, sooner or later, you're gonna know somebody around here that needs killin'. When that time comes, you just tell us and we'll take care of it."

I swallowed hard before I answered. "I hope that I'll never have to do that," I said. "I expect I can take care of any situation that might come up, but I appreciate y'all looking after me and all." And then I changed the subject.

I wondered at the time if it was some kind of test or something, a way to determine if I really thought I could handle the job and abide by the law at the same time.

Some of the Rangers that passed out of the service about the time I came in had worn the cinco peso in the 1920s and 1930s. They were, in turn, trained by a past generation of Rangers who maybe had ridden with McNelly, John B. Jones, and possibly even Rip Ford. The old men I knew had played a rough and dangerous game on the border, where the shooting seldom stopped, or during Prohibition, when Texas was torn in half. In 1966, some of them still carried the scars from these violent years. The Texas Rangers were my childhood heroes. I found that I couldn't judge these hideworn men. It just wasn't my place when I was thirty-one and new on the job they had once mastered. But they worried me a little. I forgot to mention this in the book.

I talked a little about Captain Allee, about how he emerged out of this same violent generation, about how he was hell-bent on the old style of justice, evolved as little as it was only one generation after the closing of the frontier. Captain Allee took pride in assaulting criminal defense attorneys. He once cracked a Mexican American labor organizer over the head. He pistol-whipped George Parr, the Duke of Duval County. I know that he believed he did all of this in the name of law and order and for the sanctity of the Rangers and for the honor of the men who wore the badge.

Like I said, he lived long enough to see himself vilified in the press and among politicians for busting the 1967 United Farm Workers strike in Starr County. After retirement, he even smacked a convenience store clerk who impugned his integrity. People loved it as a scene in *Lonesome Dove*, but they couldn't tolerate that kind of behavior in real life. Not anymore. Captain Allee never understood that. He could be meaner than a barrel of rattlesnakes, that's for sure, but I never once questioned his judgment in the field. Never once. I knew he belonged to an earlier time. And now, so do I.

Captain Allee made folks nervous toward the end of his career, I guess. Just a few months before he retired, we were confronted with the La Raza Unida school walkout. Local tensions simmered. We all sensed trouble. Senior Captain Clint Peoples blew into Uvalde one night around nine P.M. and gave me a call. I went down to his hotel at his request to visit with him. He started in by telling me what a great man Captain Allee was, which told me right off that I was getting whitewashed. Peoples had never really liked my captain, but I believe that he respected him.

Senior Captain Peoples reminded me that Captain Allee was retiring soon and he didn't want anything bad to go on his record from any incident that might happen. My captain had an unblemished record, Peoples said. He then said that he knew that the Captain and I were close, but in truth we were no closer than he and the rest of Company D. Peoples asked me to talk to Captain Allee and encourage him not to do anything violent during the school walkout.

I looked at him and said, "Captain, you've got to be kidding me! I'm not going to tell Captain Allee one thing! He does the telling in this company. You're the Senior. You tell him."

Senior Captain Peoples never said one word to Captain Allee that I'm aware of in regard to the Uvalde school walkout. He drove on back to Austin. We did have a little trouble but it didn't get out of hand. There was one Ranger who attempted to agitate Captain Allee, at least he did until I got a hold of him alone. Uvalde was my town, in my territory, and those were my people out on the streets. I made it clear to this bird that no other Ranger was going to stir up any shit around here, especially when it came to setting off Captain Allee, and leave me to clean up the mess. I told him I'd hold him to account if trouble broke out because of what he whispered in that old man's ear. But this wasn't enough of a book to go into all that.

I should have told you more about Tol Dawson. He was one of my closest friends in Company D. All man. You should have known that he had to wait to get into the Rangers when some political appointee brother-in-law backslapper got in ahead of him. The Rangers should always be picked on their merit, on the man. And Tol finally got in on that alone and never looked back.

If you'd have known him, you'd know that he always had these big, bright teeth that he always flashed in a big grin. The worse things got, the bigger the smile. He loved the stress, the challenge, the beat of the Brush Country that he alone heard. He was right beside me when we charged up the stairs during the jailbreak at Carrizo Springs. I'll be damned if he wasn't smiling as those bullets ricocheted off the concrete walls.

Afterward, when we had all of them jailbirds on their bellies out on the lawn, Tol asked the resident deputy to point out the son of a bitch that jumped him and got all of that started. When the deputy did, Tol walked over and snatched the felon by the hair and said, "Look at me! I want to know your face for the next time we meet." And that man should be glad that they never did.

Sometime in the early 1970s, Tol Dawson was scheduled to testify at a criminal trial in Pecos, Texas. Along the way, the defense called Tol a liar to his face, and that was probably the only day he wasn't wearing that smile. As soon as Tol got off the stand, he walked right up to the lawyer's table, leaned over, and said right in his ear, "When this is over, I'm gonna whip your ass!"

Tol waited for maybe two hours while the local sheriff did everything he could to talk him out of it. "I told him I'm gonna whip his ass," Tol said. "And he needs to know that I'm a man of my word." Sure enough, when that lawyer came out, Tol spanked him good. But the attorney never pressed charges or filed a complaint. And although Tol Dawson was hauled in front of Colonel Speir to answer for his conduct, I don't think the DPS brass punished him.

People don't admire that sort of response anymore. Today, you'd be sued, prosecuted, skewered in the press, and ostracized by the Department of Public Safety. But in the 1970s there were still enough men left who lived by the old code to understand that a private disagreement between public figures had been settled and done. And what criminal defense lawyer doesn't need his ass whipped every now and then? Now that's what I call an adversarial system.

Tol's dead now. I miss him terribly. And I didn't do his memory justice in this little book. He'll probably want to whip my ass for that when we meet at that great Ranger gathering at the river. Tolliver Dawson. I didn't do him right in this book. Not by a long sight.

I didn't talk near enough about my captains. I covered Captain Allee a little, but I hardly said enough about John Wood and Jack Dean and Gene Powell. God, they were good men. John Wood served as our sergeant before he took Captain Allee's place. We got along very well.

I had once received a telephone death threat at my home in Uvalde. The next day, John Wood and Jim Peters showed up to help with a potential riot situation. They took a liking to my new straw hat, so we headed down to Slater Western Wear to get them each one just like it. We were the same height and build, and while we walked around the streets of Uvalde, we all wore the same hat. They weren't happy when they found out about the death threat.

I never thought about it until they said something. Truth is that I told that anonymous son of a bitch that I'd meet him anywhere at any time, and that was the last I heard from him. But Captain Wood gave me a hard time about dressing up him and Peters as my doubles to fade the heat.

Once Company D had a barbecue for all the men and their wives. About dusk, Shirley and I headed home. We were young then. She was wearing some sort of hot pants outfit. We got to fooling around and trying to keep the state unit on the dirt road at the same time. With all that going on, I couldn't navigate across the narrow stock tank dam, and we plunged into muddy water that rose halfway up to the door.

My fellow Rangers helped me out of this jam with no questions asked. A wrecker towed the vehicle back to Uvalde for repairs. Set me back $200 to clean the car's interior and decontaminate the motor, which is a lot to pay for fooling around with your wife, but Captain Wood never said a thing about it to me. I heard later that Clint Peoples wanted to fire me over this incident, but he couldn't get past Captain Dean, because back then the captains called the shots when it came to matters of personnel. God, I loved it when the Texas Rangers were like that! The captains ran the company— so far as it needed running. Even Peoples couldn't get to me back then.

Col. Garrison hunted down individuals first and foremost to serve in the Ranger ranks, and once he found them, we were treated like individuals. In my time the man mattered most. I'm sorry, but the Ranger service ain't like that today. And the more Rangers are all like each other, the less they are as a group. Uniformity was not what earned the Rangers their legend.

Captain Gene Powell was one of the more level-headed men I ever knew. Whenever he faced a tough decision, he said, "Let me sleep on it." By the next morning, he knew what to do and he was always right.

After the Gary Ball shooting, Captain Powell drove down to Alpine with Sgt. Bob Favor. When he found out that I'd fired on the subject with ball ammunition, he personally ordered Favor to issue me two boxes of deadly hollow-points. "Can't take a chance like that again, Joaquin," he said.

When I decided to retire in 1993, Captain Powell asked me to come to his office in Midland and visit with him personally about my decision. He was swamped with his regular duties, but he shoved everything aside to *talk* to one of his men. He spent the next two hours explaining to me why I needed to stay on for just a few more years. But I'd already slept on it, and he understood.

"To hell with a supervisor," Captain Allee always said. "Men follow a leader." But this book should have made it plain that although these captains were born leaders, they were also my teachers and my friends. I loved and respected them all. Time and time again they backed my decisions in the field. They excused my mistakes. And, best of all, they kept Austin off my ass and let me do my job. Like me, they're all gone now from the Ranger service. Texas will never see the likes of John Wood, Jack Dean, and Gene Powell again behind the badge. And this book never had a prayer of doing them justice.

I should have said somewhere in this book that my wife Shirley wanted her husband to rise in the Ranger ranks. I think it bothered her that I was technically a *private* in the Ranger service. A private is the lowest rank in the military, but in the Rangers it was the workhorse, the man who got the job done, the officer who knew his people and his country and could be left alone to do his job, which I did. I loved being a Ranger private. But Shirley didn't understand that and kept after me to take the sergeant's exam.

Twenty-eight applicants showed up in Austin for the written test. I scored the fourth-highest mark, which was a pleasant surprise. It looked like I was a shoo-in for a promotion, which scared the hell out of me, since it meant I would soon be chained to a goddamned desk. I was agitated when I appeared for my scheduled oral examination. I tugged at my tie as I answered the questions as honestly as I could.

"Would you move to Houston if we promoted you to sergeant?" a board member finally asked me.

"I wouldn't move to Houston if you made me director of the DPS," I said.

I ranked twenty-seventh out of twenty-eight in the final tally. Damn those oral exams! It must have been my rural accent that gave me away. I pity the poor delusional bastard who scored lower than me. Or maybe his wife was sweating on him, too, and he strolled in there and told them to kiss his ass and slammed the door behind him. Maybe that was why. Anyway, they sent me right back to Uvalde to hunt for cattle rustlers and horse thieves. And you know what? They did the right thing. Shirley got over it, and I should have said as much in this book if I were really going to say it all. I tried to, but there is always more. Always.

I should have talked more about my fellow Rangers if this memoir would have been any account at all. I'd have to start by admitting that I once hit a DPS trooper. I damn sure did. I bounced him off the wall right there in the eight-foot-square polygraph room, right after he failed his test. We both knew then that he was a thief. He had recruitment poster good looks, but he was rotten to the core. I told him that he had a future, but not in law enforcement, and that it was time to get right with the department about his thieving and then move on to better things. He denied it. And that didn't sit well with me.

I ended my portion of our discussion by telling the trooper that he was a disgrace to the department and nothing but a damn liar. He jumped up from his chair and called me a liar, too. That was the wrong thing to say to a Ranger trained by Alfred Allee Sr. He found that out quick. He pushed himself up off the floor, wiggled his jaw from side to side to see if it still worked, and said, "Now you're in more trouble than I am." And he was right about that.

The phone went dead after I reported the incident to Captain Dean. He finally said, "You did *what?!*" After all the review and subsequent departmental reaming, I was suspended for three days without pay and placed on six months' probation. The humiliation of it nearly ran me out of the Rangers. I got over it. But when my check came for that month, it was short $300, and that bites hard into the budget for a family of four.

There was nothing to do but suck it up. I had no regrets. If Col. Garrison had been alive, he'd have insisted that one good punch wasn't near punishment enough for that lying, thieving son of a bitch and the shame he brought on the Texas Department of Public Safety. But those days were gone, and although I didn't know it at the time, the thing most feared by Austin bureaucrats is a lawsuit, even one filed by a lying, thieving son of a bitch. A friend told me that if the same thing happened today, they would fire you. And he's probably right. But they didn't fire me back then. The bureaucrats treated me like I had the plague instead and shorted me $300.

Two days after my check arrived, Captain Jack Dean called me into his San Antonio office. Thinking that I was in for yet another round of ass chewing, I was anxious to get it over with and get back to work. Instead, Captain Dean presented me with a check for $300. Every man in Company D had pitched in to make up for my suspension. They backed me up when Austin dressed me down, and I'll never forget that. I drove home in tears to Uvalde with the $300 check in my hand. Had you been with me that day, you would know why I loved the men I worked with in the Rangers. I don't know if I made that clear enough in this little book. I don't even know how to say something like that—that I *loved* those men.

I should have said more about Glenn Krueger, like maybe about the time I coiled a dead five-foot-long rattlesnake under his chair at a gathering at the Y. O. Ranch. We were sipping a little whiskey after hours (except for Glenn, who never drank hard liquor), shooting the shit. I waited for an hour for Glenn to discover the rattler, but he never did. So finally—and this wasn't near as good—I said, "Hey, Glenn. What's that under your chair?" He hollered like a stuck pig and splashed his Big Red soda all over everybody. I later found that snake in my overnight bag, but that wasn't the end of it.

Next morning, I couldn't locate my pants. I hunted the Y. O. for close to an hour before I finally saw both pairs of slacks flying from the flagpole. I stormed into the mess hall an hour late, looking to settle up with Krueger. Captain Dean told me that Glenn had business elsewhere.

I squared things up a few months later at a Company gathering in McAllen. We met for procedures and firearms training. Texas Governor Mark White attended, which was an honor for us. We enjoyed a great barbecue together for the gathering's finale. And then Captain Dean escorted Governor White to Glenn Krueger's waiting state vehicle. It was a brand, spanking new Chevrolet Impala, shining in the sun like a new dime.

I couldn't see Governor White and Captain Dean approaching Krueger's new car from a small rise to the north of them where I was standing. This was unfortunate, because I released a triple chaser tear gas grenade just before they crested the hill. My delivery was perfect. The first explosion went off just north of Krueger, standing by the open door near another Ranger, Bob Steele. The second erupted directly under the vehicle, and the last just a few feet past it. Both Rangers and Krueger's car were completely engulfed in tear gas.

I laughed watching Glenn and Steele as they doubled over and retched from the gas until I saw the governor approaching with Captain Dean. That image of my boss walking along with the Big Boss robbed me of all of my joy. The Captain was quick on his feet and diverted the governor to another vehicle, which I appreciated, since I had a wife and two kids to support.

But White had a sense of humor, and so did Dean, so nothing much came of it except Krueger had to drive home to Beeville with his head sticking out of the window. He claimed that for months afterward, every time he turned on the air conditioner it gassed him a little. That's better than the flagpole thing, but they were both good if you were there.

My friend Glenn and his wife Jackie passed on as I proofread this book. I loved them. They're gone.

To be any good at all, this book should have mentioned my friend Bob Favor, the most dogged man-tracker of my times. He once trailed an escape artist all the way to Canada before he arrested him again. I don't know why I didn't get around to Senior Captain Lefty Block, the hardest-working Ranger on the force. Lefty punched in at his office at Brownwood at four each morning and was still on the job at ten or eleven at night. Lefty didn't get paid for all that time, but he didn't care. Or Bobby Upchurch, a good and reliable man, who spent more time working horseback with me than any other. Me and Bobby corralled a lot of rustlers.

I should have described how Captain Jim Riddle finessed confessions from suspects. He didn't hit them, scare them, or intimidate them in any way. He led them down the road to self-awareness, I guess you'd call it, to dredge up powerful feelings of guilt and remorse. I watched him several times reduce a suspect to his knees to either cry or pray, it didn't matter which. But after talking to Riddle, a man wanted to make things right if he had it in him to do so. If you wanted to witness a master interrogator at his work, you should have seen Captain Jim Riddle. He died of a heart attack in the 1980s. The department couldn't possibly replace him. At least, not during the twenty years it's tried.

I didn't talk about Bill Gerth, a Medal of Valor winner who risked his life in a shoot-out to save a DPS trooper. Or maybe Doyle Holdridge, from Laredo, who tracked down Sheriff Ben Murray's killers in fewer than twenty-four hours. Joe Harrison once lay out in the brush for three straight days on an extortion case. He wouldn't come in till he got his man. He got him. He damn sure did. Or maybe Lee Young, the bilingual Seminole African American Ranger. Lee is a force to be reckoned with in the field, and I was proud to serve with him. Texas has a little bit of every ethnic culture, and the Rangers had the best Texans. Lee Young was one of them, and that should have been said. Damnit, I should have told you about Lee and his great heritage and what a damn good Texas Ranger he is.

If you think that white collar criminals are too sophisticated for the Texas Rangers, watch what happens when Vietnam vet C. J. Havrada gets on their trail. Or maybe we should have talked a little about Lt. Jim Denman, out of Pecos, who's got no back-up in him. He's got the makings of another Johnny Aycock, and he's still on the force, still in the field.

Before he made Ranger, Johnny Allen was placing an arrested fugitive in his car, when a crazy man attacked him from out of the brush with a butcher knife. Allen had almost no time to think. Instead he reacted by drawing his weapon and firing twice—the result of department training. The assailant fell at his feet. Ranger Tol Dawson investigated the shooting. I asked him later about his determination.

"Allen screwed up," Tol said.

I thought, here we go. Another public relations fiasco. "What did he do wrong?" I finally asked.

"He waited too long to drop the son of a bitch," Tol said, with that big old grin on his face. I miss Tol's grin.

Johnny Allen is a top Ranger. He's still out there.

This book never said a word about Ray Martinez and Rudy Rodriguez, the absolute top investigators in the Ranger corps. Together, they're a criminal's worst nightmare. Or even Joey Gordon, Ranger pyrotechnics expert, who had the balls to refute the FBI determination about the Branch Davidian fiasco in Waco. He knew it didn't happen like the Feds reported, and he said so. I should have said also that if the Rangers had handled the Branch Davidian investigation, there would have been no bloodshed. The Feds came looking for a fight in Texas and they found one and then they lied about who provoked whom. Ranger Joey Gordon helped put things right. If you didn't know that, you do now, but I couldn't find a place for that discussion in this book.

You ought to know about the Ranger in El Paso, my young friend, Hank Whitman. Few things make me feel as good as watching Hank work his caseload. He's running all the time, like I used to do. And like me, he loves the job.

I should have told you a little about my friend Clete Buckaloo. A former DPS narcotics agent turned Ranger captain, a born leader who knows the woods as well as the cities, a genius in traditional tactics, a gifted diplomat and able administrator, he probably doesn't know that he is the man most fit to lead the Rangers in the twenty-first century.

After I told Clete that you couldn't make Ranger in my day without being able to shoot a rock thrown into the air, he shot box after box of ammunition trying to learn how to do it. I finally fessed up, and we both had a good laugh about it. I don't worry about the Rangers much with men like Clete still serving in the ranks. He shoots pretty damn good, too.

And how could I have gone so long without mentioning Virginia Holman, the Company D secretary? I turned in reports on paper towels, torn feed sacks, cheeseburger wrappers, and butcher paper, and somehow she wove them into clear, pristine, official-looking documents. She hated when I did that to her, but she always fixed it. I loved working with her. She's retired now, but she probably didn't get reports on feed sacks after I left. I think maybe I'll e-mail Virginia and give her a heart attack.

I could go on about these people, what they did, how special they are, what it meant to me to serve with them. But I don't have room in this

Border Patrol Supervisor
Lance Sterling Jackson

book. You won't find enough about these men here, and I apologize to them for that. This is a small book about only one Ranger. I'm sorry, but there is only so much I can say. I should tell the Rangers that I knew and loved that they gave my life meaning. I knew fulfillment because of them. Because of the work we did together. And because we did our work in Texas, a land I was born loving. I would have died for my fellow Texas Rangers. And them for me. And all of us for the people of Texas. I should have told them all of that before I walked away. But they know. I believe that they always knew.

And last, I should have said more about my youngest son, Lance Sterling Jackson, about the pride I feel watching him wear a lawman's uniform to work each day. He's on the job, like his daddy before him, in the service of his people. There aren't words to express the love I feel for that boy and the joy he's brought to his mother and me. I could never write a book that could come anywhere near describing how powerfully I feel those emotions.

It just can't be done. Not by me.

I READ ONCE that the greatest tragedy that can befall a man is to never know who he really is. Thanks to the Texas Rangers I knew no such misfortune. My timing was perfect for who and what I was and where I came from. My career was a gift from God, the same God whose only son once said, "Blessed are the peacemakers." I saw myself as a peacemaker. I saw myself as blessed. I was born a Texan, by God! I was at my best when I was a Texas Ranger.

When I look back, I no longer remember the reasons why I quit. What's important to me now is why I stayed so long—why I loved it. I could never really put my finger on it, but I think it was truly love. I was happy wearing the badge. I knew real contentment serving the people of Texas. Nothing made me prouder than doing a good job. And looking back, I think that I did. At the very least, I hope this book did a good job of explaining that.

And there was one other thing about being a Texas Ranger that perhaps is best explained in the following story: Someone once asked former Governor Ann Richards if she could put her finger on her very best day in that office. She responded almost immediately that once she was visiting one of the great old ranches in Texas. I had my differences with Queen Ann, but she loves the outdoors, and she loves Texas, and so as I look back, maybe we weren't so different after all. Incidentally, I've come to realize that if Ann Richards wanted women in the Rangers, she should have pinned a badge on herself. She would have made a good Texas Ranger.

Anyway, Governor Richards got off by herself on this ranch. She wanted to be alone at sunset, to watch the crimson and golden light bathe the hills of live oak and mesquite. Who wouldn't want to see that? As she settled in, she realized that one of the ranch's cowboys was standing behind her with his hat against his chest, waiting in silence to speak with her, watching the sun set over that ranch just like he'd done most every day of his life.

Governor Richards knew something about this old cowboy. She knew that he'd been born on that ranch, and that he had been raised there, and that he had worked his life away between the fences of that rough, stark, beautiful country. Some people might figure an old cowhand to be an ignorant man, but Ann Richards didn't think that. She saw him standing there and still he said nothing.

"Well, hello," she said, and she gestured for him to join her. And when they were standing beside each other and looking at the sunset, she said, "Isn't it marvelous?"

"Oh, yes ma'am," the cowboy said. "It sure is." And then he fell silent again, and the governor knew that he had come all the way out there to say something to her and wasn't sure when it was the right time to say it.

"Is there something you'd like to tell me?" the governor asked him to relieve him of his burden.

"Yes, ma'am, there is," he said, swallowing hard. "I just wondered if you know how lucky you are. I wondered if you realize what you've achieved in life. I wanted you to know that I can't imagine a greater honor in this world than being the governor of *Texas.*"

"You know something, mister?" she said after she paused a moment to think about it. "I can't either."

And then he turned, slipped his worn hat on his head, and walked off the way he came. Governor Richards was moved to tears by a simple cowboy and a few simple words. She was suddenly struck by the *privilege* of serving Texas and her people. Years later, when asked about her single greatest day as the governor of the Lone Star State, she immediately thought of her conversation with the old cowboy.

And so it is for H. Joaquin Jackson. It was not within me to aspire to high office, to win accolades on the sporting fields or riches in business. I could never have been a great lawyer, teacher, minister, or scientist. Farming would have done worse to me than it did to my father. The best I could ever do in life was to wear a badge. I was a lawman. I was a Texas Ranger. And for me, there was no greater honor than to serve this great state. What a life I've lived! And it was handed to me for nothing more than the asking. God, how I loved being a Texas Ranger!

Every day that I wore the star was a great day. I made mistakes. I had disappointments. I got my heart broken more than once. I got shot at and I shot back. I encountered ingratitude. I experienced betrayal. I saw a lot of tragedy. I endured a lot of personal pain. But I would go through all of it again if I could be that Texas Ranger I was back in 1966, riding beside a living legend, Captain Alfred Y. Allee Sr., driving 110 miles an hour through country we both loved on our way to a riot.

Never let the son of a bitches bluff you out, Joaquin. By God, Captain, I don't believe I ever did. I swear that I gave the badge everything I had, just like I promised you I would. And I would do it all again for you, and for Shirley and our two sons, for the Rangers living and dead who were my brothers, and for Texas. In an instant, I would do it all again. Always and forever for Texas. Why couldn't this book have said at least that?

Why should I burn up one page of this book bemoaning the fact that Texas changed? Well, of course it changed. And it'll change plenty more before it's all said and done. It will nevertheless become that "fine, good place to be." I swear it will. But maybe, just as the character in *The Searchers* said back in 1956, it needs my bones in the ground before that happens. Me and all of my kind. So be it. That time will also come. But I've got a while yet. A good damn while. Bank on it.

Somewhere in this book I should have thanked God for letting me be a

Texas Ranger. I thank Him for allowing me not only to live my life with dignity, humility, and grace, but to serve my people. I am so grateful for the gift of serving *Texas*. I could never imagine a greater honor. No, there is no greater honor. Not for me. I could not have known a better life. And this book didn't even come close to saying that as powerfully as I feel it in my bones, and in my heart. In every beat of my heart. Not even close.

Su Amigo Siempre,
H. Joaquin Jackson
TEXAS RANGERS (RET.)

Joaquin Jackson and Homer P. Garrison Jr., April 1, 1966

In Black and White

CAREER STATISTICS

JOAQUIN JACKSON, TEXAS RANGER—27 YEARS OF SERVICE

Year	Cases Murder	Burglary	Robbery	Other	Total Hours	Felony Arrests	Convictions	Number of Years	Property Recovered	Miles Vehicle	Hours Air	Hours Horse
1966	1	20	0	13	2,945	15	2	5	$25,214	37,027	350	28
1967	3	40	1	15	3,923	35	12	52	15,665	42,230	100	20
1968		29	4	47	3,886	35	39	174	8,500	45,443		18
1969	3	16	2	16	3,733	35	8	43	11,697	39,810	200	31
1970		20		31	4,064	41	12	67	13,768	36,777	555	24
1971	2	20	1	39	3,699	37	12	38	26,735	34,984	23	18
1972	2	39		85	3,296	37	8	48	152,371	35,503	945	16
1973	3	37	7	45	3,032	33	21	63	49,900	31,783	100	21
1974	3	30		38	2,897	31	10	61	270,712	28,850		27
1975	6	18	7	62	2,886	28	2	18	65,878	28,560	400	19
1976	11	19		55	2,700	24	6	28	70,540	31,765	6	20
1977	1	31			2,404	20	23	76	34,550	24,720	15	13
1978	4	12		26	2,523	25	26	65	26,000	22,495	76	12
1979	3	23		15	2,637	10	14	84	69,650	24,640	13	16
1980	5	31	1	30	2,311	20	4	84	40,973	21,580	12	
1981	3	26	1	33	2,637	16			527,350	26,350	2	15

Year	Cases				Total Hours	Felony Arrests	Convictions	Number of Years	Property Recovered	Miles Vehicle	Hours Air	Hours Horse
	Murder	Burglary	Robbery	Other								
1982	2	74	2	100	2,424	25	53	351	181,610	24,985	9	11
1983	4	31		27	2,174	24	7	17	268,724	22,767		14
1984	1	33	2	30	2,341	24	14	145	94,424	27,250	12	19
1985	7	56	3	24	1,895	39	31	233	160,500	23,120	19	17
1986	4	32		24	1,851	21	25	151	196,302	28,592		12
1987	6	4	2	17	3,521	23	1	5	64,074	68,052	38	10
1988	16	6		36	3,727	13	7	52	98,654	63,929	68	14
1989	10	4		63	3,954	23	10	126	164,708	73,582	33	15
1990	2	53		52	3,886	28	23	597	124,144	55,023	38	16
1991	2	24	2	18	3,832	12	27	316	40,300	50,476	83	14
1992		10		54	4,016	16	6	90	79,632	60,828	50	32
1993				10	2,791	9	2	6	4,400	44,478	12	8
TOTAL	104	738	35	1,005	85,985	699	405	2,995	3,186,975	1,055,599	3,147	492

Compiled by W. Jade Keith and Kim Keith, August 2003

Letter from the Reverend

COPY

Asbury United Methodist Church

3500- Pershing Drive
Offices: 3501 Hueco Ave.
El Paso, Texas 79903
Telephone 915 - 566-1654

CHARLES R. GRAFF
Pastor

September 15, 1986

Ms. Janice Rece
Texas Ranger Hall of Fame
Box 2570
Waco, Texas 76702-2

Dear Ms. Rece:

Yesterday (September 14, 1986) there appeared an Associated Press story about Ranger Joaquine Jackson in the El Paso Times. In that story the following is said;

".....Coffman envies Jackson's early days in the Ranger service. 'Civil rights and new laws have changed things. You can't threaten to kill anyone anymore if they won't talk. Intimidation used to be a powerful investigative technique,' Coffman said."

The article then goes on to tell how Jackson tempered his colleague's remembrance of things past.

I would like to relate an experience that I had with Joaquine Jackson in 1968 that shows just how wrong Coffman is and how correct Jackson was and is. I have a keen interest in Texas Ranger history because my Great-grandfather (Drayton Matthews) served in the Rangers in 1858 and 59 under John Ford and Ed Burlison. Perhaps this remembrance can be slipped in some file and some day will provide fodder for a historian doing research on the Rangers of today. Here goes.....

In 1968 I was a young lawyer just a year or two out of law school practicing law in Brownsville, Texas. Our law firm was doing a great deal of criminal law practice and as a young fellow those were exciting times. Our job was made far easier by the slipshod investigative techniques of many of the area Peace Officers. These were the years just following the Miranda decision and it seems that Peace Officers, or at least those we dealt with had yet to figure out how to investigate and gather evidence within the framework of the United States Constitution. The law enforcement community groaned loudly under the burden of Miranda and it was said by some that there was no way you could get a confession under those restrictions.

There was a series of thefts of mercury from gas well meters in Cameron county. Mercury was commanding a high price and there was a real problem with these thefts. The local authorities were unable to catch the culprits and the Rangers were asked to assist in the investigation. The Rangers were successful and two brothers were arrested. The brothers had a Harley Davidson motorcycle and used this to get around in the country to commit their crime and make their escape. Our law firm was retained to represent the brothers.

I was drinking coffee at the stand-up bar in the rotunda of the old Cameron County Courthouse when Ranger Joaquine Jackson walked up to me and spoke. He asked me if I was one of the lawyers that was representing the brothers. I said yes I was. He then told me that it was his intention to go over to the jail at one in the afternoon and question the brothers. He said that he wanted me to know so that I could be present if I wished or confer with my clients on this matter. He was businesslike but very polite.

This was a first for me! Never before and never since had a Peace Officer informed me of his upcoming interrogation. They usually tried to play a cat and mouse game with the Defense Attorneys and this straight forward approach was something new. I was impressed and thought to myself that Jackson had just cooked his own goose. The brothers were professional criminals and were at least a match for Jackson.

I had something else to do at one in the afternoon and did not perceive Jackson's one o'clock activity to be much of a threat. But as a safeguard I went by the jail and spoke with the brothers. I told them that after lunch this big tall fellow named Joaquine Jackson was going to come over and try to interrogate them. I added that he was a Texas Ranger and his only purpose was to put them in prison. Both of them had previously served time in prison and they knew what prison was all about. I told them to say nothing....not even to tell their names or respond to questions. "Just sit and look at him...don't even speak to him," I said. I then reminded them that they had been through this kind of thing before and asked if they thought they needed me there to help them keep their mouths shut. Their response was that they knew the ropes and certainly didn't need any help to resist the questions of a Peace Officer. Confident that Jackson could do no harm, I went my way.

About mid-afternoon of the same day, the secretary came in and told me that Ranger Jackson was in the office and wanted to see me. She ushered him in and he placed his briefcase on my desk and opened it. He handed me the carbon copies of the signed confessions of the Vorhees brothers. He once again in a very businesslike manner told me that I was entitled to have copies of these confessions. With that and a short goodby he left! I have never seen him since.

I was stunned! I was shocked! How could this happen? Convinced that he could not have obtained these confessions without violating the rights of the brothers, I rushed over to the jail so I could photograph their bruises, so that I could begin to try and break their confessions. When I got there there were no bruises or marks on the brothers. I began to question them....looking for a violation of their rights or anything I could use to have their confessions thrown out. "Did he beat you?" I asked. "No." they replied. "Did he threaten you?" I asked. "No," they replied. "Did he promise you a lighter sentence or try to make a deal with you?" I asked. "No," they replied. "Then why....why did you sign that confession? Why did you even talk to him?"

They looked down at the floor and finally one of them looked at me with a tear in his eye and said, "He is the nicest man I have ever met." The conversation disclosed that he had told them that it was about time for them to get their lives straightened out and this was their last chance. I don't know how it worked out for them, but at that time, in that place, that is what they intended to do.

I have always considered that the finest piece of police work that I have ever seen. Intelligence, sensitivity, creativity, and a knowledge of the human animal accomplished what bluster and brute force could never have accomplished. Those that say they can't be effective Peace Officers within the framework of the United States Constitution have never seen Joaquine Jackson at work. He is a first-rate role model for what modern Peace Officers should be.

In 1970 I left the practice of law and became a Methodist Preacher. I still from time to time reflect on that part of my life and one of the bright spots was seeing Joaquine Jackson practice his profession. May his tribe increase!

Yours truly,

Charles Graff

Acknowledgments

T HE AUTHORS WISH to express their heartfelt appreciation to Charles, Judy, and James Tate for inspiring this project and ordering David to talk to Joaquin. Thanks to Johnnie Wilkinson for ordering her son to do what Charles Tate said. I love you, Mom. You would have made a great literary agent. Thanks also to Shelton and Sunny Smith for their faith and support and friendship.

Thanks to Cliff Tienart for being a faithful friend. Cliff's done it all and has seen even more.

Special thanks to our expert geologist, C. E. "Gene" Mear, for helping us draft the geology preface to the chapter on the Colorado Canyon shootings. Gene has never grown tired of the great mystery. We love listening to his stories. Thanks to Kim and Jade Keith for their work on Joaquin's career statistics.

Thanks to experienced Far Flung Adventures (Texas River and Jeep Expeditions) River Guide Jon Bohach, who took us through Colorado Canyon on the anniversary of the Heffley murder/shootings. Jon knows the river like an old friend. He also mediated navigational disputes between Wilkinson and stowaway Hornfischer. That should have cost extra.

Thanks to the following legendary Texas writers and journalists for opening their hearts, books, and archives (and anything else we could rip off): Joe Nick Patoski, Don Graham, Annie Dingus, Jan Reid, Mike Cox, John Morthland, Jesse Sublett, Larry McMurtry. We plundered published work by Joe Nick, Jan Reid, John Morthland, Walter Prescott Webb, John L. Davis,

W. K. "Kip" Stratton, John Knowles, Elmer Kelton (his insightful e-mail discussion of the 1950s drought), and José Angel Gutierrez.

In researching *One Ranger*, we relied upon *Texas Mountains* by Joe Nick Patoski and Laurence Parent; *The Making of a Chicano Militant* and *A Gringo Manual on How to Handle Mexicans* by José Angel Gutierrez, Ph.D.; "Johnny on the Spot," by John Morthland, as it appeared in *Texas Monthly* (December 1998); "Big Bend Is Better Than Ever," by Joe Nick Patoski, *Texas Monthly* (March 2002); "The Last Romantic Outlaw" by Jan Reid and Alan King, *Texas Monthly* (August 1973); and Jesse Sublett's excellent account of the Rangers as posted on http://www.texasmonthly.com. In our short sketch on Ranger history ("Order before Law"), we quoted briefly from *The Texas Rangers: Images and Incidents* by John L. Davis.

Thanks to Bobby Hasslocher for encouraging us to write this book. Thanks to my sister and brother-in-law, Dorothy and Jim Moring, for a lifetime of unconditional love and support—not to mention contributing research, discussions, and old photographs. I love you, sis. David loves you, too. Thanks to Wayne Weimers, Charles and Johnnie Brogdon, Johnnie and Estelle Aycock, Johnny Rodriguez, Jamie Sue Hill, "Jake," and José Angel Gutierrez for lending us their time and talents as we drafted the book. They all entrusted us with personal information, and we hope that in return we did them justice. Thanks to Robert Draper, who proposed the book's title. We're grateful to him.

Thanks to Christine Stophka for research assistance and suggestions. Thanks also to Enrique Madrid of Redford, Texas, for spending half a day teaching us more about the border culture and history of "the Devil's Swing." Thanks to Todd Allen, Mike Blakely, and Jim Hornfischer for hanging out with us when we needed a laugh.

Thanks to San Antonio police car enthusiast John Anderson for helping us with the specs on the old 1966 Plymouth Fury featured in the Prologue. Thanks to Isaac Scales for telling us even more. And special thanks to Dave Arnold of www.copcar.com for running down the original spec sheet on the old 1966 Pursuit package itself. Thanks to Ronald G. Delord for jumping in there when things looked bleak.

Thanks to our friend, legendary photographer Dan Winters, for allowing us to use his work. Dan's a great guy. And what a talent. Special thanks to Dr. Philip L. Leggett and his gracious wife, Janet, for their care and hospitality. Thanks also to Dr. Joseph S. Galati.

We are so grateful to Sarah Nawrocki for editing early drafts. Thanks to

Chandler Ford for following behind Sarah. You both did a beautiful job. Thanks to our readers—Bonnie Bratton, Barbara Minton, Jeanne Jard, Charles Tate, and Shelton Smith.

Thanks to William J. Scheick for twenty years of encouragement and support. "You're going to do *what?*" he said. Why, a Ranger book, of course. And after he understood that, he focused his considerable intelligence on how to help us. It's a lucky writer who has a friend like Bill Scheick in his corner.

Thanks to "them gals in California," as Joaquin calls them, Anna Cottle and Mary Alice Kier of Cine/Lit Entertainment and Management, for walking every step of the way with us. Thanks to talented literary agent Jim Hornfischer for believing in this project before anyone else did.

Thanks to our splendid team at the University of Texas Press: William Bishel and Joanna Hitchcock. We are especially grateful to Dave Hamrick for championing this project. We discussed the book for maybe one minute at the Texas Book Festival and Dave said, "Hell, let's do it!" There was no better home for this book than UT Press. We are forever grateful for this wonderful opportunity.

We don't know what we'd do without Shirley and Bonnie, whether we're writing a book or doing anything else. They are the loves of our lives and the spirit behind the story. Best of all, we've got some great times ahead. We love you, girls.

H. Joaquin Jackson and David Marion Wilkinson
Alpine, Texas
March 2002–March 2004